Walter Cronkite

His Life and Times

Doug James

J M PRESS
A DIVISION OF J M PRODUCTIONS, INC.
Brentwood, Tennessee 37024-1911

For my Mother and Father,
Bert and Charlie James,
for Helen Fritsche Cronkite,
and for parents everywhere
who recognize their
responsibility to their children

For I have known them all already, known them all :—
Have known the evenings, mornings, afternoons,
I have measured out my life with coffee spoons ;

T.S. Eliot
The Love Song of J. Alfred Prufrock

Contents

Introduction

Captain Walter "Wally" Schirra

I LEFT THIS PLANET three times. Once in Sigma 7, a Mercury spacecraft, then on a rendezvous mission in Gemini 6 and finally, on an 11-day Apollo earth orbital mission. One commentator who insisted that he was not a space fan, Walter Cronkite, had become a friend by then. After I retired from the U. S. Navy, it seemed only days had passed before I was sitting on the "left hand" of the famous Walter Cronkite, commenting as a co-anchor.

One newspaper ad for the CBS network stated, "Follow the Flight of Apollo 11 to the Moon—with Walter-to-Walter coverage" (I always wondered who got the top billing).

The privilege of knowing Walter C. is to realize that he is not acting. What you see is what you get, sorta like show business people say—"John Wayne played John Wayne." If Hollywood stars spent as much effort preparing for their movies roles as Walter does for a broadcast, every movie would deserve an Oscar and every TV show an Emmy.

Walter and his team of experts had volumes of background material ready for each mission I helped broadcast. I was a regular "left hander" for Walter through all of the subsequent Apollo missions, 11 in all. I shared a small part of "his life and times" during those days, and I realized how committed he was to his profession. His day at the CBS news studio, the famous West 57th Street of New York City, started by 0800 and rarely ended by 2000 (simple math with these military hours yields a 12-hour work day!). Every item was checked and double-checked for accuracy prior to his broadcasts. I know — for even I, with years in the space program, had to check with NASA, Houston.

The perfectionist of CBS News is also a warm and loving family man. Betsy, his first and only wife, keeps him in line during their joint appearances (as does mine!). I particularly admire her comment in response to a badly chosen remark by Walter at a retirement dinner. He stated, "After my retirement, I would like to cruise on a 65-foot sailing yacht with a 16-year-old mistress." Betsy's immediate retort, "Walter, you may acquire a 16-foot yacht, you have a 65-year-old mistress!"

Too often, celebrities miss the main stream of life. Walter Cronkite, in the past and the present, is an icon of our times.

Preface

An Homage to Walter Cronkite

IN 1974, WHEN I BEGAN working on my doctorate, my admiration and respect for the notable CBS newsman was such that I chose as my dissertation topic "The Journalistic Career of Walter Cronkite." I found Mr. Cronkite immediately receptive to my request for an interview, although he clearly spelled out that I would be permitted one hour only and no more. The staff at CBS News was cooperative beyond my expectations; likewise were John Chancellor, Frank Stanton, Richard Salant, and the late Bill Downs and Harry Reasoner.

I had made appointments with Messrs. Reasoner and Chancellor and Dr. Stanton. All were so generous with their time that no clocks were kept running; I asked questions until I was satisfied. The interview with Mr. Salant was a last-minute affair, but quite productive. Mr. Downs submitted a tape with answers to questions I had provided. Though Eric Sevareid had agreed to meet me in Washington if he had the time, our schedules could not be coordinated. His willingness to help was appreciated nevertheless.

I was especially captivated by Mr. Cronkite's remarkable mother, Mrs. Helen Cronkite, presently 98 years old and still living in Washington, who had me into her apartment and was most generous with information about her famous son. Her bedroom was stuffed to overflowing with memorabilia: under the bed, in the closets, and protruding from her secretary. (I was as excited—in the words of an old Fred Allen routine—as a blind dog in a meat market.) In her living room hung a nearly life-size painting of her son sent Cronkite by an adoring fan. That she would permit me to take one of her family albums to choose pictures for the dissertation, as well as for this commercial venture, was more than I could have hoped for. Over the years, we have exchanged notes and Christmas cards, and she has sent me clippings she thought might interest me. Cataracts make reading difficult for her, but telephone calls every few months have kept the friendship alive. Her mind is still clear and her spirit remains strong.

I dedicated this work to Mrs. Cronkite, as well as to my mother and father and other parents who care enough about their children to sacrifice for them and lead them by example. I have thanked Mrs. Cronkite often for the role she played in shaping the values and creating the drive her famous son demonstrated. She readily admits she is distressed by the seeming lack of concern modern parents show for their children and feels, as I do, that dedicated parenting would remedy many of today's societal ills. Her son is her immeasurable contribution to the world.

*   *   *

After submitting the dissertation and receiving my Ph.D. in communications from Walden University, I took my advisor's advice and began rewriting the dissertation for publication. Even though I had been keeping up with Mr. Cronkite through newspaper clippings I had saved—as well as those sent me by Mrs. Cronkite and other friends and family members—and his brief appearances on television and in *People* magazine, I felt I needed things I had failed to get the first time around, and needed for him to bring me up to date on his life since his retirement. I began the procedure of applying for yet one more interview with the great man. After two "confirmed" dates had to be scuttled because of last-minute intrusions into his schedule, I had to settle for a telephone interview.

At our first encounter, before he retired, I felt Mr. Cronkite to be somewhat tense—as much New York businessman as newsman; in the 1989 phone conference, however, I found him to be perceptibly gentler, more personable, and, frankly, warm. His speech has softened considerably since he has given up his daily newscasts, and the rich Midwestern accent matched perfectly his mother's. Even though he is trying to complete his autobiography—

a twenty-five year commitment to A. A. Knopf—Mr. Cronkite responded to my every request, including permitting me to use many of his copyrighted speeches and articles.

I am doubly thankful to such a generous man—for his remarkable life as well as for the time he took out to help me.

*   *   *

If, as you read this, you think I have gotten off the track in places, you are probably correct. There were so many side-trips with this remarkable man I could not resist the urge to include them. This was especially true in the chapter about his adventures in World War II. The biography is, frankly, a disjunctive narrative, because Cronkite's life has touched so many important events. His wife, Betsy, said she felt that living with Walter was like being a part of history. I feel I would have been remiss if I had ignored the history that was swirling around him throughout his career.

This book is the result of many years' pursuit of the career of a man I consider to be the ablest broadcaster in the history of network news. If it reads like a work of fiction, like an homage to a nearly perfect man, I believe I have not exaggerated. That Cronkite's life has been one out of a Frank Capra movie is close to the truth. His steps were steady and sure; his family bedrock-solidly behind him and his dedication to his craft absolute, resolute, and total.

*   *   *

The majority of my research was done at the libraries of Auburn University—where I taught television production and broadcasting history for five glorious years—and the University of South Alabama. Much was done at the public library of Newport, Rhode Island, during two summers I spent there with the Navy, and in the microfilm library at Harvard. One morning en route to New England was spent at the special collections department of the Library of Congress. The ubiquitous purveyor of knowledge on all subjects since its founding, the *New York Times* (the CNN of its day), provided perhaps the greatest amount of usable information.

For Peggy Harbin and Cheryl Sumner, who proofread and offered helpful suggestions on the project, I offer my profound thanks. To Arnold Schwarz, who copied the photographs from Mrs.

Cronkite's family album, I am appreciative, and to the friends and family members who offered clippings, notices, and telephone calls whenever Mr. Cronkite appeared on television, I am thankful.

I was humbled by the ready acceptance of Captain Walter Schirra to read my manuscript and write an introduction to a book about his friend. As it turned out, Mr. Cronkite was to be Captain Schirra's house guest the day after our first telephone conversation.

Even though Mr. Cronkite has had several secretaries over the years of this biography, three have been especially kind in their assistance. Ann Whitestone was the first. It was she who set up the various tours and private screenings at CBS when I interviewed Mr. Cronkite. She also arranged for me to be on the set for Mr. Cronkite's *Evening News* telecast. Further, it was she who gave me the name and phone number of Mr. Cronkite's Park Avenue ophthalmologist (at his suggestion) for a serious eye problem I was having at the time of the interview. Lisa Beatrice was the next secretary I called so often when I was trying to set up the second interview. We called each other over a two-month period, and even though the office interview became a telephone interview, I appreciate Lisa's personal involvement.

Suzi Grainger is the third—and current—assistant to Mr. Cronkite who has provided substantial help to me, even though I was calling her when she was new to the job and unfamiliar with the pressures and demands of serving such a high-profile personality. She is thoroughly competent and professional, yet has given me warm and kind attention, for which I am humbled and thankful.

I cannot conscientiously ignore the tremendous assistance I have received from my publisher, John Ishee, his wife Myra, and their son Mark. John was so incredibly helpful that I doubt this project would have evolved without his personal attention and worthy advice. The excellent work of editing and design by Rupert Palmer is likewise appreciated.

Doug James
Mobile, Alabama
1991

Tribute

An Appreciation of
Harry Reasoner

BECAUSE OF his humanity, his contribution to broadcasting and because of the part he played in helping me write this biography of Walter Cronkite, I feel the sudden passing of Harry Reasoner deserves notice.

Mr. Reasoner was with ABC when I interviewed him to gather material on his famous former alter-ego. Even though he was scheduled to go on the air shortly after my interview, he was totally relaxed and showed no anxiety whatever during the hour or so we spent together. He made it plain that he was prepared to let me stay as long as I wanted to.

I had always been a fan of Mr. Reasoner's. I especially appreciated his wit, eloquent essays, and unassuming manner. I was greatly amused at the way he more or less dismissed the Nixon White House staff members, particularly Spiro Agnew, during our interview. He felt they were corrupt opportunists who, while espousing law-and-order, were desecrating the Constitution and wrongfully turning the American public against journalists who were sounding the alarm against the excesses of the Nixon administration.

I had planned to ask Mr. Reasoner to read a copy of my Cronkite biography, to contribute an endorsement, as he recovered from his surgery. As his long hospital stay became longer, I began to realize he was more ill than most of us knew. His death was truly a shock, and I fear his unique style of reporting the news will never be duplicated. That is probably as it should be.

I appreciated Harry Reasoner, as millions of Americans did and am grateful for the hour I spent with such a gracious and natural gentleman.

D.J.

"And That's the Way It Is"

The CBS Evening News with Walter Cronkite

To seek the public's favor by presenting the news it wants to hear, is to fail to understand the function of the broadcast news in a democracy. . . .

I am overcautious to the point that people think of me as kind of remote, and they accuse me of not giving myself, of being too slow in friendship. . . . I would like nothing better than being an Irish bar drunk, making friends with everyone.

—*Walter Cronkite*

THE DAILY thirty-minute network news program, *The CBS Evening News with Walter Cronkite,* that was seen by home viewers before Cronkite's 1981 retirement, was rather like the proverbial tip of the iceberg. What follows is a description of "the way it was" behind the scenes when Walter Cronkite was the managing editor of his daily news program.

To an outsider, the scene in the CBS newsroom at 6:30 p.m. is bedlam. Typists, production personnel and others involved in the impending telecast are working feverishly at desks or dashing about the studio performing last-minute details to have all in readiness when the cameras are turned on. Non-production staff members and a half-dozen or so visitors stand around the large studio, out of camera range.

Lights hanging from the ceiling bathe the background and the center of the newsroom/studio with noonday brightness. No attempts are made to light the central figure from below or in any flattering way. A single cameraman responsible for the "bumper shots"—side shots used at the beginning of the show and just before commercial breaks—pushes his camera into place to the observer's left. An unmanned, stationary camera is located directly in front of the news desk, alongside the font—a TV monitor from which Cronkite can read the news while appearing to be looking into the stationary camera.

In the center of the noise and flurry sits Walter Cronkite, the man who will presently bring order to the chaos. He is calmly working at his curved news desk, seemingly oblivious to all that is going on around him. His coat is draped over the back of his chair and he is bent over a sheaf of papers, making notations with a ball-point pen. He has removed the glasses he wears during the day and installed the contact lenses he wears on the air. Despite efforts to develop non-reflecting lenses, he gave in to contacts, partly in response to a telephoned suggestion from a Cronkite fan, fugitive Abbie Hoffman. He supplements his vision at his news desk with a pair of Ben Franklin reading glasses before air time as he makes corrections to his copy. A stop-watch in his left hand, his lips move as he reads, timing the length of the stories he will present on the air. No staff member dares break his concentration or disrupt his solitude; until he completes his newscast, no one speaks to him unless he speaks first.

Above the activity, the floor manager suddenly calls, "Five minutes, Walter!" The visitors look at the floor manager and back at Cronkite. He gives no indication he has heard the warning but continues working on the manuscript. A new countdown time is called each minute but he shows no sign that he is aware of the warnings. When "Two minutes, Walter!" is announced, he reaches for the small dual microphone unit (one working and one back-up) that has been lying on his desk. He attaches the device to his tie as a female staff member places a pedestaled, circular mirror on the right side of his desk. He removes his reading glasses and lifts his face to the woman, who powders it lightly. He then looks into the

mirror as he runs a comb carefully through his hair. The mirror is whisked away and the floor manager calls out, "One minute, Walter!" Cronkite removes his chewing gum and drops it into a waste basket behind the desk and takes a sip of tea and honey mixture from a styrofoam cup, as has been his custom since 1972, when he had a benign tumor removed from his throat. Hidden from view under the desk are his mouthwash, non-prescription sprays and lozenges for the sinusitis, bronchitis and frequent colds which afflict him.

At "Thirty seconds, Walter!" he casually stands and straightens his tie—he likes to wear brightly-colored ones on camera. His shirt is a monogrammed Givenchy and his suit, usually a conservative pin-stripe, was bought off the rack at Saks Fifth Avenue. He is wearing his high school ring, gold cuff links with the CBS "eye" logo and a gold Rolex watch. Even though the Fashion Foundation of America voted him one of the sixteen best-dressed men in America in 1972, he dismissed the honor as being "stupid," and denies any attempt at competing for such recognition. He slips into his coat, sits at his desk again, shoots his sleeves and stares into the stationary camera as Bob Hite introduces the program before Cronkite greets his audience with his traditional "Good evening," and the *Evening News* begins.

Even though Cronkite is managing editor of the news program—some critics in the print media have ridiculed him for insisting on that title—he remains a reporter at heart; he doesn't like the term anchorman, preferring to see himself as a lead correspondent. He has written or edited every item he reads on the air and he often types his own copy with his newsman's seventy-words-per-minute speed. He disapproves absolutely of any broadcaster who "rips and reads" words cold from a teletype machine, or of anyone who would read copy written solely by others. Cronkite familiarizes himself completely with the news happenings he will include in his program, from start to his signature "And that's the way it is" closure, which his mother claims credit for—she says it is an expression she has used all her life and her son picked up from her.

Cronkite is at the West 57th Street CBS News Building, a converted dairy processing plant, at 9:30 or 10:00 each weekday morning. He used to take the Lexington Avenue subway and the 42nd Street bus to work each morning, but fame had its drawbacks and public transit became difficult. For years he took a cab, or was driven in by his wife, because, he charged, their dog Buzzy wanted to go for a ride. "I guess the real test will come when the dog dies," he once joked. His complaints that "Barbara Walters doesn't have to stand in the street, waiting for a cab," paid off, and CBS began providing him with a limousine.

He steps carefully over the dog droppings which cover the sidewalk in that residential part of the city, goes inside through the front entrance and, in his long, loping gait, strides with his head thrust forward and staring straight ahead, through the small lobby, past the receptionist and the two security guards standing on either side of the inside doors and disappears into the labyrinthine corridors that lead to the newsroom.

His office, smaller and more modest by far than his NBC or ABC colleagues', is little more than a glass-walled, book-lined cubbyhole with venetian blinds, which has been built, obviously as an afterthought, into one corner of the newsroom. In 1962, when he assumed his managing editor position, Cronkite sponsored a major overhaul of the physical arrangements, converting the studio into a combination studio/office/working newsroom, which puts him closer to the news. Previously, he had to shuttle between office and newsroom throughout the day and then walk a long distance to the television studio.

His office is furnished simply: his desk and chair face a sofa and matching overstuffed chair arranged against the outside wall of the long, awkward, rectangular room. Behind his desk is a wall-to-wall bookcase which reaches to the ceiling. Encyclopedias and such publications as *Facts on File* fill the bookshelves. On the bookcase ledge are mementos of his travels and gifts from viewers: a framed color photograph of himself and Alexander Solsynitzen, a stuffed piranha with its tail missing, a ceramic Angus bull and a child's cardboard lunar-landing module. He shared with family and friends many of the gifts he received. "Most of this stuff is god-awful junk. But a lot of work went into these things. How could I just heave them away?"

An oil painting of the *Wyntje*, his first sailboat to bear that name, hangs on the wall across from the sofa. Over the door opposite his desk are three TV monitors of various brands for post-

Evening News viewing of the three network news shows, a practice all the networks follow.

Just outside his office door sit the two secretaries who write his letters, screen his telephone calls, receive his guests and mail, order his lunch and mix the honey and tea mixture he sips to soothe his throat during the telecast.

The staff of thirty-five has been at work since 9:30, transcribing the news and viewing the films that have been arriving through the night, from CBS correspondents and the major commercial news-gathering agencies. On a typical morning, Cronkite collects the information his staff has prepared for him and sits down with his executive and associate producers to consider possible stories for that evening. In composing a news format, Cronkite told Peggy Hudson for *Senior Scholastic* his network doesn't "balance the news by putting in so many grams of Republican news, so many grams of Democratic news, so many grams from New England, *et cetera.* Balance is being sure, over the long run—maybe not even in one day's broadcast—that all sides and all points of view have been given a fair exposure."

At noon each day, Cronkite holds a telephone conference with other CBS News bureaus in Atlanta, Chicago and Los Angeles. He extracts information from his colleagues in those key American cities and makes suggestions for possible follow-ups or a different approach to a story. He is on the telephone at intervals all day, calling other CBS newsmen when specific stories are breaking in their areas; or he sometimes calls key politicians or government officials as various situations require. Of Cronkite's phenomenal news sense, former CBS president Fred Friendly once remarked, "There's a fellow with clay on his feet. He doesn't sit around waiting for someone else to do his leg work. He goes out and gets the information and writes it himself."

As staffers rewrite stories taken from the major wire services, they are expected to check the sources. Cronkite interrogates the writers like a martinet as to the article's accuracy: "Did you check this out? Are you sure of that?"

By the same token, when Cronkite makes an assignment for a story, he expects his orders to be carried out. Once, for example, when he instructed an assistant to send Marvin Kalb to interview some Arabs in Washington, regarding perpetual rumblings in the

Middle East, the assistant balked, reminding Cronkite that Kalb was Jewish, and sending him to an Arab gathering might not be wise. Cronkite repeated the order in a flat voice that left no doubt as to what he expected: "I want him to talk to the Arabs." Kalb was dispatched.

Peggy O'Neil, writing for *Life*, reported, the same bulldog tenacity for securing news from the Middle East was displayed immediately after Egypt's President Nasser's death. The Egyptians had declared a communication black-out, preventing news from leaving the country and foreign correspondents were being turned back at the airports. Cronkite decided to cover this story himself, but lacked a visa to enter the country. Undaunted, he hired a German pilot to fly himself and his camera crew to Cairo. At the airport, he was stopped by an Egyptian official who would not admit any travelers who identified themselves as reporters. Cronkite's stature and professional statesmanlike mannerisms confused the man: "You vee eye pee?" he asked uncertainly. Seizing the opportunity, Cronkite responded with authority and a trace of dramatic irritation, "Yes, vee eye pee." The official waved him and his crew past the check point.

Following the initial sessions with his producers, colleagues and other staff members about possible stories for the *Evening News* program, Cronkite returns to his office and reads over the mail his secretaries has selected for him. He receives over 600 pieces of correspondence each week. He routinely refuses invitations to open shopping centers, as well as offers for matrimony, both of which arrive with amazing regularity. He confessed to interviewer Dick Cavett that he was frankly amazed at how many marriage proposals he received and how serious the women seemed.

One of the most bizarre offers for marriage came from a German woman living in the western United States. She mailed Cronkite a check for $1000 and a parcel containing cuff links engraved with *Ich Liebe Dich* ("I love you"), a toilet kit and even a pair of pajamas. An enclosed letter instructed Cronkite to meet her in Munich, where he would help her reclaim some property that would be theirs to share. Cronkite immediately returned the check along with a letter, diplomatically explaining, since he was already happily married, he would be unable to honor her request. Before he could return the package, however, it was stolen from his office. The woman's daughter wrote him an angry letter demanding the return of the parcel. Cronkite informed the daughter that the items had been given to charity, ending the strange affair.

He usually has a light lunch at his desk—"the Cronkite Special," his secretaries call it—which consists of cottage cheese and a pineapple slice on a lettuce leaf. While he is eating, he makes more telephone calls and, for additional perspective, reads over the newspapers he regularly subscribes to: the *New York Times,* the *Washington Post,* the *Wall Street Journal* and the *Christian Science Monitor.*

More conferences are held throughout the afternoon with the writers and four typists who are preparing transcriptions of the wire service material. As new stories continue to arrive, the projected line-up of the evening telecast is constantly re-evaluated and amended. Some items may be dropped as others are added or perhaps the order is reversed. The format is intentionally kept flexible to allow the last-minute changes which keep the news program current.

The middle of the afternoon is reserved for taping special television or radio broadcasts, including interviews to be used on the program that evening. At this time, Cronkite may prepare a tape for a network special or for some charity like the *New York Times'* weekly news review for the blind or he might make a network promo, which, he says, "drive me out of my goddam, everloving mind."

By 4:30, Cronkite's shoes have been shined, even though they won't be seen on camera, he has run an electric shaver over his face, the schedule of news stories is becoming firmer and, by 6:00, he is at his news desk with the copy he and the producers have agreed on for the *Evening News.* Each story has been double-spaced on a separate page and he reads over each one carefully, consulting writers, producers, reference books or staff personnel as he needs additional information. At 6:15 the studio lights are turned on, he is given the final line-up of the filmed or taped segments of the program and the countdown begins.

When late-breaking items or other air-time changes in the program are required, the staff is trained to make them. One of the most memorable switches occurred the evening Cronkite received a telephone call during a commercial break: When the newscast resumed, the camera revealed Cronkite leaning back from his desk, listening on one of the desk phones. He casually looked at the camera, raised his hand as a sign he knew he was being waited on, a gesture that heightened the suspense and he continued listening for a few more seconds. After hanging up the phone, he explained that former President Johnson had just died en route to an Austin, Texas, hospital.

Often the direct feed lines from remote locations are poorly patched or technically unusable, in which cases Cronkite will calmly interrupt and fill the viewers in on the details; he promises to try again, or he dismisses the attempt altogether. Despite the snarls that might present themselves while he is on the air, Cronkite's leadership prevails and all traces of anxiety melt when he is at his desk. When a group of homosexual activists stormed the studio, the engineers cut quickly to black and played a commercial. When Cronkite reappeared, he continued as if nothing abnormal had transpired.

(Once when Harry Reasoner was sitting in for Cronkite, he was signaled to continue with the next news item, rather than pausing for a commercial break. An alert producer had realized that the planned commercial for an anti-diarrheal medication began with the words: "Harry's got diarrhea.")

If there is some doubt about using one particular story over another, the decision may wait until after the broadcast begins, often in anticipation that supplementary material or film will arrive to enhance or clarify the story. Those judgments are made by Cronkite during commercial breaks or filmed reports, when he might tell his staff, "Let's drop this Cyprus story and use the one on alcoholism instead." The directors and the font operator quickly make the change in scripts and the program resumes. The news piece which follows another break might concern a terrorist bombing, but Cronkite isn't satisfied with the scanty information and asks a staffer, "Where in London did this bombing take place?" The staff member replies, "I'll find out," and hurriedly talks to a messenger, known as "Marco Polo," who rushes from the studio. Cronkite may turn to yet another assistant who had approached his desk even before the break began. They confer briefly. Marco Polo returns and whispers to his sponsor. Cronkite turns to her and she says, "In

Soho." The floor manager calls, "Okay, Walter. Here we go!" Cronkite faces the camera again, calmly ignoring the hurried conferences or the personnel moving on-camera in the background or the tapping of a typewriter revising a story. He smoothly takes up where he left off before the break.

CBS affiliate stations have the option of using the telecast live or taping it for airing at a later time. Even though the half-hour news program is "in the can," or finished, the staff stands by for another half hour in the event that "flubs," technical mistakes or important late-breaking news stories require a retake, as in the case of the capture of fugitive Angela Davis. CBS News learned of her apprehension at 7:20 EST. Cronkite and crew went back on the air and retaped an entirely new show in order to include the Davis story. There have been other rarer instances of stories requiring the taping of as many as a half-dozen updates in a single evening. Regardless of how many programs are taped, one or six, Cronkite seldom leaves the CBS News building before 8:30.

His delivery in his rich baritone voice is, according to one contemporary writer, "close enough to flawless to be a little frightening. While no one is waiting for him to come up with an occasional 'Nick Dixon,' people are sometimes exasperated with his everlastingly unruffled composure."

The television audience sees Cronkite at the end of a long and usually hectic day, at his weariest. It is his responsibility to write, orchestrate and conduct the news team and to project freshness and involvement in the program, even though he has been working since late morning. Except for vacations, strikes, rare illness or special assignments, the indomitable newsman is at his post each evening.

In 1975, he suffered for several months with a back problem resulting from an injury incurred during a tennis match. He was still bedridden with the injury when the fall of Vietnam began. CBS sent a limousine with a therapist to pick him up: he was not about to miss that story. "Not," he told David Shaw for *TV Guide*, "after covering it for what seemed like half my adult life." Fortified with cortisone and pain-killers, he was literally strapped into a specially-built chair as he conducted a two-and-a-half hour telecast. He was in constant agony and he had to be helped to his feet at the program's conclusion, but he anchored the special without apparent discomfort and his audience never suspected his misery or that he "did the fall of Vietnam, strapped to my chair."

The longest involuntary absence from his desk took place during the thirteen-day AFTRA strike in March 1972. For that period of time he was replaced by Arnold Zenker, a CBS junior executive with no previous television camera experience. Zenker made such a favorable impression "sitting in the slot"—as the news desk is called—that after the strike, Cronkite smilingly signed on with, "Good evening. This is Walter Cronkite, sitting in for Arnold Zenker."

Cronkite is a perfectionist and he quickly became known as a kind of desk-pounding prima donna at CBS. One news producer said, "He's a 500-pound gorilla who always gets what he wants." He will refuse to run filmed stories that are of less than professional quality. When a program fails to go smoothly, Lamont Lansing reported in *People,* "he can uncork a temper that would get respectful attention in a Marine command post." Cronkite admits when he does lose control, he becomes "pretty awful and irrational," but, as he expects only the best from his staff, he is no easier on himself: "I get quite upset when I feel that other people have failed for one reason or another to do their job, but I get even more upset when I fail to do mine."

A story is frequently written about Cronkite's wrath that happened while he was covering the tragic events of November 22, 1963. He was in his New York office when word was first received from Dallas that President Kennedy had been shot. Cronkite rushed to his news desk and went on camera at 2:33, still in his shirt sleeves, to report the story as it came in from Dallas and reactions to the assassination from around the world: "From Dallas, Texas, the flash—apparently official—President Kennedy died—at one p.m., Central Standard Time, two o'clock Eastern Standard Time—some thirty-eight minutes ago." For the first time in his journalistic career, he lost his composure on the air. After reporting President Kennedy's death, he bit his lip and his eyes filled with tears.

He remained at his news desk for the remainder of the afternoon. As he was going back to his office after that exhausting, emotional labor, he looked around for a telephone to call his wife. He picked up a phone that was ringing and was subjected to the fury of an irate woman who demanded that "You people at CBS

"From Dallas, Texas, the flash — apparently official —

"President Kennedy died — at one p.m., Central
Standard Time — some thirty-eight minutes ago."

do something about Walter Cronkite. It's a disgrace that a man who has been trying to get John Kennedy out of office should be on the air talking, at a time like this!" Cronkite took a deep breath and replied, "Madam, this is Walter Cronkite, and you are a goddammed idiot!" and he slammed down the phone.

Later, in an interview with Oriana Fallaci for *Look*, Cronkite admitted losing self-control on occasions and, when reminded of the previous incident, confessed, "Unfortunately, that Park Avenue lady drove me mad. It was the first voice that I had heard after four-and-a-half hours on the air. I am not proud to have invoked the Lord's name in losing my temper."

Cronkite believes a program's effectiveness is hindered by the time limits imposed on it. When he increased the length of the *Evening News* from fifteen to thirty minutes in 1964, he felt he had made significant strides long overdue, but during his stay as managing editor, he pushed for a full hour of news, preferably at the 10:00 hour. For years he hammered on the same theme: a thirty-minute broadcast is too brief and shallow for a complete understanding of our complex world. He once demonstrated his point by having a news director paste a transcript of an *Evening News* show over the front page of a copy of the *New York Times*. The script covered less than eight columns of the newspaper, causing Cronkite to comment: "The number of words spoken in a half-hour evening news broadcast—words spoken by interviewees, interviewers, me, everybody—came out to be the same number of words as occupy two-thirds of a standard newspaper's front page. We are a front-page service. We don't have time to deal with the back pages at all." He received little encouragement from his executive bosses or advertisers for such a move, but held on to the belief that "It will come, but not soon." It came, of course—but on CNN, not CBS.

In his many speeches, Cronkite frequently calls on the newspaper industry to recognize its responsibility to television viewers. He believes since network news can treat only the headlines, newspapers must entice television audiences to read newspapers for the complete stories. A 1975 survey revealed that as many as seventy per cent of the Americans who were polled rely on television almost exclusively for their news. His speeches and articles encourage viewers to read newspapers, books, and opinion journals and not to rely on television only because, as he told Peggy Hudson, "We don't tell everything well in television news. We need a high school course in teaching kids how to read news or watch television. An intelligent, well-educated public will not select a newspaper or magazine or television program that necessarily tells it like they want it to be." When he first took over as managing editor, he wanted to end each program with the admonition, "For further information, read your local newspaper."

Unfortunately, it appears that the number of Americans depending primarily on newspapers for their news has decreased over the years. One 1989 report claims 67 percent of Americans now rely on networks or local stations as a major source for their information.

Cronkite is encouraged, however, by the statistics which indicate many disadvantaged Americans—who cannot or will not read—have been excited by television news. He feels by introducing this segment of the population to the fact that someone is interested in their problems, they might themselves work toward solving those problems.

Since he could not get his news program expanded to a full hour, Cronkite decided there were other ways to keep his viewers informed. In 1976, he conceived the idea for the popular CBS "Bicentennial Minute" specials, which featured sixty-second capsule reports on events leading up to the colonies' declaration of independence from England. The one-minute report was so well-received that CBS adopted it for its regular news format, inserting little news items into its regular day-long programming. The concept has since been picked up by the other networks, local stations and now even children's shows have news briefs. In addition, many CBS historical features now conclude with book titles to consult as they exhort viewers to "Read more about it."

It has always been Cronkite's desire and philosophy to be as totally achromatic in his news coverage as possible. He told Richard Gehman for *T V Guide* he defends his political neutrality and refusal to editorialize on the air by stating, "CBS is against opinion broadcasting. There's a good case to be made for it, but it's always been this network's policy to be objective, to present unbiased analysis. It's erroneous to suggest that there's a strong censorship in the network. The CBS policy has always been to avoid use of the word 'commentator.' I go along with that—there's plenty of room for analysis in what we do."

Despite opinions to the contrary, Cronkite steadfastly denies that he is a pundit. He let that title and honor go to his network's former resident philosopher and essayist, Eric Sevareid. Cronkite feels his own neutrality created the believability and trust his viewers prefer. Unfortunately, it also projected an unintentional coolness or aloofness to some. His executives privately encouraged him to demonstrate more of his wit and warmth on his news programs. He would have liked to appear more personable and admitted to Isabella Tavers in a *Look* interview, "If there were some magic elixir that would make the show more popular, of course, I'd be willing to go along." As for kidding around the way most news teams do—"happy news," he calls it—he would never have been a part of that. Deeply embedded in his mind was the memory of the disastrous *Morning Show,* and he had no desire to retread that ground. He told those who tried to get him to exercise more levity on the air, "I'm not shy. I don't like people who take themselves seriously, most of all myself. But I don't think my type of irreverent humor belongs on a news show. There are 5,000 young disc jockeys with more talent that I have." He would occasionally end his newscast with anecdotes, however. One such story was of a collegiate wrestler, one gram over weight before a match. The solution, reported a smiling Cronkite, "He spit out his chewing gum."

Because of his adherence to strict objectivity, his politics have often been the topic of parlor conversation. Cronkite admits he has voted for Republicans as well as Democrats in national elections, but has never divulged who and when. He prefers to think of himself as a true liberal, that is, one who is not bound to doctrine or committed to a particular point of view. Since he feels he could not be a good Democrat only or a good Republican only, he considers himself an independent, admittedly slightly left of center politically, yet with some conservative views. He opposed the busing of school children to achieve racial balance in the public schools, for instance. Despite his sympathy for America's blacks, he disagreed with the civil disobedience policies of Martin Luther King, Jr. Further, he shared in Richard Nixon's philosophy of law and order but was very disappointed that the former president failed to uphold it by example.

Vietnam 1968

Absolute neutrality is a human impossibility and there have been times when Cronkite has unintentionally violated his preferred objectivity when presenting the news. Ralph Renick, a television news director at Miami's WTVJ, recalls one vivid example of Cronkite's non-verbal editorializing: "I'll never forget the expression on Cronkite's face after his program ran a film of Negro children being beaten by whites in Grenada, Mississippi. He positively recoiled. That hurt look was the most powerful kind of editorializing." Fred Friendly agrees, once remarking, "When the news is bad, Walter hurts; when the news embarrasses America, Walter is embarrassed; when the news is humorous, Walter smiles with understanding."

Perhaps the most extraordinary example of Cronkite's public stand on a controversial issue was at the height of the increasingly unpopular Vietnam war. In 1968, he traveled to Southeast Asia to learn for himself what was going on. He acknowledged privately he was turning against the war, but as he told Ron Powers for a *Playboy* interview, "When I went over there, I didn't know what I was going to report back, actually. I didn't go over to do a hatchet job. I didn't go over to be anti-Vietnam. I had been very disturbed over the lack of candor of the administration with the American public, about the constant misleading statements as to the prospects of victory—the light-at-the-end-of-the-tunnel stuff. I thought—and I still think—that was the most heinous part of the whole Vietnam adventure.

"Then, after the Tet offensive, Johnson, Westmoreland and McNamara were saying we had won a great victory. 'Now we've got them; this was their last great effort.' And it was clearly untrue. That's why I felt I finally had to speak out and advocate a negotiated peace."

After returning from his disturbing trip, Cronkite called on a number of influential politicians to share his objections to the war. Over a long, private luncheon with Robert Kennedy at the senator's Fairfax, Virginia home, Cronkite discovered how deeply opposed Kennedy was to the war. Cronkite tried to convince him on the spot to announce his candidacy for the presidency. Senator Kennedy, on the other hand, was equally impressed with Cronkite's hatred of the war and tried to persuade him to run for office. Senator Kennedy eventually did seek election, of course; in part to voice his opposition to what had generally become known as "Johnson's war."

After the luncheon meeting, Cronkite began assimilating what he had seen in Vietnam and what he had heard in Virginia and compared it with what he had seen and heard coming out of the White House. He listened to his conscience and decided to do something he had never done; he expressed a personal, pointed, anti-administration opinion on the air. He felt "It was time for me to cash in on all this trust people say they have for me." In March 1968, on a special television report—not on his *Evening News* program—he told his audience of his disillusionment with the American policy regarding Vietnam. He urged the U. S. government "to negotiate, not as victors, but as honorable people who lived up to their pledge to defend democracy and did the best they could."

He continued his thesis later, this time on the *Evening News,* declaring, "We have been too often disappointed by the optimism of the American leaders, both in Vietnam and in Washington, to have faith any longer in the silver linings they find in the darkest clouds. It seems now more than ever that the bloody experience of Vietnam is to end in a stalemate."

Author Frank Mankiewicz believes that Cronkite's "clear-eyed reflections" after the Tet offensive made the antiwar movement respectable. "How could you believe LBJ and Westmoreland if Walter Cronkite said it wasn't true?" he asked. General Westmoreland spoke out openly and often condemning Cronkite's unprecedented newscast, and never forgave him for it.

The aftershock of Cronkite's comments were, perhaps, more than he might have expected or even hoped for. Harry Waters of *Newsweek* wrote: "To many, it was as if Lincoln himself had ambled down from his Memorial and joined an anti-war demonstration." Washington was caught totally offguard by Cronkite's assault and, immediately, telephones were ringing all over town.

President Johnson, who was watching the telecast in the White House on a custom-built special triple-screen television receiver that enabled him to view all three major network news programs simultaneously, reportedly turned to his press secretary, George Christian, and remarked, "Well, if I've lost Cronkite, I've lost Middle America." The statement was not an idle one. President Johnson respected Cronkite's honesty and recognized his tremendous influence on his audience.

David Halberstam, a Johnson White House insider, wrote that "it was the first time in American history that a war had been declared over, by an anchorman."

Bill Moyers, another of Johnson's press secretaries, suggested that Cronkite's report was such a setback to the administration's Vietnam policies that Johnson solidified his resolve not to seek re-election in 1968.

Cronkite today doubts that his opinion convinced Johnson to decide to retire, but he believes he might have been wrong in airing his thoughts in such a public way. Richard Salant supported the program, however, because Cronkite had been to Vietnam and had seen the war first-hand. "[Cronkite] felt very strongly about it. I gave in, but he was very unhappy about it."

In the rare instances that Cronkite did express his or his network's opinions, he was careful to label them as such, limiting his comments strictly to matters he considered to be of grave importance to the American public. Examples of these opinions included charges of news management by the White House, cost overruns on the space program, or the misuse of communication satellites.

When, in 1990, Andy Rooney made unflattering remarks about blacks and gays and was suspended from *60 Minutes,* Cronkite defended his friend. Diane Reischel, in the *Dallas Morning News,* wrote that Cronkite feels the affair demonstrates how self-conscious broadcast news has become: "We should by no means become insensitive to the feelings of minority groups of any persuasion. But, on the other hand, we have to be careful not to become so overly sensitive that we lose our sense of proportion in dealing with these stories."

One special documentary that received deserved praise was the *CBS Special Report: D-Day Plus Twenty Years* Cronkite hosted in 1964. He and his guest Dwight Eisenhower revisited the shores of Normandy where the former Supreme Allied Commander re-evaluated the massive World War II assault against Nazi forces. As Cronkite gently directed General Eisenhower's recollections, a historic time capsule was recorded for posterity. As the two walked along the beaches or drove a jeep over the battlefields and through the American cemetery, the former president paid tribute to the

hundreds of Americans who fell in battle there. Especially unfor-
gettable and moving was the final helicopter-mounted camera pull-
back shot of the General and the former war correspondent, seated
on a low stone wall, the markers on the American graves behind
them ever widening, until the two men were lost in a sea of white
crosses and stars of David.

*   *   *

Throughout his long journalistic career, Cronkite has interviewed most of the world's leaders, including every U.S. president
from Harry Truman, whose courage he admired greatly, to Ronald
Reagan, whose presidency he dismisses as "an unthinking time"
when the country was under the spell of a likable personality.

On June 17, 1974, he flew to Zurich, Switzerland, to be the
first member of the free world's press to interview Soviet dissident
and author, Alexander Solzhenitsyn. Cronkite was enormously
pleased with the meeting and for years, the photograph of the two
men together was the only one he displayed in his CBS office.

If he were to single out one genuine "scoop" in his sizable list
of spectaculars, Cronkite would probably have to name the role he
played in opening the dialogue between Menachem Begin and
President Anwar Sadat of Egypt, who, next to West Germany's
Willy Brandt, was the world leader he most respected. Israel and
Egypt had been enemies since the time of Moses, but Cronkite
thought the two men could help change their countries' history of
hatred one for the other.

For three weeks, after Begin indicated he would welcome a
visit from Sadat, some members of the three U.S. networks who
knew the principals personally tried to persuade the two leaders to
put their ancient grudges behind them and agree to a meeting.
Cronkite was successful in his efforts to get them to prepare a
video-taped exchange of ideas to be aired on CBS News. Cronkite
was also able to extract an agreement from Sadat to visit Israel to
discuss peace negotiations if, the Egyptian president told him, the
invitation were formally given. Prime Minister Begin passed along
to ABC's Peter Jennings the hoped-for invitation and it was then,
via a live satellite hook-up with the two Mid-Eastern leaders, that
an insistent Walter Cronkite persuaded Sadat to say he would go
to Israel. It was a monumental accomplishment and ABC News

president Roone Arledge spoke for the millions who saw the event as a possible solution to the centuries-old disputes in that world hot-spot: "CBS ought to be congratulated. It was dynamite TV!"

Cronkite modestly played down his part in arranging the meetings: "I don't see anything so extraordinary about it. It was just a normal day's work in news gathering. I don't think a journalist should become involved in high-level diplomacy, but it is a journalist's duty to pursue his diplomatic pronouncements. I wasn't trying to get this meeting started. My official attitude is, 'I couldn't care less about it,' though I can't help believing it will be important and helpful. Maybe we were catalysts. But then, maybe they would have gotten together without us."

Cronkite and ABC's Barbara Walters were among the correspondents who flew on President Sadat's presidential jet from Egypt to Tel Aviv for the historic meeting. It was evident that the Egyptian president enjoyed enormously the company of his television news celebrities. He provided them with a light meal of roast beef sandwiches, cheese and coffee, along with an exuberant exchange of conversation and jokes during the flight. The following month, Cronkite, his wife and mother were special guests at a luncheon for Prime Minister Begin at Israel's embassy in Washington.

More praise for Cronkite's skill as an interviewer came about as a result of the three milestone telecasts with former President Lyndon Johnson, for which CBS News was critically said to have paid $300,000. The meeting was taped at the LBJ ranch just ten days before Johnson's death. The two Texans were old friends, despite Cronkite's overt objections to the Vietnam War that Johnson staunchly defended in the interview. That he refused to repudiate any of his public statements on the Asian war was, in Cronkite's words, "one of the disappointments of the interview." Cronkite had hypothesized, once Johnson was out of office, he would say something like: " 'Well, there were some points where I think we went wrong; there were some things I did I wish, looking back on it, I hadn't done.' But that never happened, either in personal conversation or in the interviews."

By Cronkite's own admission, perhaps the worst interviews he ever conducted were the two with Chicago Mayor Richard Daley. During the infamous 1968 Chicago Democratic Convention, newsmen and networks were fair game: twenty-one reporters were clubbed by policemen so severely that several had to be hospital-ized. Mike Wallace was bodily thrown off the convention floor and Dan Rather was grabbed by one of Daley's security guards. After an unpleasant verbal exchange ("If you're not going to arrest me, take your hands off me!"), Rather was then punched in the stomach and knocked to the floor by Daley's "security guards," as millions watched on live television. Cronkite, who sat helplessly in the CBS news booth during the Rather episode, said angrily of Daley's goons, "If I may be permitted to say so, Dan, I think we've got a bunch of thugs here." Cronkite further charged that the convention officials were trying to prevent the free flow of information from Chicago to the rest of the country.

Chet Huntley said much the same thing in a commentary he made on NBC radio during that hot August in Chicago: "The hos-tility toward any kind of criticism, and the fear of telling how it is, has become too much, and it becomes our duty to speak out. The significant part of all of this is the undeniable manner in which Chicago police are going out of their way to injure newsmen and prevent them from filming or gathering information on what is going on."

The innumerable acts of violence perpetrated by the Chicago police against members of the press, as well as the obvious planting of Daley stooges on the convention floor, made the Democratic Convention a nightmare for all who were trying to cover it. The *New York Times'* editorial staff wrote: "Not since the gangster days of a generation ago has the reputation of the city of Chicago been so tarnished as it has been during the past week while playing host to the Democratic National Convention."

It was at this time that Cronkite chose to meet the Chicago mayor on camera. He requested the first interview with Daley, which was looked forward to by colleagues who were counting on Cronkite to present their grievances to the arrogant, ruthless politi-cal demagogue, but "Cronkite was not much of an adversary," one disappointed contemporary angrily wrote. "As Mayor Daley de-fended his 'security guards,' even chastising CBS in what was an interminable monologue . . . Cronkite, with eyes darting, fidgeted with his pencil and ended up commending the politeness and gen-eral friendliness of the Chicago Police Department. Daley lied and Walter Cronkite became a cowering reporter."

Cronkite felt the stings from all quarters—primarily from himself, the way he had let Daley manipulate him and the interview, and from his colleagues who had come under the iron fist of Daley's Chicago and whom he had let down. He was unable to reconcile himself with the knowledge that he had performed uncourageously. In an uncharacteristically weak defense that Daley "had not been objective and that he, as a newsman, had backed away from the important issues in his attempt to remain neutral," Cronkite admitted, "I'm a softball pitcher when it comes to interviews." He had failed and no real purpose had been served during the Daley encounter.

Cronkite requested another interview with the intention of playing a harder game, but without embarrassing his guest, as has always been one of his rules.

The follow-up interview was also a failure. As Cronkite reflected on the second disastrous meeting, he said he had felt the climate of the convention made objectivity an impossibility and he feared he would "get involved in a debate, a dialogue with Daley. My intention was to give him a platform, which I felt he was entitled to, to state his position," but the situation again seemed to be beyond his control. "I was, to begin with, nonplused and flabbergasted by [Daley's] arrival. It was not scheduled for that time. He walked into the studio with his phalanx of followers with no advance notice to me at all. I looked up and there he was, climbing into the seat. I started by doing exactly what I'd intended to do, turn it over to him, and, as we got toward the end I couldn't hold my peace any longer and I began asking him questions and then I realized I had violated my own rule. I was deeply involved emotionally. I was seeking desperately to maintain my own objectivity . . . and I got angry and . . . it was very, very badly done."

On September 1, top executives of ten of the nation's largest newspapers and television networks sent a string of protests to Mayor Daley regarding the official maltreatment of newsmen. The convention was ended, unfortunately, and the complaints fell on deaf ears.

The pressures of the 1968 convention manifested themselves on Cronkite in yet another manner—he resigned on camera. One of the CBS executives thought he was using the word "erosion" too often and passed him a note to cease and desist. Cronkite passed back a note: "I quit!" and was on his feet, removing his headset. He had reached for his jacket and was heading for the door before cooler heads calmed him down and led him back to his anchor chair.

He later admitted he wouldn't have really quit: "I was never going to get to the door." Some felt he may have been responding to a subconscious, post–1964 convention resentment (the year he was replaced by Roger Mudd and Robert Trout) he harbored against CBS.

*   *   *

The polls have repeatedly indicated the trust viewers have felt for Cronkite over the years, but what of his colleagues, both at CBS and at other networks? The writer interviewed many of Cronkite's contemporaries in an effort to learn some of the reasons they and the viewers have had such faith in him and to discover the attributes they believe have contributed to his position as Dean of network newsmen.

Richard Salant, president of CBS News from 1961 until 1978, has known Cronkite since 1952, when the former joined the network. They frequently play tennis and socialize together, and Mr. Salant jokingly added, when he was interviewed in 1974, he had a daughter who once had a crush on Cronkite's son, Chip. The following extract from Mr. Salant's comments reveal some of his feelings for Cronkite's success: "His outstanding characteristic as a journalist is that he is a thorough professional. He is something a great deal more than a reader [of the news]—he is a journalist. He is objective, both in his on-the-air appearances and in his management role. He is competitive in the old journalistic sense. He wants to be first if he can, to be more accurate than anybody else.

"He not only is the anchorman on the *Evening News,* but feels, quite properly, that he should never lose touch with the reportorial areas—that he should get out in the field and cover stories first-hand.

"Walter has gotten where he is because, well, because he is as good as he is, because he is as professional as he is.

"Walter's not only a great professional journalist; he is a delightful companion. He's just fun to be with, he and his wife both."

Bill Downs was even more straightforward in expressing his regards for his World War II correspondent chum: "He's a goddammed good newsman! He's responsible, hard-working, imaginative. He knows where to go for stories and has built up his contacts and sources and I think he's proving that now, and the reason he's the most trusted man in the United States, according to one poll, is that he's trustworthy. It's that simple."

Dr. Frank Stanton was president of the CBS network for twenty-eight years. He naturally had high praise for his star newsman, and believed, in order to assay properly Cronkite's qualities, "You have to start with his general competence. This is a highly selective business that he is in, and the competitive process has a lot to do with the position where he is today. And that goes back to his ability to communicate with people. It starts out that Walter's a damned good communicator—and not all journalists are good communicators. He has journalistic skills of considerable magnitude—and he's an excellent communicator."

Harry Reasoner achieved national fame as Cronkite's alter ego when the latter was on vacation or special assignments. In their years together at CBS, Reasoner grew to respect Cronkite's expertise and competence and with his usual tongue-in-cheek wit, said: "The basic thing is, you don't believe Walter Cronkite would lie to you any more than Heidi would, and that is as true of his colleagues who know him, as the people in general. He's a solid, professional reporter.

"And he's also interesting in that he's the first major figure to come into the television age. Murrow's status was incomparable, but Murrow was created by World War II and radio, even though he came on into television. But Walter, after he left the wire service reporting, moved along into television. He's a television man and he knows how to use it.

"Walter is not a commentator. He believes as strongly as I do in being objective. I suppose if you watched him regularly over the years—from out in the country somewhere—you would have the feeling that he hates bullies where he finds them in the United States and elsewhere in the world. He hates liars. He hates pretension and he hates phonies. He is determined to report these things where he finds them. But he does as much as he can—I think successfully—to keep his personal opinions out of his broadcasts."

In a similar sentiment, the *New York Times* observed, "People know that newspapers can make mistakes. But they are convinced that Walter Cronkite has never lied to them."

Ron Powell wrote: "Good old Walter Cronkite, with that damn corny little mustache and those sad bassett-hound eyes . . . talked plain language to twenty million Americans every night on the news . . . looked less like an Eastern intellectual than a Tulsa general practitioner, [and had] the extremely annoying habit of popping up in opinion polls everywhere as the most trusted man in America."

It was the 1966 Oliver Quayle survey that showed Cronkite to be the most trusted figure in America. According to the thesis of a *Time* cover story the same year, he was "the single most convincing and authoritative figure in television news." If these conclusions are to be believed and if television is the powerful force most experts believe it to be—for good or for ill—and if Victor Hugo was correct in his statement, "Nothing is so powerful as an idea whose time has come," then Walter Cronkite had at his fingertips more power and more potential for influencing more people than any person who ever lived. Novelist Kurt Vonnegut wrote in 1981, "Walter Cronkite could have been president of the country just as George Washington in his own day could have become king." Even Lyndon Johnson predicted that "if Cronkite said on television what he said on the radio he could be the most powerful man in America."

When the news services mistakenly reported that Cronkite had agreed to be John Anderson's 1980 vice-presidential running mate, he raised hopes of the electorate and frightened serious contenders. The terrifying thought that a non-aligned, totally honest candidate might be running for political power was more than many PACs or politicians could handle.

It is to Cronkite's everlasting credit that he obviously recognized the might he possessed and, more importantly, the responsibility he had during the nineteen years he was anchorman for CBS News. Despite his undisputed and potentially unlimited power, he consistently, rigorously and conscientiously refrained from overstepping the boundaries he had set for himself.

In giving his viewers just the news, straight and unadorned, Cronkite believed they would form their own opinions. Even though the following comment was made in the wake of Watergate, it typifies his simple basic philosophy of his role as a reporter and, indeed, all newsmen: "Our job is to hold up the mirror—to tell and show the public what has happened and then it is the job of the people to decide whether they have faith in their leaders or government."

Kenn Venit, vice-president and senior consultant for Primo Newservice, Inc., believes news program viewers like to see news anchors as surrogate family members. In particular, Venit reports, viewers want people they can trust and feel comfortable with; they want to feel that they are being read to directly, and they want to feel emotions are being shared. Walter Cronkite's projected image met and unquestionably surpassed the standards of Venit's research. His approach was not so much a cold and disembodied television network news reader as a caring and concerned Victorian father, who gathered his family around him in the parlor after dinner to read the newspaper aloud and explain the day's events.

Venit stresses the word "comfort" in explaining why some newscasters seem to be more successful than others. "The tone of voice that an anchor uses and the inflection and body language send signals to viewers. And as viewers receive them from people who get through to them, those are the people they most prefer to watch." Few would maintain that Walter Cronkite did not meet all the foregoing criteria.

The results of Cronkite's attempts at strict adherence to objectivity have been enormous. Even in 1990, nine years off the air, according to another "Ratings Poll," which tested the popularity of 102 broadcasters, he was still voted the most likable news person in the country.

When he was doing his nightly news program, Cronkite once remarked, "Every day somebody says to me, 'My mother won't believe anything until Walter Cronkite says it's so!'" Then, as now, he is the platinum yardstick by whom newscasters are measured.

The unabashed devotion and confidence his viewers displayed led one television critic to declare, in a rather generous moment, "Viewers rarely recall or relish a Cronkite statement. They believe it instead." Jack Paar carried this theme a sacrilegious step further on his NBC *Tonight* show by jokingly confessing, "I'm not sure that I believe in God, but I do believe in Walter Cronkite."

"I Was the Newsroom"

The Young Reporter

I never had the ambition to be something. I had the ambition to do something.

—Walter Cronkite

WALTER Leland Cronkite, Jr., was the only child of a St. Joseph, Missouri, dentist, a descendant of one Herck Siboutzen Krankheyt, a Dutchman who settled in New Amsterdam in 1642. Walter's mother, Helen Lena Fritsche, was a descendant of Germans who emigrated to the United States in the nineteenth century. Her grandfather had the dubious distinction of owning the first cigar factory west of the Mississippi River, in Leavenworth, Kansas.

When President Woodrow Wilson reluctantly committed American troops to fight in the First World War, Dr. Cronkite joined the army as a First Lieutenant with the 140th Infantry. Born November 4, 1916, Walter was only seven months old when his father took his commission and was ordered to Kansas City, Missouri, where Dr. Cronkite was to be stationed as a dental surgeon during the remainder of the war and, coincidentally, where Mrs. Cronkite's family lived. The new location so suited the Cronkites that they remained there after the war; Dr. Cronkite established a private practice and the family lived in Kansas City for ten years, until 1928.

Dr. Cronkite's specialty was restoration dentistry. In those days, there were few laboratories dentists could turn to for prosthetics. The work was done by the doctors themselves or by their trained assistants. Since Dr. Cronkite chose not to hire assistants, he did all his own work: casting gold inlays, making molds, dentures, and all the myriads of fine, detailed sculpting required of a skilled dentist. Because of Dr. Cronkite's heavy work schedule, he was rarely home except at night, when Walter was getting ready for bed. If Walter wanted to see his father or talk with him, he had to visit him at his office.

There was never a close father-son bond between the two. Walter, nevertheless, would sit around in his father's laboratory, chatting about his friends or his dogs or sports, not expecting much response from his father and dismissing the one-sided conversation as necessary because of his father's concentration on his work. Even when he was home, Dr. Cronkite preferred to read his books rather than talk with his son. Walter resigned himself to the fact that his father was not particularly interested in building any sort of relationship with him. Because of Dr. Cronkite's preference for intellectual and professional pursuits, and his predeliction for solitude, there were few family outings, picnics, or things of that nature. Walter's mother redoubled her efforts to see that her precocious son's needs were met and that his insatiable curiosity was satisfied.

In 1928 the Cronkites moved to Houston, where Dr. Cronkite had accepted a teaching position on the faculty of the University of Texas Dental School. He also set up a private practice, which would keep him even more isolated from his family.

The shifting of locales precipitated a dramatic and even traumatic change in ideologies: Texas in the 1920s aggressively exhibited a more intense atmosphere of racial prejudice than Kansas City had. Even at the age of seven, Walter was becoming more aware of the overt hostility southern whites felt toward blacks and Mexicans. He had read in the newspapers and magazines and heard whispers about the hatred and violence that had led to arson, false witness, castrations, shotgun murders, and public lynchings. He had been protected from first-hand knowledge of such social injustices in Kansas City, but in Houston he would be graphically exposed to the harsh feelings held by many middle and upper-class whites toward ethnic minorities.

It was Walter's mother more than any other single person in his early years who quietly preached to him the gospel of objectivity, liberalism, and tolerance, but one of the most powerful episodes in the young man's pragmatic education was demonstrated by his father.

Soon after arriving in Houston, Ron Powers wrote for *Playboy*, the Cronkites were invited to a small social gathering at the home of a wealthy and influential Texan. The scene of the reception was on the large front porch of an elegant Victorian house. The conversation was polite and the company congenial. The host had ordered ice cream from a local shop and, as was the custom in those days, it was delivered by a boy on a motorcycle. On this occasion, the delivery boy was black, not in itself unusual, but since there was no alley in that exclusive neighborhood, the delivery was made at the front of the house. There was an unwritten law then that "inferiors" always went to the back of a white person's house. The Cronkite's host became livid with rage at this open and unthinkable breach of Southern decorum. He jumped to his feet, raced to the boy and hit him in the face with his fist, shouting, "That'll teach you niggers to walk up to a white man's front door!"

The Cronkites watched the scene in disbelief and horror. Dr. Cronkite was stunned and outraged at the demonstration of racial hatred and violence. He sprang to his feet and announced to his wife and son that they were leaving. Dr. Cronkite was so furious that Walter thought his father meant the family was leaving Houston, not just the party.

Years later, when he was reminded of that unpleasant incident, which was indelibly impressed on his mind, Cronkite recollected, "My father was very definitely a liberal in those days, or at least a populist. Most people get more conservative as the years go on, but that was not true for him."

Powers also related another experience similar to the episode on the front porch that involved Cronkite on a more personal and tragic level. He was working as a drugstore delivery boy with two other boys his age, both of whom were black. The three became good friends, but since they knew well the feelings in Houston about such relationships, they judiciously restricted their association to the confines of the drugstore. There they were free to joke and laugh and shoot craps in the back room or match pennies in the alley behind the store.

Walter, at age 4,
modeling a leather
coat ...

... and a Buster
Brown suit.

Studio portrait at
age 6, Kansas City

Boy Scout in 1929
with Lady

One night, one of the boys was making a routine ice cream delivery in a white neighborhood. Leaving his bicycle at the curb, he had to walk between two houses in order to reach his customer's back door. Again, there was no alley, or "neutral zone" for the young man to use, so he walked across the customer's back lawn. A next-door neighbor saw the black intruder in the all-white neighborhood, raced for his shotgun and killed the delivery boy with not so much as a warning. The man, claiming he thought the boy was a peeping Tom, was never seriously questioned nor punished for the cold-blooded murder. A white man did not have to defend his thoughts or actions against blacks in the South. Cronkite recalls that "this guy was no more a peeping Tom that I was—maybe less. Of course, if he'd gone to the front of the house, the guy who ordered the ice cream might have shot him." Retelling the grisly events of that day in his young life still brings a shudder and a sigh: "I almost never got over that."

*   *   *

During her son's formative years, Mrs. Cronkite took her parental responsibilities seriously. She recognized Walter's precocity and spent a great deal of time with him, actively encouraging his mental and social development. She secured him a part in his first play, "Kitten Tom Goes to Court," at age four, and filled her family photo album with pictures of him throughout his childhood.

His early years were not unlike those of other middle-class children his age: he played games with neighborhood children, climbed trees, swam and played football. Dogs were frequently kept as family pets, two favorites being Lady and Patch, both wire-haired terriers. Walter spent hours dressing them in old clothes and funny hats and teaching them tricks. He especially enjoyed having Lady pull him on roller skates down the sidewalk in front of their house. Some neighbors complained to Mrs. Cronkite that the little dog was being mistreated, that the leash was choking her. Mrs. Cronkite politely disagreed with them and didn't stop the practice because, she remembers happily, "They both enjoyed it so."

During his Houston years, the family lived a distance from Walter's grandparents, who were still in Kansas City. Many summers of his childhood were spent with his mother's parents, where he was surrounded by cousins, uncles and aunts. One uncle in particular, Mrs. Cronkite's brother Ed Fritsche, developed such a warm and close relationship with Walter that Uncle Ed became somewhat a surrogate father to him. Fritsche was a salesman whom Cronkite fondly remembers as being "the most gregarious man I've ever known in my life. He charmed everybody, and in two minutes, he was a deep, close friend of theirs and knew their personal history: their ages and marital status of all their children. He knew where they lived and everything else. He was a very incredible man in that regard."

Going to church was part of Cronkite's growing up, being what he calls a "Presbyterian-Lutheran kind of Calvinistic background." He strongly defends the importance he believes religion has made in the way he approaches life. He told interviewer Martin Cohen that his parents were extremely loyal to their religious convictions and applied those beliefs to their personal codes of conduct. His Sunday school attendance, Bible reading and church participation were not idle activities for him either: he was expected to practice morality at home, too. The principle of honesty was of prime importance to his parents and quickly became paramount in his personal conduct.

Cronkite told a *Parade* interviewer of the time he convinced a local druggist to let him buy a watch on credit. When his mother learned of it, she took the watch from him, paid the druggist the dollar Walter owed for it, and kept it until it was paid for.

"Don't you see?" she asked him, "You don't know how you're going to earn the money. There's no outright dishonesty here, but you're flirting with it. It's one of those gray areas, Walter. Be careful of gray—it might be grime." Throughout the years in his personal life as well as broadcasting the news, Cronkite remembered his mother's admonition—to avoid the gray—pulling back from the presentation of only half the facts.

His father embraced Unitarianism about the time the family moved to Houston, but Walter was not especially interested in a religion which appeared to him to be that loosely defined. With encouragement from his parents to find a church which met his own needs, he set about visiting various churches in his hometown. A couple of years later, when he was twelve, he joined a Boy Scout troop that met in an Episcopal church. Most of the members of his

Walter's Father in
World War I Uniform

Walter's Favorite
Uncle
Ed Fritsche
Pebble Beach, 1951

troop attended that church and, as time went on, his interest grew in that religion and he eventually became an Episcopalian.

All through his public school years, Cronkite was considered a good student. He had a quick mind and an inquisitive nature that spurred him on in his intrinsic need to know about things. Apart from assignments at school, he read widely from many types of literature. As a youngster, he was a constant reader: "I picked up anything that was around. I read everything, from my father's medical books to the typical boys' stories: *Boy's Life* magazine, the Mark Tidd stories, the *American Boy,* Tom Swift, Tom Slade and more serious stuff. I was always a newspaper reader, which was kind of unique in those days."

While enrolled at Sidney Lanier Junior High in Houston, Walter was a member of the traffic patrol and the band. At various times he played drums, clarinet and saxophone. He preferred the latter two instruments and still owns a saxophone. He occasionally entertains the Walter Mitty thought of brushing up on it so he can accept the occasional invitations his orchestra leader friends offer to perform publicly.

Athletically, young Walter was strictly of the sandlot league. He played baseball and football in neighborhood games, but was never good enough to make school teams, except once. He tried out for and made the track team at San Jacinto High School, but before he could compete, he pulled a groin muscle so severely that he had to drop off the team. Later on, he began playing tennis, a sport he still enjoys.

When the family bought a combination radio-phonograph-recorder, Walter enjoyed standing before the machine, microphone in hand, pretending to be a sports announcer, broadcasting imaginary football and baseball games. His mother served as his cheering section, encouraging him in a childhood exercise for an activity that he would actually engage in briefly in his checkered career.

Once, when he was about three, his mother, as most parents do, asked him what he wanted to be when he grew up. He answered enthusiastically, "I want to be a motorcycle cop, so I can arrest people!"

Since his father, grandfather and a paternal uncle were dentists, it would seem natural that Walter might follow that profession, but there was no pressure from his family to choose that or any

High School
Graduation Portrait,
1933
San Jacinto High
School
Houston

With Mother in
New York City
Mother's Day, 1954

particular vocation. He was grateful that he was not expected to join in what was, by then, a family tradition. He did not want to be a dentist and today dismisses the notion entirely by flatly declaring, "I had no desire to look in people's mouths."

As he was growing up, Cronkite admits he was intrigued by many possible job choices. About the time he began junior high school, the *American Boy* magazine ran a series of fictionalized short stories on careers and he became fascinated by an article about mining engineers. The idea of exploring and taming rough country in faraway places excited him, so he determined to follow that profession. It was not long, however, before he gave up that dream when the hard and cold reality of physics began giving him trouble; he couldn't even figure out the principle of the pulley. He considered other areas: laboratory researcher (inspired by his father's line of work), law, and even becoming an Episcopal minister. He laughingly confesses that the latter two choices appealed to him "because of a certain sense of ham in me."

It was in a high school journalism class that Cronkite began showing a genuine and lasting interest in a possible career. His teacher recognized his fine sense of awareness in his environment, a vivid imagination, a healthy curiosity about so many things and a good writing style. She encouraged him to work on the school paper and the yearbook. Journalism, he happily discovered, permitted him the opportunity to follow actively his divergent interests.

In 1933, he graduated from San Jacinto High. He didn't order a class ring because he didn't care for its design. His parents told him to choose one he liked and they would buy it for his graduation gift. He selected a gold one that he still owns and it is the only jewelry he wears.

*   *   *

In the fall of the year he graduated from high school, Cronkite enrolled at the University of Texas in Austin. He resisted the urge to major in journalism because by then his interests had switched to politics. He chose political science as a major and economics as a minor, but read Henry Beetle Hough's *Country Editor* at night—a work that was a bible and an eventual career road map for him.

Young Cronkite jumped fully into college life: he pledged Chi Phi fraternity; played intramural sports; was active on the university

newspaper, the *Daily Texan*; joined the campus dramatic organization, the Curtain Club; and participated in student government activities. Since he had refused any financial aid from his parents, he
took two concurrent jobs to pay his tuition: as a sports announcer
for a local radio station and campus correspondent for the *Houston
Press*. A little later, Powers writes, he took on yet another job, this
one in a bookie joint. In discussing his brief stint in that ignoble
position, he recalls he was instructed by one of the managers to 'Sit
back here in this room and, as this stuff comes in, you read it out
over the P.A. system.' Well, I'd never been in a place like this
before, so I gave them the real Graham McNamee approach on
this, describing the running of the race and all. A mean character
ran the place—a guy named Fox—and he looked like one. He came
dashing into the room and asked me, 'What in the hell do you think
you're doing? We don't want entertainment! We just want the
facts!'" By mutual agreement, Cronkite and the Fox parted company.

During the two years he worked for the *Houston Press,*
Cronkite was asked to expand his assignments by covering the capitol beat for the news bureau of the Scripps-Howard syndicate,
which owned the *Press*. In order to keep up with his studies, remain
active on campus and fulfill his journalistic obligations, he had to
stay in constant motion. He slept little and studied less. Each night
he wrote his column for the college's daily paper, attended classes
in the mornings and then dashed over to Austin to cover the proceedings when the legislature was in session. His political science
professors anxiously awaited his return each afternoon for a report
on capitol business. They were teaching theory, but he was dealing
directly with real-life Texas politics.

Inevitably, the killing pace Cronkite had set for himself began
to take its toll: he was spending more time on his reporting assignments than he was on his studies. He missed classes and his grades
suffered. In his junior year, he arrived at the point where he was
going to have to decide if he wanted a degree or a vocation.

In 1935, a diploma was not required for many good jobs. He
knew he was not going to be a doctor, lawyer, or engineer, so he
correctly believed he could survive without a college degree. Too,
he felt if he could pay his own way at the university, as he had been

doing, he had proven he could make a living as a reporter. After carefully weighing his options, he dropped out of school.

At the time, the decision did not bother him much, but he lived to regret it in later years. He confessed in a 1963 interview that he "could have bent the books a little harder, but covering the state capitol was a lot more exciting than studying political science in school. Besides, since I never went to class, I was getting awful grades." In 1974, he told Dick Cavett in a televised interview it was not just his failure to graduate that bothered him. He explained, "I got so busy being a newspaper man that it all seemed worthless back at the university, which was a mistake. I'm sorry I did that. I'd like to have had a couple more years of intensive formal education." In a 1977 *McCall's* article, daughter Kathy recalled a similar discussion with her father after she had decided to drop out of school. He told her that the absence of a degree had always made him feel a little inadequate, that he had turned down several offers to teach at various universities, particularly back at the University of Texas, because of his youthful mistake. When his daughter reminded him that even without a college degree he had become the greatest newscaster in America, he replied, "Yes, but if I had gotten a formal education, I could have been the Kaiser!"

*   *   *

After leaving college, Cronkite took a full-time position with the *Houston Press*. As a cub reporter, he was given countless routine assignments he felt were of little significance. He was also made religion editor and assistant to the amusements editor. The fragmented, tedious duties made him feel he was not being challenged, but he was still young, energetic and reasonably philosophical, so he kept plodding along. Even though he spent most of his work days chasing fires and covering standard hometown news stories, there were, however, a few memorable moments to break up the otherwise mundane job. Once, when he learned where Clyde Barrow—of Bonnie and Clyde fame—was hiding out from the law, he conned his way into the gangster's hideout. There, while Barrow and his partners in crime kept a sharp lookout for federal agents, young Cronkite shared a beer with the infamous bank robber as he got his story.

Soon the sedentary assignments at the *Press* began to bore him. He had dropped out of school to be where the news was breaking, and Houston, he decided, was not the place to be. He began looking about for employment elsewhere. While visiting his grandparents in Kansas City in 1936, he came to the conclusion that the pastures looked greener in radio. He learned of an opening for a news and sports editor at KCMO, a 100-watt station in Kansas City. He went for an interview, was impressed by what he saw and took the job on the spot, even though he hadn't even resigned from his job in Houston. Excitedly, he wired his mother (who had divorced Dr. Cronkite earlier that year) the following telegram on May 30:

Dear Mother:

Have taken a $15 a week job effective on Wednesday. Promised $25 per week within short time. Combined news and announcing. Looks like good setup. Will write details tomorrow.

Love, Walter

In the early days of radio, reporters and announcers were rarely sent to news or sporting events for live coverage. Since remote broadcasts were too complicated and expensive for small stations with limited budgets to cover, a standard procedure for covering games was universally followed: An announcer sat in a booth at the station as the sport was being played. Wire services assigned men to the game who sent play-by-play copy to their subscribers. Teletype machines at local stations printed the action, allowing announcers to read the game on the air. All things considered, the procedure was a rather dry and boring one, but totally acceptable in those pre-television days.

There was never any temptation for Cronkite to follow the popular "rip and read" practice that was standard then and is still used today. For an imaginative closet thespian like Cronkite, the challenge of recreating actual ballgames on the air, as he had done as a child for his mother, was a *tour de force* never heard of in Kansas City, nor anywhere else, for that matter. Working with a sound effects man, a prodigious knowledge of sports and a phenomenal talent for improvisation, he introduced Kansas City to football—Cronkite style. He choreographed his sportscasts with the care and finesse a Balanchine uses in working out intricate ballet maneuvers. In his quest for realism, Cronkite asked the schools whose games he would be covering for photographs of their stadiums, recordings of their bands, weekly plans for bleacher-stand card stunts and the names and numbers of their athletes. He didn't stop there. To "color" his announcing, he frequently called the wives of Kansas City's well-known sports fans to find out what their husbands would be wearing to the games. As a particular game progressed, Cronkite would exclaim over the cacophony of recorded football bands and crowd noises in the background, "Why, there's Dr. John Smith in his new camel's hair coat!" Then, over the din, he would shout, "How d'ya like the game so far, Doc?" or, "Hey, there's ol' Billy Brown in his new gray fedora! What did you think of that play, Billy?" Once, when the wire service broke down, he ad-libbed for a full twenty minutes until the lines were restored.

(Much has been written about another sports announcer who began his career in a way similar to Cronkite's. His career took him beyond broadcasting, however, to modeling, the movies, and, eventually, the White House.)

Cronkite, who quite obviously reveled in his make-believe ball games, reconstructed the sporting events with such authenticity and enthusiasm that he became an overnight sensation with the KCMO audience. He gained such a following and reputation that the Federal Communication Commission, likewise, took notice. It wasn't quite sure if what the zealous sportscaster was doing was strictly legal. It objected openly, but could not censure his broadcasts since it was never able to determine just what laws, if any, were being broken.

As involved as he had become in radio, however, Cronkite didn't stay interested for very long because, among other reasons, he felt radio news was too shallow. His departure from KCMO was hastened after a dispute with the station's management over the broadcasting of a fire that had not been verified, but had been phoned in by the station manager's wife. It is to Cronkite's credit that the story proved to be false. He began early avoiding "the gray areas."

In retrospect, Cronkite's pronouncement of radio's superficial nature was not an unfair assessment. In the 1930s, that medium offered lighter, entertaining, vaudeville-born programming, designed to help lift the spirits of Americans weighed down by the otherwise oppressive Great Depression. Radio's general accessibility and ability to offer financially-strapped listeners a no-cost laugh or diversion to escape momentarily the harshness of life did not go unnoticed or unappreciated. The direction radio should take past levity, however, was not certain. The Federal Radio Act of 1927 and the Communications Act of 1934 seriously limited radio's scope and, in effect, denied it the freedoms promised in the First Amendment. In many ways, the frustrations Cronkite felt in 1930 are the frustrations he and his colleagues feel today: Freedom of the Press does not apply to radio or television.

                              *   *   *

By 1937, twenty-year-old Walter Cronkite had graduated from high school, dropped out of college, worked for a major newspaper, witnessed the divorce of his parents, and quit his newspaper for a radio station. Either of the jobs he had held were possible careers for him, but he was frustratingly dissatisfied with his short professional life to this point. Admittedly, he was a dreamer, but still a pragmatist. He was assiduous, but knew when and how to relax; ambitious, yet not ruthless. Even though he was confident there was a niche for him somewhere in broadcasting or print journalism, he was unable to determine exactly what it was he wanted. For the next sixteen years he searched unstintingly for his destiny—a quest that ended in 1953. Jumping from job to job, city to city, state to state and even continent to continent, Cronkite embarked on a modern odyssey that Richard Gehman appropriately entitled "The Wanderings of Walter Cronkite."

After leaving KCMO, Cronkite returned to Texas, taking a position with the United Press, staying just long enough to open a bureau in El Paso. A few months later, still in 1937, he gave radio another shot, this time at clear-channel station WKY in Oklahoma City, where he worked again as a football announcer. Two months later he made another decision, this time to leave reporting and announcing altogether. His first non-reporting job was as a publicity agent for Texas-based Braniff Airways. For a year, he worked in the

Kansas City office, but he missed journalism too much to stay away from it. In 1939, he rejoined the United Press, where he was assigned, initially, to the Kansas City bureau.

It had been in Kansas City that he finally began to feel some pieces of his personal jigsaw life fitting together. He was employed by the UP as a night editor whose job it was to edit stories from the national trunk lines from the east and west coasts for transmittal to subscribers over all of the United States. He claims today he "didn't just work in the newsroom; I was the newsroom." Working against the clock was one of the constant pressures he had to learn to handle. Speed was important but accuracy was essential. He felt the Kansas City post was one of the most difficult he ever held: "I don't think there's a tougher job than that. In effect, I was making up the front pages for the small dailies." He might well have added that the experience prepared him for his later CBS position as managing editor of the *Evening News,* which made virtually the same demands.

Adding to his growing sense of place during his stay at KCMO in Kansas City was meeting his future wife, Mary Elizabeth Maxwell, a former Agriculture Queen from the University of Missouri. "I spotted Betsy the day she applied for her job," Cronkite remembers. "My desk faced the hallway, so I could look out and see people as they came in. As soon as I saw her, I was intrigued."

Like her future husband, Betsy was in the news business. She got the job Cronkite saw her apply for, being hired to write radio commercials. They were forbidden by the station to fraternize but they became acquainted with each other when she asked him to read a cosmetic advertisement with her on the air:

He: You look like an angel that fell from heaven.
She: I do?
He: You do.
She: It's because I use Richard Hudnut beauty products.

Betsy also edited the women's page for the *Kansas City Journal-Post,* where one of her assignments was writing a column for the lovelorn, "Ask Hope Hudson," Kansas City's version of "Dear Abby." In lighter moments when they were secretly dating (still against company rules—they considered their courtship a daring adventure), the two would write each other's assignments. Cronkite took impish delight in answering letters for the newspaper's female readers, who requested help in solving personal problems.

He transferred again to Texas, but they continued their relationship through long letters. The two young journalists fell in love and began making plans for the future. He would visit her in Kansas City as his schedule permitted. "I would never have gone to visit him," Betsy recalls. "It would have created a scandal!"

She had told him she wanted to quit her job after they were married and devote herself fully to being a housewife. Unfortunately, his salary was inadequate for any such marital plans at the time, so they agreed to postpone their wedding date until he was making $35 a week. The letter-writing romance continued until he received his sought-after raise, and they announced their plans to marry.

The wedding took place on March 30, 1940, in Kansas City's Grace and Holy Trinity Episcopal Cathedral. After a three-week honeymoon in Mexico, the couple returned to Kansas City, where he had taken another job.

Thus, at the age of twenty-three, Walter Cronkite's life continued to take shape. He was married to a kindred spirit who understood his ego and his journalistic needs. Even though the new Mrs. Cronkite was capable of being a successful newswoman in her own right, she was content providing her husband the support he would require to realize his potential. In addition, the years he had spent with the United Press had convinced his company he was a professional in the truest sense of the word, his having boldly demonstrated time after time there was no assignment he could not handle.

The newlyweds settled into their new home on Locust Street in Kansas City, Middle America. There was painting to do, furniture to buy, curtains and draperies to hang. Little did they or any of their contemporaries realize that in less than two years their domestic tranquility would be shattered. Cronkite would be removed from his country for ten years, covering a global conflagration that would shatter their lives and the world—and change them forever.

Addendum

In an effort to understand more how chance or "luck" might have played a hand in Cronkite's charmed life, it may be helpful to consider the evolution of radio broadcasting itself. Since it and he grew up together, the influence of the newscasters and direction radio took had a great impact on his life and career.

*   *   *

Before World War I erupted, "wireless" pioneers — the brilliant entrepreneur and inventor of the wireless, Italian-born Guglielmo Marconi; rapacious and controversial Lee de Forest, American inventor of the audion tube, an early amplifier; the Canadian refiner of the vacuum tube, Reginald Fessenden; American developer of FM radio, Edwin H. Armstrong; and underrated and obscure Nathan B. Stubblefield, who sent the first wireless voice through the air in 1892 — were all making significant advances in what would eventually be known as radio. Similar work was progressing concurrently on the even more spectacular television process, which would transmit wireless moving pictures accompanied with synchronized FM sound.

By the time the United States entered World War I, only seven months before Cronkite's birth, Marconi had sold hundreds of his wireless sets in Europe. Before the "Great War" broke out in Europe, Marconi's enterprise had moved into the North American market, where there were more than 400 ship-based wireless stations, 100 shore stations and more than 1,000 amateur wireless stations operating.

The advent of the war abruptly ended the casual and insouciant manner which had characterized radio's early growth. What had previously been considered an eccentric's plaything became a powerful military weapon with lethal potential. To prevent the passing of secret messages to the Germans, the U.S. Navy, which controlled all American wireless regulations at that time, ordered every amateur station shut down. The navy then nationalized the larger facilities for its own transmission and reception of signals and established military wireless installations at major universities to teach sailors to use the new medium. The smaller stations that had been shut down were dismantled and a moratorium was placed on all broadcasting patents.

Following the signing of the Treaty of Versailles in 1919, which formally ended the hostilities, the navy continued its regulation of the wireless in the belief that radio's sole function was as an instrument for maritime communications. In 1920, however, because of legislation originating in the United States Congress, the navy grudgingly relinquished its domination of wireless operations and radio passed into the hands of private owners.

With the November 2, 1920, broadcast of the Harding-Cox presidential election returns over Westinghouse-owned station KDKA in Philadelphia, the era of commercial broadcasting was inaugurated.

The practice of commenting on the news via radio was initiated by H. V. Kaltenborn in his controversial and short-lived series over New York City's AT&T-owned station WEAF (now WNBC), in 1923. Other famous pioneer radio announcers and news commentators who followed Kaltenborn included Elmer Davis, Lowell Thomas, Edwin Hill, Walter Winchell, Boake Carter, Raymond Graham Swing, Gabriel Heatter, Drew Pearson and Graham McNamee. All of these newscasters were well known to young Cronkite. He admits he imitated them as a youngster and they were an inestimable influence on his career.

To large degree, the progress of radio news' early years of reporting was hampered by established and unscrupulously powerful newspapers that felt threatened by the immediacy and personal appeal which radio could offer and they could not. The owners of these papers exerted pressure in high places to the extent that radio stations, suddenly and without explanation, found themselves cut off from the services of the three major news-gathering agencies: the Associated Press, the International News Service and the United Press International. The ensuing news service embargo on the wireless stations lasted from 1933 until 1935, when the United Press took the initiative and restored its service. The other agencies followed soon after.

In all honesty, it must be admitted that the paranoia of the newspapers was not without substantial grounds, for, from 1920 to 1970, the number of daily newspapers in the United States declined by fourteen per cent, as radio and later television emerged as the foremost source of informing the public. By 1973, some sixty-five per cent of Americans interviewed by a Harris Poll disclosed that they received the majority of their news, especially political information, from television.

Radio continued to grow and develop during the 1920's and 30's, attaining what has become known as its "Golden Age." That dominance ended in 1952, however, when the new medium, television, took over.

"Of Course I Want to Go"

The War Correspondent

Writing is an exhausting and tearing thing. Most of the correspondents actually worked like slaves. Especially was this true of the press association men. The result was that all of us who had been with the war for more than a year grew befogged. We were grimy, mentally as well as physically. We'd drained our emotions until they cringed from being called from hiding. We looked at bravery and death and battlefield waste and new countries almost as blind men, seeing only faintly and not really wanting to see at all. I am not writing this to make heroes of the correspondents, because only a few look upon themselves in any dramatic light whatever. I am writing it to let you know that correspondents, too, can get sick of war—and deadly tired.

—Ernie Pyle

THE PRACTICE of sending messengers into war zones is probably as old as warfare itself. The fate of the soldier who ran the twenty-six miles to Athens, bringing news of the Greek victory at Marathon, is well known. One ancient king had put to death the bearers of news of lost battles. In more recent times, the correspondents were as likely to meet their deaths on the battlefields as were the soldiers.

The American Civil War was reported by such men as artist Winslow Homer and photographer Matthew Brady. These chroniclers and their lesser-known colleagues quite literally risked life and limb to inform the civilian populace of the progress of the various battles. With paintings, sketches, photographs, bulletins and stories sent via the telegraph—which was used extensively during the War Between the States—courier or whatever other means were available to them, these pioneer war correspondents performed their duties with seeming indifference to the dangers constantly threatening them.

World War I was covered in somewhat the same archaic fashion, except that hapless pigeons were trained to deliver messages from the front. The wireless was not used initially, because getting the device into the field was a problem. Marconi developed a "portable" radio for the Italian army, but it was so large and cumbersome it had to be transported on a large flat-bed truck.

By the time the Spanish Civil War erupted, Meyer L. Stein wrote, "live" reporting was a reality. From the comparative safety of a Spanish haystack, H. V. Kaltenborn narrated segments of the fighting in 1936 to herald the advances the Columbia Broadcasting System had made in the wireless. Kaltenborn continued his experimental radio broadcasts on a daily basis for five weeks. Other correspondents from various networks followed suit with sporadic live broadcasts during that bloody prelude to World War II, but few felt that there was a need to expand radio's role in reporting war news.

As the entire European, African and Asian continents erupted into war, the civilian populations anxiously awaited reports from the numberless war zones. American Jews desperately sought news from Germany; gentiles feared for their European cousins as the *Wehrmacht* rolled across the continent; Americans of Asian descent sought news from China as Japan launched its bloody conquests. To help win the information war, the number of correspondents swelled to fulfill the demand.

The men and women who accepted their overseas reporting assignments joined Allied forces as non-combatants, although bombs and bullets were impartial and all too frequently ignored the neutrality of the reporters. Not only were they victims of indiscriminate enemy attacks, the newsmen were often captured, tortured and executed. Of the numerous war correspondents killed during this period, the most famous and universally mourned was Ernie Pyle, who was shot by a Japanese sniper as the indefatigable reporter was covering the war in the Pacific. In the recent war in Vietnam, some twenty newsmen, among them Sean Flynn (Errol Flynn's son), Welles Hangen, Terry Reynolds, Alexander Shemken and Dan Stone were among the killed or missing in action.

From the long list of prestigious American journalists assigned to the European theatre during World War II, with the possible exception of Pyle, it is doubtful if any shared the professionalism or the uncanny perception of Edward R. Murrow. In 1937, at the age of twenty-eight, Murrow was given the position of European Director of CBS. Upon arriving in England, which was to be his base of operations, he faced the responsibility of rescuing radio from the deplorable abyss to which it had sunk.

Radio, as has been noted earlier, was not considered a serious news medium, but a device to entertain the masses with inconsequential drivel. "Radio was not an accepted part of the world of journalism," wrote Murrow biographer Alexander Kendrick. "Radio purveyed news, of a sort, on the periphery of its daily serials and musical programs." Murrow would change all that.

Cronkite, too, Ron Powers reports, has shared some thoughts on the influence Murrow had on radio, on himself in particular and other newsmen in general. "There's no question about it, he's definitely the father figure of this industry, and should be. At the time he was becoming prominent during World War II, there was a great question about which way broadcast news would go. The press services weren't selling their services to broadcasters, for instance, because they didn't believe radio was serious enough to be a proper customer.

"There was an awful lot of clatter of showmanship in radio broadcasting. The telegraphic ticker, the Walter Winchell approach, and a lot of the deep-voice announcer types, reading copy prepared by someone else.

"Ed squared that away pretty quickly, by setting a tremendous example, fighting for the truth, honesty, integrity, and all the proper things.

"What we owe Ed is just absolutely immense."

*   *   *

As the European war heated up, American flying hero Charles A. Lindbergh and the U.S. Ambassador to the Court of St. James, Joseph P. Kennedy, like Britain's Prime Minister Neville Chamberlain and the exiled Duke of Windsor, wanted to make peace with Hitler. Fistfights broke out between Americans of differing opinions as many fell under the influence of these naïve pacifists. Congress was sharply and bitterly divided as President Roosevelt called for mothballed World War I ships to be reactivated to answer England's call for aid.

Murrow felt that unless his countrymen knew the full horror of Nazism, the Storm Troopers might very soon be parading down Pennsylvania Avenue. Consequently, his crisp and often elegant prose was ever brutally honest in his eyewitness coverage of the unprovoked, unrelenting and deadly German raids on London. The first-hand descriptions on "London After Dark," broadcast during actual bombing and rocket attacks on the great British capital city, conveyed vividly to Americans the harsh realities of war. The result of those CBS radio reports was that Americans rejected pacifism and recognized Hitler's bloodthirsty Third Reich for the wicked force it was.

Radio's importance as a news medium was quickly realized and established itself in the nation's consciousness. A record was set for hours of news broadcasts on December 7, 1941, when the Japanese bombed Pearl Harbor. The following day, thousands of Americans crowded around their sets to hear President Roosevelt's call for a declaration of war against the Japanese empire for the day, he said, "that will live in infamy." On D-Day, four years later, the record was broken again. On CBS radio alone, seventeen regularly scheduled programs were pre-empted for a total of five hours of war news in a single day.

*   *   *

A special uniform distinguished the early correspondents from military personnel. The original issue consisted of a standard British officer's olive-drab uniform as the basic unit. There were no indications of nationality, in an attempt to keep the reporters neutral.

In World War II Correspondents' Uniform

Further distinguishing features included a green felt strip with the words "Foreign War Correspondent" embroidered in gold letters sewn to the uniform's upper left sleeve. A two-inch circle of green felt with a gold "C" trimmed the standard officer's hat. A regulation helmet was issued for protection during battle conditions. After the United States entered the war, changes were made for the American correspondents: an American officer's uniform was used, complete with nationality device and officer's insignia on the hat. The "Foreign War Correspondent" patch was sewn to the coat's left pocket and a "C" armband to the upper left sleeve.

On combat missions, each journalist was limited to 125 pounds of personal baggage and a musette bag for carrying a portable typewriter and other writing supplies. Each man was expected to carry enough typing and carbon paper to last for ten days. Since the censorship restrictions required four copies of each story to be filed and distributed to various military officers where possible security leaks were checked, the paper supply often had to be quite large.

Censorship was one of the real headaches which vitally hampered the work of the correspondents. The American Office of War

Information, headed by Elmer Davis, former radio newscaster and personal friend of President Roosevelt, placed exacting standards on the news permitted to leave war zones. The Allied censorship officers worked closely with each other, protecting information that could be helpful to the enemy: numbers and locations of troops, casualties and the like. A reporter or soldier in a war zone would write what seemed to be an innocuous story or letter, only to have it censored with a razor, leaving the page looking like a piece of Swiss cheese.

Neither radio nor Edward Murrow were exempted from the stringent censorship restrictions. When he first requested to make live broadcasts from London, permission was denied. It was feared that some vital information might be inadvertently, or even intentionally, leaked to the enemy.

It should be noted here that those fears were not idle ones. Several correspondents had already been reprimanded for violating the censorship restrictions. There were isolated cases of temporary suspension of newsmen or dismissals. Once, as the Allies were about to invade Paris, a previously-recorded account of the event by CBS correspondent Charles Collingwood was played over the air, but before the actual invasion took place. The newsman and his network were embarrassed and remorseful over the unfortunate event, the Allies furious because they believed security precautions had been violated. After tempers cooled, however, Collingwood and CBS were forgiven: the incident was dismissed as a technical mistake involving bad timing, not an intentional or damaging act of subterfuge.

Not one to be easily dissuaded, Murrow recorded ten pilot broadcasts to demonstrate the effectiveness of live reporting and to testify to his ability to respect the rigorous censorship codes. His request was once again denied. He then appealed directly to his friend Prime Minister Winston Churchill, but to no avail. Murrow even asked some of his influential American friends to work on Churchill. Finally, enough pressure from undisclosed high places (possibly from President Roosevelt) was applied and Murrow was at last permitted to begin his live broadcasts.

Murrow inaugurated his descriptions of the bombings from his special vantage point high atop the BBC building, a location kept secret until after the war. A censor sat in a chair nearby, his finger nervously poised above a squelch button on a special voice-delay device in the unlikely event the respected newsman should say anything compromising. The button was never pressed.

*   *   *

A total of 1,646 American news correspondents and photographers, the overwhelming majority of whom were men, were to cover the war from the first rumblings in 1936 until its end in 1945. Of that number, 37 were killed and 112 were wounded; 203 Purple Hearts and 108 Silver Stars for heroism were awarded.

Many who distinguished themselves during the war went on to greater things at war's end. William L. Shirer would record his experiences as one of the most probing chronicles of the Third Reich. From his base in Berlin for much of the war, Shirer kept the United States and its allies informed of worsening conditions inside Germany. In those pre-satellite days, he sometimes used a complicated radio hook-up via New York, in which he and London-based Murrow conducted informal discussions on the air. Other notable correspondents serving during this period included novelists Quintin Reynolds, John Steinbeck and Ernest Hemingway; established newsmen Clifton Daniel (who later married President Truman's daughter, Margaret), and James B. Reston; CBS's Charles Collingwood, Eric Sevareid (who arrived at his Indo-China base by parachute), Howard K. Smith, Robert Trout, Richard C. Hottelet, John Daly (who would achieve greater fame hosting television's popular *What's My Line?*) and Bill Downs; NBC's Merrill Mueller; ABC's George Hicks; Andy Rooney, who worked for the military's *Stars & Stripes,* and, of course, Walter Cronkite.

Newsmen in London and Paris worked in buildings protected by sandbags and military guards. Inside the structures, the reporters slept on cots and kept plentiful supplies of food, water, emergency lanterns, and candles for the long hours they were expected to maintain. Both the United Press—"Unipressers" or the "Down Hole Club," as they were variously called—and the Associated Press correspondents worked round the clock; their bureaus had insatiable appetites for war news and never knew closing hours. During the first two weeks of the war, the writers moved 80,000 words a day, about twice the normal peacetime rate. Their readers in the States devoured the war stories hungrily, significantly boosting the circulation of virtually every newspaper in the country; as America became more involved in the war, the buying and reading intensified proportionally.

*   *   *

At the time the Japanese struck Pearl Harbor, Walter and Betsy Cronkite were living in New York City, where he was working at the UP's foreign office. The entry of the United States into the war would provide the initial impetus to expose Cronkite to the world and the world to Cronkite.

When he was informed by the United Press that he would be sent overseas to cover the war, Cronkite and his young wife shared the same thoughts and fears and sudden change of plans which were fragmenting homes all over America and the world. Betsy, being the patriotic free spirit she was, decided at once to join the WASPs, the women's air corps. She even began flight training, but soon opted to return to journalism. After seeing her husband off to the war, she returned to Kansas City to stay with her parents as she worked for the Hallmark Greeting Cards Company, helping publish a serviceman's newspaper.

Cronkite's by-lined articles would be run concurrently—or exclusively—in several U.S. newspapers that subscribed to the UP's wire service: the *New York Times, Herald-Tribune, World Telegram* and *PM,* a New York-based tabloid. In writing for a wire service which supplied news for several papers, Cronkite had an immediate advantage over correspondents who represented only one paper or journal or radio network. In situations where the military could carry only one writer on a specific mission, a wire service reporter was preferred because of the number of media he represented.

The wire services, naturally, wanted as much mileage from their reporters as they could get. As a result, their people became journalistic gypsies, traveling constantly to where the action and stories were. At various times during the course of the war, for example, Cronkite was assigned to cover the U.S. Navy, Army, Marines and Air Corps, the Royal Air Force and Navy, Field Marshal Montgomery's headquarters and the Royal Canadian Army.

Cronkite's first assignment, in 1942, was to report the fighting in the North Atlantic during the dark, confusing, early days of the war.

After the Germans invaded France, the French military was sharply divided: the Free French followed anti-Nazi Charles de Gaulle, the pro-Nazi Vichy French Pierre Laval. The Free French's navy had been forced to scuttle its own fleet at Toulon to prevent capture by the rapidly advancing Nazis; many patriotic officers and men elected to go down with their ships rather than be taken prisoners. The Free French also blew up their own drydocks, coastal batteries, and as many other military installations as time permitted before the ravenous *Wehrmacht* could seize them.

The Allies were having little success in repelling the aggressive German forces in northern Africa. Field Marshal Erwin Rommel, the resourceful, unrelenting and intrepid "Desert Fox," smashed his way through British forces in the North African desert.

Lieutenant General Mark Clark had been dispatched to Morocco by General Eisenhower to assess the situation and locate a Free French general the Vichy troops would rally around. He was transported by a U.S. submarine and taken ashore by British commandos under the cover of darkness. The water was so rough as he was being brought to shore that General Clark removed his trousers and money belt for easier swimming in the event the boat capsized. The vessel was indeed turned over by the heavy seas and all aboard had to swim ashore. The general's trousers and money belt were likewise washed away and, once on land, he had to spend the night shivering in his underwear. He was given a pair of trousers the next day and, remarkably, his own were found, *sans* the money belt and shrunken by the sea water. The episode was one of the lighter moments in an otherwise tense situation. Even Britain's King George VI joked about the event one morning when Generals Eisenhower and Clark were invited to eat breakfast with him. When General Eisenhower introduced Clark to the monarch, the King asked, "Oh, yes, you're the chap who lost his trousers, aren't you?"

Clark, then 46 and the youngest major general in the army, was promoted to lieutenant general and awarded the Distinguished Service Medal for his success in negotiating with the Free French. (The trousers, by the way, are on permanent exhibit at the Smithsonian Institution in Washington.)

"The situation," General Clark said in a telephone interview with the writer, "was highly fluid. Everybody was shooting at everybody."

By some humorless irony, when American civilians stateside were flocking to movie theatres to watch the anti-Nazi intrigues of Humphrey Bogart and Ingrid Bergman in Morocco's *Casablanca,* or Bob Hope, Bing Crosby, and Dorothy Lamour's frolicking on *The Road to Morocco,* Cronkite was actually "on location" in that African city. It was from Morocco he filed his first important by-lined story exclusively for the *New York Times.*

Even though the Allies were victorious in the air battle, code-named "Torch," the state of chaos which characterized Morocco during that time was so total that Cronkite's story was delayed for seventeen days before publication, until the facts could be sorted out.

Knowing that a big battle was to take place, the newsgathering agencies sent their best and most seasoned reporters—the legendary Ernie Pyle among them—to get the story. Cronkite, "the new kid on the block," was the first correspondent to file a report. His page-four article was introduced by a stateside editor who explained that Walter L. Cronkite, as he was known then, was attached to the U.S. Atlantic Fleet. The readers were also told that Cronkite was the only American reporter to witness the bitter and decisive three-day battle in the air and on the ground for possession of Port Lyautey, Morocco (now known as Kinetra).

The conflict was not with the Germans, as one might assume, but an air war between U.S. Navy and Army Air Corps planes and the Vichy French air force, supported by the French Foreign Legion. To keep the Vichy French out of the city, the Americans had rigged their planes with special depth charges that exploded on impact when dropped on ground forces.

The following is an abridged account of Cronkite's first communique as a war correspondent:

The battle of "Depth Charge Junction" turned the tide in the bitter three-day battle for Port Lyautey and gave the American invasion forces possession of this city and its valuable airdrome.

The battle was fought at a junction five miles south of Port Lyautey, along the broad highway leading to Rabat, over which the French tried in vain to move tank columns and mechanized forces to aid the beleaguered garrison here.

The tanks and troops of the Moroccan garrison at Rabat—the most decorated garrison in all Morocco—twice tried to blast a way past the junction and twice they were turned back by the combined fire of naval shell fire, depth bombs dropped from low-flying naval scout planes and American tank columns rushed down from the northern beachheads.

All had a part, but it was the naval plane squadron that led the attack, and it was their depth charges that gave the junction its new name.

Their attacks slowed the columns [of French tanks] until, first, naval shellfire could be brought to bear, and, later, dive-bombers and the American tanks could join the fray.

Their action was deemed to have played an important part in enabling the combined amphibious forces of the United States Army and Navy to capture today this colonial city of 17,000, mostly Europeans, and its modern seaplane and land plane airdrome.

. . . The French Legion and crack Moroccan rifle and cavalry battalions fought viciously against the Allied occupation and the American forces had to blast their way inland with all the weapons at their command.

The Americans had held their fire under instructions from the High Command, which until the last had hoped for peaceful French cooperation. Fire from 150-mm cannon . . . and machine guns lining the ridge overlooking the beach ended that hope and the three-day battle was on.

For two days the American forces were stuck on the beach . . .

American mastery of the air . . . gained the first day . . . and the inability of the French to send reinforcements . . . finally wore down the French."

The Moroccan situation settled, the Allies turned their attention to Rommel's *Afrika Korps*—a bloody campaign waged primarily by the British. Once Rommel's drive was successfully repelled, the focus of the war turned to Western Europe. England was in a death struggle with German forces using occupied France as a launching site for daily bombing runs on London and other heavily populated or industrialized cities on that fortress island. Cronkite followed the action when he was reassigned to London, the base of operations for him and the small staff which had now been assigned to him.

*   *   *

Newsmen are known for their clannishness. They may work for different papers or networks, but their common basic interests bind them tightly together. There was still a semblance of social activity in London when Cronkite arrived there, even though much of it was literally underground. The USO performed occasionally; Bob Hope had already launched what would be a half-century of entertaining troops with his first British tour in 1942.

Not long after Cronkite arrived in England, he met Ed Murrow and other London-based correspondents and was soon raising a few glasses with them at the pubs along Fleet Street, bombing raids and special assignments permitting. Murrow, a sort of Pied Piper for CBS, had signed on Eric Sevareid, John Daly, Charles Collingwood and many others. Cronkite didn't yet have what was considered a brilliant prose style, but he was certainly good and, importantly, he was fast. Murrow was so impressed by the stories of Cronkite's bravery—not to mention his good reporting—he made him an enticing offer to join CBS, promising him $120 a week. (Even then, Andy Rooney recalls, Cronkite was the one "racing the other guy to the telephone booth to get his story in first. He was like all the old movie characters. He was the ultimate reporter.") Cronkite was flattered and confessed the invitation was tempting, but made no immediate commitment. When the United Press heard of the Murrow offer, it immediately gave Cronkite a substantial raise, from $57.50 to $92 a week—and he remained with the UP.

It was while he was stationed in London that Cronkite first met Major General George Patton. The meeting was not a particularly pleasant one for the rookie war correspondent, however. General Patton found Cronkite's rumpled uniform and scuffed shoes offensive and reprimanded him for his appearance.

*   *   *

The day-to-day living in London was uncertain at its best, hazardous at its worst. Somewhere in the consciousness of virtually all who lived in the city was the realization that as they lay their heads uneasily on their pillows at night, the morning could find them orphaned, widowed, childless, mangled, or even dead. Nearly daily, the Germans made high-level bombing raids or sent their dreaded V-2 buzz-bombs roaring into the skies, killing some 20,000 during the Blitz alone.

The emotional and physical damage on the civilian population was endless, maddening, and, in some cases, devastating. "Blitz fatigue" was a common ailment which sent overstrung Londoners into the countryside for brief respites from the interminable and relentless siege. When the sirens sounded in the city, warning of the approach of bombers or rockets, the occupants, from Royal Family to costermonger, dashed underground like moles. As many as 60,000 Londoners a night took refuge in subway tunnels, basements of buildings, or the repressed elegance of private and exclusive clubs or hotel bomb shelters, which afforded relative safety but not necessarily peace of mind. It was not unusual for many to leave their shelters after a raid and return to where their homes had been, only to find a massive, smoldering crater as a reminder of the cruel and relentless efficiency of the German *Luftwaffe*.

The correspondents, of course, shared the same fears and fate as did the British subjects. Cronkite's flat took a hit during one bombing raid. The damage was rather severe, but he was safely underground when the bomb struck.

As time passed, there was no easing of the tensions in England or on the Continent. Many British children were sent to Canada or the United States for the duration of the war, while their parents remained stoically behind.

Even though correspondents had little emotional attachment to the land, they, too, chose to remain. Even though their salaries were adequate, it was not the money that kept them at their typewriters. It was their commitment to perform the jobs they did best: reporting to their readers or radio audience the ugly face of war, as well as the acts of bravery they witnessed nearly daily. It was with deep dread that Cronkite and his colleagues hourly risked peril to file their stories. Climbing into a jeep or aircraft for a "routine" land run or flight over Allied or neutral or enemy territory was always tense. There was never any guarantee of a safe or uneventful mission, but the trips were made and the reporters were there. Cronkite was no exception. Besides the uncounted regular sorties he flew, he went on eight bombing missions over Germany during the fiercest days of the war.

Cronkite's maiden bombing mission was in 1943. Sixty-seven B-17s, each laden with more than six tons of bombs, left an airfield outside London for what was hoped would be a routine high-level bombing run over the target city of Wilhelmshaven, an important German seaport. As the formation of Flying Fortresses neared its goal, surface batteries opened fire on it. Since their massive payload prevented the planes from climbing higher to distance themselves from the ground fire, there was no defense from that type of attack. The men had no recourse but to fly on, praying that they would not be hit. To add to their misery, a squadron of *Luftwaffe* fighter planes materialized and closed in for the kill. As the pilots of the lumbering bombers flew doggedly toward their mission, their flight crews manned every available gun in a desperate effort to repel the hornet-like German attackers. At one point in the exchange, Cronkite took over a .50 caliber machine gun to assist in the successful effort to drive the invaders away.

Cronkite's B-17 was not hit by enemy fire, although others in the squadron were not so fortunate. Thirteen U.S. planes were shot down during the attack, resulting in death, injury and capture for many Americans on that run. Unknown to Cronkite until the next day, among the killed was his friend and colleague, *New York Times* correspondent Robert Post. Post's plane had taken a bad hit, requiring all personnel to bail out. Post had been seen parachuting from the craft, but he was killed by surface fire before he hit the ground.

The remaining members of the squadron continued to Wilhelmshaven and dropped their combined massive and deadly total of 300 tons of bombs on the enemy shipyard before returning to command headquarters in England, grateful to be alive.

Cronkite climbed out of his plane and headed across the airfield to the debriefing room when he was joined by Homer Bigart, a correspondent for the *Herald-Tribune*. Bone-tired and emotionally drained, Ron Powers writes, Cronkite brightened when he saw his friend.

"Homer," he announced in a giddy, frivolous moment, "I think I've got my lead." Walking with his arm dramatically raised before him as if he were reading his words from a theatre marquee, he continued, "I've just returned from an assignment to hell. A hell at 17,000 feet, a hell of bursting flak and screaming fighter planes." Bigart, who stuttered badly, listened in amusement, but then realized his friend might be serious. He stopped and put his hand on Cronkite's arm and exclaimed, "Walter! Y-Y-Y-You wouldn't!" Cronkite laughed heartily and the two proceeded to the debriefing.

That night in his room, as he sat before his typewriter to reconstruct the day's harrowing events, Cronkite's report followed his original thoughts closely. The following account appeared in the February 27, 1943, *New York Times*:

Hell 26,000 Feet Up

American Flying Fortresses have just come back from an assignment to hell—a hell 26,000 feet above the earth, a hell of burning tracer bullets and bursting gunfire, of crippled Fortresses and burning German fighter planes, of parachuting men and others not so lucky. I have just returned with a Flying Fortress crew from Wilhelmshaven.

We fought off Hitler's fighters and dodged his guns. The Fortress I rode in came in without damage, but we had the element of luck on our side.

We gave the ship repair yards and other installations at the great submarine and naval base on the North Sea a most severe pasting. As we swept beyond the target and back over the North Sea from which we came, we saw great pillars of smoke over the target area.

Six of us represented the American News Services, newspapers and radio, "The Writing Sixty-Ninth"—a seventh correspondent could not go because of illness and the plane taking another had to turn back because of technical difficulties.

Actually, the impressions of a first bombing mission are a hodge-podge of disconnected scenes like a poorly edited home movie—bombs falling past you from the formation above, a crippled bomber with smoke pouring from one motor, limping along thousands of feet below, a tiny speck in the sky that grows closer and finally becomes an enemy fighter, a Focke-Wülf peeling off above you somewhere and plummeting down, shooting its way through the formation; your bombardier pushing a button as if he were turning on a hall light, to send our bombs on the way.

Our bombardier was First Lieutenant Albert W. Diefenback, 26, of Washington, D.C. His job began at that thrilling moment when the bomb bay doors swung open on the lead ship and on down the line to us.

That signaled that we're beginning our bomb run. Then we swept over Wilhelmshaven. There were broken clouds, but through them appeared a toy village below which was really a major seaport, and I thought:

"Down there right now people are scurrying for shelter—which means interrupting work on vital submarines and ships and dockyards."

Lieutenant Diefenback's left hand went out to the switch panel alongside him and almost imperceptibly he touched a button and said calmly over the communication system:

"Bombs away."

That was it. Our mission was accomplished—our bombs were on their way to Hitler.

In 1944, General Eisenhower and the Allied Commanders began preparing their plans for operation "Overlord." Comprised of U.S., Canadian, Dutch, French, and Norwegian ships and men, it would be the largest armada ever assembled in the annals of warfare. The historic assault the world would know as D-Day brought together nearly 3,000,000 military personnel, thirty-nine divisions and 11,000 aircraft. The fleet and its 2,500,000 tons of supplies constituted the men and material the Allies hoped would bring about the liberation of France, and eventually Europe, from the clutches of Nazi Germany.

Late on June 5, 1944, the eve of D-Day, Joe Morris wrote in *Deadline Every Minute,* Cronkite was in his London flat, in his pajamas and about to go to bed, when he heard a knocking at his door. He threw on a robe and opened the door where an Air Corps public relations officer was anxiously waiting. "Mr. Cronkite, there's a good story breaking. I think you'd better come with us."

Without a moment's hesitation, Cronkite responded, "Just a minute, while I get some clothes on." He dressed hurriedly, grabbed his gear, ran to the officer's staff car and the two drove off.

In the security of the moving car, the officer explained more about the impending operation. "The invasion of Europe is about to start. We're sending a B-17 bomber over the coast at low altitude as a spearhead and can take only one correspondent. We drew lots, and you won. Of course, if you don't want want to go, just say so."

Cronkite knew there was to be a massive Allied attack on the coast of France. Everybody, even the Germans, knew it; the exact time, place, and size of the operation, however, were the critical unknowns. To prevent any specifics from leaking out, officers of all branches of the services—regardless of nationality—who had any information that might be pieced together by the Germans, were being rounded up and locked in bars at that very hour, where they would remain until the troops reached Normandy. To confuse any espionage agents who clandestinely followed newsmen about, some correspondents were sent on fictitious assignments. Consequently, the D-Day landing was generally considered to be the best-kept and, at the same time, the most widely-advertised secret of the war.

There were, regrettably, isolated examples of disclosures of the invasion that could have had damaging effects on the success of the venture, but fortunately probably never reached enemy ears. One of the most publicized offenders of disclosure was Major General J. F. Miller, who, after having too many drinks at a cocktail party in London, made the mistake of talking about the date of the invasion. He was shortly thereafter summoned to Allied Supreme headquarters where he was personally reprimanded and demoted to the permanent rank of Lieutenant Colonel by West Point classmate General Dwight Eisenhower. He was also told to pack his bags and catch the next military flight back to the States.

"Of course I want to go!" Cronkite told the Air Corps officer. Every Allied correspondent in Europe wanted to witness this greatest of all united assaults and Cronkite was no exception.

"Good. I'll take you to headquarters now for your instructions."

Cronkite was driven to a building where he joined seven other newsmen who had been selected to cover the mammoth landing. Each was given a visa from General Eisenhower. The instructions written there and signed by Eisenhower were specific: "No correspondent may quit the overseas theatre during the validity of this overseas visa without the express permission of the Supreme Commander."

The actual invasion began with a signal from General Eisenhower's command post, a trailer deep in the English countryside. With the push of a button on his desk, the B-17s left their airfields and dropped tons of bombs to soften up the German shore defenses; over 14,000 sorties were flown by the Allies. By dawn, the ships, large and small, lined up in the English Channel to begin their assault. Artillery from the larger craft pounded the beaches before the amphibious vehicles bore in the infantry. For two days, the Allies poured on all the resources they had, never giving an inch, pushing the enemy slowly and steadily back across France and Belgium, back to their *Vaterland.*

Most of the journalists covering the landing observed the action from ships or waded ashore with the invading troops. Of all the correspondents who were involved in the landing, only one was killed: Arthur Thorpe of the British Telegraph Exchange. Others had close brushes with death, and among the injured were Henry B. Jameson, Roger Greene and Robert Miller. As Cronkite's "luck" had it, he was provided a grandstand view of the operation from the relative safety of a plane from the 303rd Bomber Group.

George Hicks of ABC radio received enormous praise for his coverage of the D-Day bombardment. Reporting directly as an eyewitness from the bridge of the U.S.S. *Ancom,* he kept listeners enthralled with his live broadcast of the action. The other media correspondents, including Cronkite, were unable to file their stories so immediately. The print media stories arrived at their respective papers from one to four days after the invasion was launched.

Despite elaborate plans the other radio newsmen had laid to transmit coverage from the center of the action, some were unable to complete their assignments as intended. Water from rough seas damaged many radio transmitters, while others were completely swept away before the men reached the beach. A few of the more resourceful and successful reporters resorted to the World War I practice of filing their stories using carrier pigeons.

An unknown Army Signal Corps cameraman, Russ Meyer, filmed the landing at Normandy and, for several days, the fierce ensuing action. His camera work was an extensive and superb piece of work; so good, in fact, a great deal of it was used as newsreel footage in the popular 1970 film *Patton.* Meyer would gain fame after the war as the leading entrepreneur of the "Vixen" genre of so-called "soft-porn" movies.

The civilian response to the success of the Normandy invasion was overwhelming. President Roosevelt had led the nation in prayer over the radio as General Eisenhower had begun the operation. New York's Mayor Fiorello La Guardia broadcast a prayer service from his city hall office; Mayor Bernard Samuels of Philadelphia tapped the Liberty Bell with a wooden mallet before leading a prayer over the radio for patriots at home and servicemen overseas. In England, King George VI called his subjects to thanksgiving services after the landing. Fifty thousand Americans attended a similar gathering at Madison Square Gardens. Major sporting events were canceled and department stores were closed to permit New Yorkers to attend thanksgiving services at churches and synagogues all over the city.

The large Times Square crowd that gathered to read the messages on the electric sign on the *Times* building was unusually and inexplicably quiet. Elsewhere in New York that momentous night, the sixty-nine spotlights which had been used to illuminate the Statue of Liberty before the war were turned on for fifteen minutes. Her torch blinked out "V" for victory—for the Allied troops and the people of France, upon whose shores the battle was being fought and who had presented the statue to the United States in 1886.

*   *   *

As a result of Operation Overlord's *coup de maître,* the Allies had created the momentum to place the Germans on the defensive at long last. Generals Eisenhower and Omar Bradley and Field Marshal Montgomery continued the northward drive to hasten the Nazi's withdrawal from France, Holland and Belgium.

There was considerable debate and disagreement among the three Allied officers as to the most effective method for seizing the bridgehead at Arnhem, in the Netherlands. If the retreating Germans could be cut off and forced to surrender, perhaps the end of the war in Europe could be expedited. Various suggestions were proposed, but Supreme Allied Commander Eisenhower rejected them all because of their complexities. He wanted a simple, forthright pincer movement that could be mounted and executed in a matter of days.

To avoid hard feelings among the Allied High Command, particularly with the testy Montgomery, General Eisenhower was strongly advised by President Roosevelt—who usually gave his generals free reign in developing strategies to fight the war—to use the British plan. Monty's called for a complex and massive paratroop drop behind enemy lines. Despite the fact he privately believed the proposal was unreasonably ambitious, Eisenhower reluctantly permitted the British to have their way—a horrible and costly mistake for the Allies.

General Matthew Ridgway was in charge of the entire paratroop drop, assisted by Generals Jim Gavin and Maxwell Taylor. The First Airborne Army was placed under the command of American General Brereton, who was instructed to prepare his troops to strike at Arnhem. The 82nd U.S. Division was to capture the critical bridges at Grave and Nijmegen, while their American 101st Division colleagues were to secure the road between Grave and Eindhoven. The British XXX Corps, led by the Guards Armoured Division, was to force its way up the road to Eindhoven and from there proceed to Arnhem under the protective canopy the airborne troops would provide. The complicated operation, named "Operation Marketgarden," would require split-second timing for success.

Cronkite, by now seasoned and considered one of the best combat correspondents in Europe, had been informed he would accompany the 101st Airborne on a flight whose destination and mission were, at that point, unknown to him. With the failure of so many planned D-Day radio broadcasts and the long delay in publication of his own Normandy invasion account fresh in his mind, he began rethinking communications. In an effort to shorten the length of time required for a report to get from its source to London and thence to New York, Cronkite consulted the communications officers of the 101st Airborne. He knew the division had its own radio channel for transmitting military messages to its base at Reading, England. The resourceful newsman proposed that he be permitted use of the Army's radio channel when he landed, destination still unknown. The Reading radio operator could then relay Cronkite's stories to the United Press bureau in London for distribution to the States. After some discussion, it was finally agreed to permit Cronkite limited use of the channel—a total of 100 words. The confident reporter felt he could distill the essentials to those requirements. The story would be brief, but transmitted at the speed of sound, the immediacy he desired would be a reality and a plus for the UP. He could send a detailed story later.

*   *   *

When he was informed he would be traveling with the 101st Airborne Division, Cronkite naturally assumed he would fly in a conventional aircraft, land on a conventional airfield and from there be transported to the war zone by jeep, as was the SOP, or standard operating procedure. On the morning of September 17, 1944, however, Cornelius Ryan wrote in his epic *A Bridge Too Far*, he found himself on a British airstrip filled wing-tip to wing-tip with gliders—500 of them. His stomach knotted up, his mouth became dry as he surveyed the scene and contemplated the mission he had agreed to go on. Directed to one of the wood-frame and cloth gliders, he climbed aboard with a growing sense of trepidation. He tumbled into a cloth seat alongside fourteen stone-faced, combat-ready airborne troops, single-file on each side.

As he felt the tow-line from the powered plane ahead of him tighten and the little craft bump along behind, he began having serious thoughts about returning from this mission alive. The tow-plane was cleared for take-off and they were pulled slowly into the air. The noise of the rushing air outside the glider's cloth skin began to grow louder, causing him to fear the little plane would be ripped to shreds by the violent air currents. He looked nervously about at the impassive and silent men. They were occupied with their own thoughts, perhaps sharing his fears, and offered no consolation. There were no side windows to allow him to see what was going on outside, so the jittery journalist concentrated his gaze dead ahead at the tow-plane and tried to calm himself.

The skies were filled with aircraft. For the 500 gliders there were 500 tow-planes. In addition, there were supply planes, fighters and bombers. From the ground, it must have seemed that every Allied plane capable of getting aloft was in the air.

When the target area was reached, the glider pilots released the tow-lines and the small crafts prepared to descend. Cronkite, still not knowing what to expect, felt another tightening of his abdomen. As soon as they had a clear path to the ground, the pilot pushed his control wheel forward and the glider dropped like a stone into a sudden, sharp, heart-stopping nosedive. The glider pilot was following the safest procedure for landing a small, defenseless craft in a combat zone; by diving straight down, the glider was less likely to be hit by ground fire. Only a few feet above the ground, the pilot leveled off abruptly and crash-landed the glider for a quick stop. This action permitted a rapid exit by the troops, again to minimize the chances of being hit by enemy fire.

Even though the landing procedure in Cronkite's glider was letter-perfect, he had made the monumental mistake of presuming the wheels under the fuselage would be used for landing. He recalled later how surprised he was "when we skidded along the ground and the wheels came crashing up through the floor!"

The unorthodox landing had shaken everything inside loose: helmets that had previously been hooked securely came flying wildly from the heads of the soldiers. The men, too, were tossed about violently, many landing in a heap on the splinters that had earlier been the floor.

Cronkite remembers, "I grabbed the first helmet I saw, my trusty musette bag with the Olivetti typewriter inside and began crawling toward the canal which was the rendezvous point." When he looked back, he was surprised to find half a dozen men crawling after him. One of them asked, "Are you sure we're going in the right direction, Major?" Cronkite let the question sink in, then removed his helmet and looked at the rank insignia painted on it; he had grabbed the wrong helmet in the glider. He explained to the men what had happened and they reversed directions, still on their all-fours, to look for the major.

By the time the helmets were swapped, scouts had returned to report they had seen no Germans in the area. The men got to their feet to get their bearings. They had landed in a potato field near a canal in Cronkite's ancestral Dutch homeland. The gliders lay in broken disarray around them: only fifty-three of the original 500 had landed without mishap. There were deaths and injuries as the gliders had descended, crashing nose-first in the Dutch soil.

Considering the wreckage of men and planes about him, Cronkite surmised that once again an "element of luck," as he put it, was with him. He threw his musette bag across his shoulder and set out on foot for Eindhoven.

Cronkite had not traveled very far when a jeep driven by a British soldier and bearing two passengers approached from behind. It slowed down as one of the passengers studied the lone figure on the road. The pedestrian had neither rifle nor back pack, only a musette bag with what had to be a portable typewriter in it, judging from the way it was swinging.

"Walter?"

Cronkite turned to see who had called his name.

"Bill!" he exclaimed, recognizing the man as Bill Downs, a former Unipresser, but then with CBS. Downs was attached to the Guards Armoured Division, a British unit. He was traveling with a British escort officer to report the progress of the American, British and Polish paratroop landing.

Cronkite and Downs had been known to lift a few pints together and Cronkite had such a reputation of being "one of the good guys"—young, unassuming, hard-working, and probably the only reporter in Europe whose strongest expletive was "Gosh!"—Allied correspondents all over the world knew him and looked him up when they were in Europe.

"Get in!" Downs said. Cronkite eagerly climbed into the back seat of the jeep and they rode off to Eindhoven, swapping tales of how they had arrived in Holland. (For whatever it is worth, Downs claimed Cronkite was still wearing the Major's helmet, although Cronkite doesn't remember it that way.)

After Cronkite located the 101st radio communications officer and sent his brief account of the glider invasion and liberation of Eindhoven, a city of 110,000, he rejoined Downs in the town square for a liberation celebration.

The mayor had come out to welcome the Allies and the natives and military personnel continued the festivities throughout the afternoon. As dusk approached, Downs and Cronkite became aware of an uncanny stillness that seemed to intensify with the twilight. Their Dutch hosts began nervously retreating to their homes, and the Dutch, British and American flags, that had been prominently displayed all day, began disappearing. Suddenly, a German reconnaissance plane roared overhead from behind a line of trees at the edge of the town. It circled before dropping illuminating flares to brighten the darkening sky.

A column of Allied vehicles had been bottle-necked all afternoon at a narrow bridge over a canal in the north end of the town and it appeared the Germans were going to take advantage of the traffic jam. It had been falsely rumored that the roads had been mined by the Germans, so the Allied vehicles were playing it safe, waiting to use the bridge instead of going around it.

By this time, however, everybody had double-timed it from the square. Downs, Cronkite and their British driver dashed to their jeep, looking about anxiously for the best place to take cover. Downs suggested, with a good deal of urgency in his voice, "Walter, the Germans are going to beat up that column that's stalled at the bridge. Let's go back to the south edge of town where it's safe, and watch the show from there."

Neither man knew, as obviously the Allied airborne divisions had not known, that they had all been dropped between two S.S. *panzer* divisions that surrounded Eindhoven. As the city had been celebrating the Allied landing, the Germans were stealthily placing troops at both ends of the town to seal it off. When bombs began falling and the sound of small arms fire was heard getting louder, the two newsmen realized their choice of a possible haven was a bad one. For about forty-five minutes, planes roaring overhead dropped bombs, cutting off the men from the town and the Allied troops, killing 65 people and seriously wounding 150 in the process.

Downs spotted a high fence which bordered a thick forest. He told his driver to stop the jeep, and all three of them ran for the fence. Motivated by the will to survive, the portly Downs was over the fence, he said, "like a gazelle." He saw his partner clear the fence and, from the corner of his eye, watched him disappear in the darkness after his excavation tool proved defective. Downs and his driver jumped into a water-filled canal that Holland had an ample number of and lay there, listening to the sounds of the heavy fighting in Eindhoven.

When things quieted down a bit, Downs dragged himself, cold and soaking wet, from his hiding place and began to look for Cronkite. He called "Cron-kite! Cron-kite!" but there was no response. At that point, he realized that "Cronkite" sounded too much like

Krankheit, which is German for "illness." He feared he might arouse a German medic and called off his search. He rationalized, "I felt Walter was sort of indestructible, so I wasn't worried too much." He located his jeep and left Eindhoven.

Most of the correspondents in that area were sharing the plush Metropole Hotel in Brussels the British had taken over for their headquarters. Upon his arrival at the hotel, Downs went to his room to clean up and change uniforms. When he came back downstairs, he ambled into the bar, still concerned about Cronkite's safety. To his surprise, Cronkite, still covered with mud but with a drink in his hand, was standing in the middle of a crowd of journalists at the bar.

"Walter!" Downs shouted with relief.

"Bill!" Cronkite responded. "I thought you were dead! I walked all through the woods calling your name!"

"I called for you, too, Walter!" Downs reassured him with a laugh and a friendly slap on the shoulder, "But if the Germans had heard me yelling '*Krankheit,*' I'd probably be in a Berlin hospital by now!"

After finishing his drink and reunion, Cronkite took a bath and began his round of interviews. Returning to his room, he was back at his Olivetti, writing the follow-up account of the Arnhem landing. Two days later, it appeared as a front-page article in the *Times:*

Sky Troops Race for Control of Bridges

The air-borne troops of Lieut. Gen. Lewis H. Brereton's sky train army made contact with a British armored patrol in the Netherlands today, some twenty-four hours after their landing in this canal-laced country behind German lines.

Glider-borne reinforcements of troops, weapons and supplies of all sorts swept down to the forces that landed yesterday in the greatest airborne operation of all time as the British forces, driving northward from Belgium, established their contact with General Brereton's men.

The juncture was effected on the outskirts of an industrial town in which German snipers are still holding out, holding to the end until they are dug out by bayonets or blasted out by bazookas.

The Germans are fighting desperately now, after their first panic fight. They are trying to hold on to the dozens of bridges vital to the progress of our armor across the canals.

It is a race against time. The Allied airborne troops must prevent the destruction of the bridges.

Sometimes the Germans—many of them of high school age—are blowing up bridges and leaving some of their own men on our side of the canals to face death or to surrender.

The Germans on the perimeter of this southern area, held by Americans, stiffened during the night. Supported by mortars, anti-tank guns and heavy artillery, the Germans counter-attacked the paratroops holding one perimeter.

The enemy gained a local success. Our men were pushed back several hundred yards to the banks of a canal. There they dug in for a finish fight. Not only did they hold their lines but they saved the bridges in the sector.

This morning, the Americans struck back against German paratroops operating as infantry and regained much of the lost ground.

By Sunday night the Germans had evacuated at least thirteen Dutch hamlets and villages. The Allies held four important bridges and three road junctions.

The villages and hamlets were freed by southern flank of the airborne forces, with whom I landed yesterday.

The Germans succeeded in blowing up some bridges, but at other places the surprise was so complete that they had no chance to complete demolitions. We have no information on the number of villages freed to the north of us by others of the thousands of paratroops and glider-borne infantrymen who came tumbling from the skies with us shortly after noon yesterday."

*   *   *

The Allied assault along the Rhine to seize the bridge at Arnhem—termed by the fighting airborne troops their "little patch of hell"—proved to be a notable failure. An insufficient number of aircraft was the primary cause for the fiasco. Other contributing factors included poor weather, inoperative radios, and the inability of the various divisions to maintain the prescribed timing essential for their individual points of attack. The British 1st Airborne Division, which had been dropped near Arnhem, historian William L. Shirer wrote, lost all but 2,163 of some 9,000 men. General Eisenhower, angered and frustrated by the disaster, told his staff, "The setback is ample evidence that much bitter campaigning is yet to come."

Others had their own irreverent thoughts on the true cause of the failed operation, however. At a 1974 reunion of the Guards Armoured Division in Eindhoven, Downs laughingly agreed with a British paratrooper who told the assembly, "The bloody Guards Armored stopped too long and too often to brew tea!"

Fortunately, the other battles of the war were enjoying successes, but despite the growing might of the Allies' inertia, the Germans obstinately refused to surrender their positions in France. In a desperate, last-ditch effort in early December 1944, the Nazis mustered nearly seventy divisions, fifteen of which were armored, along their western front. On the sixteenth of December, they launched an attack known infamously as the Battle of the Bulge. Under General Eisenhower's command, the assembled Allied military giants—Bradley, Montgomery, and Patton—slowly forced the *panzers* eastward until, eventually, as Sir Winston Churchill wrote in his historic account of World War II, "the Germans had nothing to show for their supreme effort except ruinous losses of materials and causalities amounting to 120,000 men."

Many Americans had been captured by the Germans during the brief battle. On December, in a snow-covered field near Malmedy, the frozen bodies of 129 of them were found, their hands tied behind their backs. Rather than deliver them to a prison camp, they had been executed on orders of SS officers.

*   *   *

In late December, the 101st Airborne proceeded from Arnhem to Bastogne, a Belgian crossroads town. The 101st was to seal off the surrounding highways in an effort to contain the Nazis, but three divisions of the Germans' crack 5th *Panzers* and 7th Army immediately enveloped the Americans, trapping them inside Bastogne. On December 22, General Heinrich von Lüwitz sent a surrender demand to General Anthony McAuliffe, who was acting commander of the hapless 101st, while General Maxwell Taylor was spending a few days with his family at Christmas.

General McAuliffe was sleeping when the German representatives brought the note, which had been neatly typed in German and English. The general was awakened by the disturbance and asked an aide what was going on outside his room. When he was informed of the German message, McAuliffe sat up and exclaimed in disgust, "Oh, shit!" He called in his chief of staff Lieutenant Colonel Moore and instructed him to inform the Germans he had no intention of surrendering. A few moments later, Moore returned and told the general the "by the book" Germans insisted on a written reply.

"I don't know what to say."

"How about that first remark of yours?" an aide suggested.

There was considerable laughter at this comment, but General McAuliff declined in favor of the single word "NUTS!" handwritten on a piece of paper. The reply became a headline item in the States and a rallying cry for the entrapped Allied forces.

When General Patton was given the order to break through the German's encirclement of Bastogne and rescue the 101st, Cronkite had been assigned to cover the operation. General Patton organized his troops, stood from the front seat of his jeep, pointed dramatically toward Bastogne and, with typical Pattonian flair, gave his driver the order to "Drive like hell!"

Cronkite was on a nearby hill as he waited the arrival of General Patton's approaching forces. He described the scene for readers of the *New York Times*, which ran on December 27, 1944:

Planes Supply Men Cut Off At Bastogne

Giant fleets of C-47 cargo planes skimmed over the snow-covered Ardennes hills today to drop supplies to American troops still fighting inside the Bastogne pocket in eastern Belgium.

Besieged troops, still holding the highway city, are fighting magnificently, using supplies dropped from the air, and no apprehension is felt as to the ultimate outcome of the battle.

Hundreds of the big planes flew over the battle area in a seemingly endless stream, like a school of giant winged fish. They were unarmed, but P-38 Lightning fighters hovered above them in a sky studded with anti-aircraft bursts. The planes flew down a valley at such an altitude that they were at eye level to this observer watching from a hilltop south of Bastogne.

Flak began bursting in their formation as they crossed the battlelines, but the big ships flew on steadily to drop their vital cargoes out of sight over the rolling hills.

Radio messages from the cut-off forces in the Bastogne pocket said they were in complete control of the situation, had plenty of food, ammunition and medical supplies and were killing lots of Germans.

Troops in the town, pounded for a week by the German shells, have piled up hundreds of dead Germans as they defend the approaches to Bastogne, but they have suffered terrible losses themselves. Even 36 hours ago they reported in a message that there were many injured among their ranks. The defenders are using every available basement as a first aid station.

Now the defenders of Bastogne can hear the roar of approaching American artillery even above the thundering of the German guns from the surrounding heights. But it may take some time before this secure mission can break through, before the Germans can enter the town.

Two days later, another Cronkite story appeared in the *Times* regarding the arrival of Major General Maxwell Taylor, commander of the 101st. The article included a photograph of General Taylor with the caption "He Flew to Bastogne From Washington, D.C." The short report read:

Major General Maxwell Taylor of the 101st Airborne, who was in Washington, D.C., when his division was trapped in Bastogne, flew the Atlantic Ocean and slipped through enemy lines in a speeding jeep to be with his men in the final phase of the battle—it may be revealed tonight.

The fighting General, commander of one of America's toughest divisions, left Washington Christmas Eve. He arrived inside the Bastogne pocket two days ago, after a wild dash through enemy territory in a jeep carrying him, his aide, and one other officer.

By the time he got there his men had already knocked out nearly 150 German tanks, 25 enemy halftracks and had fought off as many as 4 German divisions at one time in a desperate battle to keep the enemy from the vital Belgian road center.

General Patton's counter-offensive, which had begun December 22, met extremely heavy resistance. Too, he was concerned about the inclement weather. He summoned the Third Army's chaplain, Colonel James O'Neill, for what has become a classic Patton tale:

"Chaplain, I want you to publish a prayer for good weather. I'm tired of having to fight mud and flood as well as these Germans."

Chaplain O'Neill objected to the request. He tried to dissuade General Patton by telling him "praying of that kind would require a pretty thick rug."

General Patton responded adamantly, "I don't care if it takes the entire carpet! I want the praying done!"

On the 22nd of December, Christmas cards with the message "Greetings from General Patton" on one side and the following prayer on the other, were distributed to the Third Army:

> Almighty and Most Merciful Father, we humbly beseech Thee, of Thy great goodness, to constrain these immoderate rains, with which we have had to contend. Grant us fair weather for Battle. Graciously harken to us as soldiers who call upon Thee, that, armed with Thy Power, we may advance from victory to victory and crush the oppression and wickedness of Thy enemies, and establish Thy justice among men and nations. Amen.

The blizzard and freezing rains which had held the army down suddenly subsided and the skies cleared. General Patton later called

Chaplain O'Neill to his headquarters to decorate him with the Bronze Star.

The ensuing advance, however, was excruciatingly slow. Massive casualties were suffered on both sides. At that time, the daily B-17 bombing runs over Germany were reducing that country to rubble. The Russian front was fast crumbling. Italy had been liberated. The Nazis realized that if they lost Bastogne, they would, in all likelihood, lose the entire war. Hitler, finally convinced of the gravity of the engagements and the inevitable *Götterdämmerung* if the Allies won this decisive battle, as a desperate measure, ordered in his remaining *Luftwaffe* planes and unleashed the secret new jet plane.

On December 30, Hitler sent a note to Field-Marshal Karl von Runstedt, his coordinator of defensive forces in the Ardennes, instructing the Germans to throw all remaining forces against the enemy in order to achieve a final triumphant victory. The communique, which was read over German radio, uncharacteristically concluded by adding, "In case the *Wehrmacht* does not emerge victorious from this battle, this message must be regarded as a farewell word from the *Führer.*"

Violent, low-level attacks were made by the German *Luftwaffe* on New Years' Day, 1945. The mounting Nazi losses, however, were too heavy, curtailing further significant offenses. Germany was on its knees. The Allies' growing strength crushed any pitiful resistance the Nazis could muster. The Americans chipped away at the enemy until, at last, the German encirclement of Bastogne was broken. The agonized gesture of the Third Reich had failed to achieve the successful engagement it believed it needed to remain in the war.

Cronkite rode into the beleaguered city with General Patton's Third Army to celebrate the liberation of the 101st and the Belgians who had also been trapped. The victory, however, had a hollow ring to it. The Battle of the Bulge, which terminated in late January, 1945, had been fought at a terrible price: U.S. losses were estimated at 40,000 and the Germans reported an astounding 220,000 killed or captured.

The grateful Belgians continue to set aside a memorial day annually to honor the sacrifices made by the Allies in routing the Germans from their country.

*   *   *

The Rhine River is a natural barrier snaking along Germany's western border, and crossing it had been the goal of the Allies since the D-Day landing on June 6, 1944. To slow the movement of the steadily advancing troops, the German High Command ordered the bridges over the Rhine blown up, and soldiers placed in the towns along the river to prevent the Allies from entering Germany. The orders for the demolition of the bridges were, fortunately, not always carried out by German officers, who felt any further resistance was futile. The defenders of the bridges—frightened young boys, for the most part, since Germany's supply of men was exhausted—had been threatened with punishment by death if they did not hold their ground. Even so, they frequently deserted their posts as the Allies approached.

On the afternoon of March 7, the U.S. 9th Armored Division discovered, to its obvious delight, the Ludendorff railroad bridge at Remagen was still standing. Engineers dashed to the bridge and began cutting the demolition wires left by the retreating Germans, as one infantry platoon ran across. Several charges went off, but the bridge held. The troops and heavy war machines of the Allied forces quickly crossed the Rhine in the spring of 1945. Such crossings up and down the river's length symbolically, if not literally, marked the end of the long war.

As the end of the European war was at last a reality, a series of deaths ironically removed the principals from the scene: President Roosevelt died suddenly of a cerebral hemorrhage in Warm Springs, Georgia; Italian dictator Benito Mussolini and his mistress Signorina Petacci, while trying to escape to Switzerland, were captured and killed by Italian partisans; Adolf Hitler and Eva Braun, his former mistress and bride of less than 24 hours, committed suicide in their Berlin bunker; and Propaganda Minister Josef Goebbels (who, when Hitler killed himself, egotistically announced "I rule Germany!") and his wife poisoned their children before committing suicide in rooms next to their late *Führer.*

*   *   *

The Allied forces had brought the bloody war in Europe to an end. Members of the Nazi High Command were captured, charged with their crimes and imprisoned to await trial, even though a bitter, if not pragmatic, Churchill had pressed for their immediate execution. He wanted to avoid any lengthy period of retelling their grisly crimes.

Cronkite remained in northeast Europe, covering the surrender of the scattered German army. As the last of the Nazi were captured, he was reassigned to the Low Countries, where he had been given the task of reopening press bureaus in Belgium, the Netherlands and Luxembourg.

Nuremberg, Germany was named as the city where the trials would take place. General Eisenhower's deputy, Lieutenant General Lucias B. Clay, chose it because he believed it offered optimum security, even though it had been eighty per cent destroyed by Allied bombs.

(The writer asked a professor of German to collect whatever information he could on the trials while he was traveling through Nuremberg. He was unable to comply, however, because, the professor reported, the natives acted naïvely as if they knew nothing of the trials.)

Immediately, as the focus of the activity moved to Nuremberg, the city began filling with witnesses, lawyers, spectators and reporters. Cronkite, named chief correspondent for the United Press, would be one of three UP reporters assigned to cover what was to be the most publicized war trial in history.

Armies of workers were employed in the task of repairing or restoring the Palace of Justice, the Grand Hotel, the *Gast Haus* and other buildings which would be used by the court, prisoners, special representatives and guests. The Palace of Justice which housed the courtroom was in seriously weakened condition from Allied bombings. Even after extensive overhauling, its floors collapsed, necessitating further hasty repairs.

The press gallery, a balcony overlooking the courtroom in the Palace of Justice, would hold over 300 representatives from more than thirty countries. The United States had, at intervals, a total of ninety-six correspondents, Great Britain about fifty, the U.S.S.R. about twenty-five, and France forty, while the German press was represented by only five reporters.

Cronkite and other members of the press corps were quartered in an ancient hotel whose foreboding medieval appearance and sorry physical condition earned it the title "The Castle." After a long day of listening to hours of testimonies translated via heavy headphones and seeing films of unbelievable horrors perpetrated by the Third Reich, the reporters returned to the Castle to write their stories and socialize in an attempt to relax. Rude German doormen and impertinent waiters openly displayed their hostility toward the Allied correspondents and the trials they were covering. The third-floor bar was dimly and hideously lit with orange lights, giving it the look of a cheap bordello. A persistent Teutonic musician thumped so loudly on an old, untuned piano that work or talk was virtually impossible. Housing was in critically short supply in bombed-out Germany and reporters had to be packed ten to a room. The Castle's outdated and inadequate plumbing frequently forced the men to leave in the mornings without bathing, shaving or even brushing their teeth. Its kitchen was filthy and refrigeration so poor that food poisoning was not uncommon. It seemed one or another of the reporters was always in the hospital as a result of eating in the hotel's dining room.

In contrast with the heavy restrictions imposed by censorship boards during the course of the war, the press was, at the outset, assured of total freedom in covering the trials. Supreme Court Justice Robert H. Jackson, who served as the United States' Chief War Crimes Prosecutor, publicly proclaimed, "I believe it to be vitally important that there be no censorship on what transpires in the courtroom and no part of the court proceedings will be secret. The trial of the major European war criminals will be a public trial." He added a word of caution to the press corps, however. "I have no intention for a circus atmosphere to prevail. The idea is not to put on a show, but to hold a trial."

On the morning of November 20, 1945, the prisoners were led into the paneled courtroom from their adjoining cells to begin the proceedings. Among the twenty-one accused were Hermann Goering, Rudolf Hess, Wilhelm Frick, Joachim von Ribbentrop, Field Marshal Wilhelm Keitel, General Alfred Jodl, Hans Frank, Baldur von Schirach, Franz von Papen, Artur von Seyss-Inquart, Admirals Karl Dönitz and Erich Raeder. The men were charged with the "planning, preparation, initiation and waging of illegal wars . . . war crimes and crimes against humanity."

The trial went on for nearly a year, Cronkite and his staff sending out stories each day of the week the court was in session: of Hess's insistence that he had flown to England to take King George VI back to Germany for a peace conference with Adolf Hitler; of Goering's arrival at the trial under armed arrest but with twenty pieces of matched red leather Louis Vuitton luggage filled with custom-tailored uniforms, medals, jeweled watches and syn-thetic morphine, and his center-stage antics of laughing and nod-ding.

The final sentencing was handed down September 30, 1946. Seven defendants were given prison sentences: Dönitz, Hess, Rae-der, Funk, Speer, Schirach, and Neurath. The rest were sentenced to death by hanging, to be carried out on October 15 of that year.

Despite promises to the press for full access to all parts of the trial, the judges denied members of the press permission to witness the executions. A roar of protest arose from the journalists in Nur-emberg and newsgathering agencies around the world. Cronkite's company president, Hugh Baille, flew to Nuremberg in order to make an appeal to the Allied Council to allow the press to cover the hangings. Baille argued that many people would spread rumors the executions did not take place or that the criminals were free. The mysteries that surrounded Hitler's death had made most re-porters suspicious of the court's decision. Baille also suggested that some possible final confessions or utterances of historical signifi-cance should be recorded for posterity by members of the press. The appeals were considered and the judges relented somewhat: photographs would still be forbidden, but two members of the press who would pool their stories with the press corps could attend the hangings.

Goering cheated the gallows by taking cyanide. The remaining six convicted criminals were executed and a horror-filled chapter in human history was closed.

By the time the war trials had ended in Europe, the Japanese had surrendered and, with similar legal proceedings to follow in Japan, the war was over.

*   *   *

Cronkite and his colleagues packed up their personal effects to join their families in their home countries. For four years, he had experienced the violence, tragedies, dirt and stench of war. He had witnessed the horrors brought upon the civilian population of London by weapons launched by madmen from across the English Channel unseen miles away. He had known the impersonal and indiscriminate death the unceasing attacks wrought. He had seen bravery as well as cowardice. As a journalist, he had walked through the infernos of burning cities and observed hand-to-hand combat where human beings stabbed or shot or beat each other to death. He had seen, from high above the clouds, a sky filled with planes and bombs that brought about the indiscriminate, random slaughter of hundreds of German civilians on the ground far below. In whatever manner the carnage was carried out, the results remained the same: people killed and people died. Homes or entire cities vanished from the earth overnight. Widows were left homeless with pieces of children to claim as their families; starving, homeless men casually ate bloated, fly-blown horse carcasses in the streets. Cronkite and the men he had worked with were sickened by what they had been exposed to—man at his most bestial.

Walter Cronkite's aversion to fighting, warfare or any other form of violence is not restricted to a world war. It extends to any vestige of inhumanity of one person to another, whether on the front porch of a rich man's house in Houston, in the streets of Dallas or on the battlefields of Europe or Vietnam. "How can men go to war?" he asks rhetorically at times. "How can people who call themselves civilized even take up arms against each other? I don't understand how civilized people can carry guns."

Possibly because he despises the war he was a part of, and possibly because he is a modest man, Cronkite today declines any honors accorded him for his wartime exploits. He is firm in his insistence that he "was a great coward . . . always looking for a good story in the artillery so I wouldn't have to to out with the infantry. I was always worried about the risk of losing an arm or a leg so I couldn't dance anymore."

In a 1974 televised interview from his Martha's Vineyard summer home, Cronkite told Dick Cavett emphatically, "No! I was absolutely no hero! I had the good fortune of getting assignments with the United Press and I had a chance to run a pretty good gamut of experiences."

On another occasion, when asked about his years as a war correspondent, Cronkite paid homage to the soldiers he served with and whom he regards as the real heroes: "It didn't take any courage to do it once. If you go back and do it a second time—knowing how bad it is—that's courage."

"The Right Place at the Right Time"

The Early Days at CBS

I was just plain old lucky to be in the right place at the right time. But I think that to take advantage of luck, you've got to have some ability to do the job. As far as the ability to work on camera is concerned, that part of it was an absolute accident. I never trained for it; I'm just lucky to have it. Whatever it is, it seems to work. I was also ambitious as a young man to push myself along, not to become president of the United Press, but because I wanted to be where the story was. So I pushed to get where I could go. And I guess the whole thing just built up into a store of experience, and with experience came a certain amount of knowledge.

—Walter Cronkite

AS THE TIDE turned in favor of the Allied Powers during World War II, deep resentments and subtle hostilities emerged between Russia and the Western nations. The high hopes and euphoria of the 1945 Yalta Conference were short-lived. Those decisive high-level meetings between the "Big Three"—Roosevelt, Churchill and Stalin—promised a bright future for the post-war world. It soon became only too clear that the Soviet Union had no intention of honoring its part of the Yalta agreements. There was nervous concern from the West over Stalin's attitude toward Poland. Despite repeated letters and warnings from Roosevelt and Churchill, the Russians ignored their allies and began their subversion of defenseless Poland.

After Roosevelt's death, Churchill and President Truman attempted to resolve the problems with Stalin. At a time when full attention should have been focused on crushing the remaining pockets of Nazi resistance, the Allies were dangerously divisive.

Following Germany's surrender, the Soviets initiated a series of hostile maneuvers nearly as traumatic as the war had been. Churchill, in utter frustration and disdain for the aggression and hypocrisy of the Soviets, concluded Russia was "a riddle wrapped in a mystery inside an enigma." On May 2, 1945, Churchill sent the president a telegram in which he verbalized his apprehensions over the widening chasm between Russia and England and the United States:

". . . What is to happen about Russia?

". . . An iron curtain is drawn down upon their front. We do not know what is going on behind. . . . All kinds of arrangements will have to made by General Eisenhower to prevent another immense flight of the German population westward as this enormous Muscovite advance into the center of Europe takes place. And then the curtain will descend again to a very large extent, if not entirely."

By war's end, the difficulties with Russia were found not only at the higher levels of government; any individual, agency—anything or anybody—who had any dealings with the Soviet Union met with the same stony silence. Newsgathering services that prided themselves with the ability to provide newspapers and radio stations with information were having their share of abortive attempts at finding out what was transpiring behind that seemingly impenetrable and appropriately-named Iron Curtain.

United Press president Hugh Baille consulted with his staff about the lack of information coming from Russia. After days of discussion, it was decided that perhaps part of the problem stemmed from the reporters, themselves, who had been assigned to Moscow. Perhaps if an experienced, charming, and resourceful correspondent were sent, some chinks in the curtain might be found. Perhaps the right man could provide more information to the West than the standard Party line, which was currently the standard questionable fare. All agreed if anybody could fulfill the agency's mission, it would be Walter Cronkite.

Cronkite, meanwhile, had already resettled in the States with his wife, whom he had not seen for any considerable length of time since the war began. When he was offered the position of UP Bureau Chief in Moscow, he was none too anxious to take it. The solitary years he had spent without Betsy were lonely ones and he had no desire for another separation from her. Too, he felt he had "served his time" overseas and had no desire to be subjected to food rationing or housing shortages which typified post-war Russia. The long, cold winters were no temptation, either.

His company had anticipated his objections and was prepared to address them: he could take his wife, westerners were permitted to shop at stores used by the Party elite, he would live in a decent apartment the UP kept for its reporters, there was a sizeable American and Western European community for socializing and, finally, the winters provided wonderful opportunities for skiing and other cold weather sports.

A challenge Cronkite found hard to resist was being *the* reporter who would be able to get the truth out of Russia. He talked the proposal over with Betsy and they decided to take the assignment for two years, from 1946 until 1948.

Once again, Cronkite packed his bags and headed east. Her hopes ever high, Betsy packed 200 golf balls, planning to spend the time improving her golf game. As fate would have it, however, there were no golf courses in Moscow, or in all of Russia, for that matter. Undaunted, she took a job with the United States Information Agency, helping publish a *Life*-formatted magazine called *Amerika*. *Amerika* was a non-political informative publication, assembled in the Soviet Union and published in the United States for U.S. readers.

Western journalists assigned to Moscow traditionally lived at the Metropole Hotel. During the 1920's, however, the UP's Eugene Meyer had leased a comfortable apartment for his company and, over the years, the United Press had managed to hold on to it. Cronkite replaced Edward Shapiro, who had been there during the war and would, as it turned out, relieve Cronkite two fruitless years later.

Cronkite would be working out of his apartment where a small room had been set up as a bureau office. He had two translators, two messenger girls and a chauffeur—all Russians—to help him with his reports and get him around town. A maid, or "poor old woman," as Cronkite remembers her, accustomed to standing for hours in the interminable lines required to purchase food, helped Betsy run the apartment.

At every opportunity to wrest knowledge from inside Russia, Cronkite was frustratingly met with what he recalls as "total and complete censorship and that's very difficult to live with." Official Soviet-generated propaganda was virtually all that was available to him or any other correspondents. Eaves-dropping devices and the presence of the KGB-appointed office staff prevented Cronkite's even thinking of talking with private citizens. The stories he sent to the States were like those the newsmen before him had sent: mundane, non-political "non-news"; bits and pieces of information of no real significance. Anybody could report the drivel he was sending back.

It was a drab, gray and depressing gloomy existence. An occasional day of skiing broke the monotomy, as did a trip to the Bolshoi or the opera. Once, at the opera, the Cronkites did get glimpses of Stalin whenever he, in Cronkite's words, "poked his head from behind a curtain that hid him from the crowd."

When their two years were up, Betsy was pregnant and neither of them wanted their first child born in a Soviet hospital. There was no temptation for either of them to remain. Cronkite knew when to call it quits. Until the advent of *Peristroika,* some forty years later, there was little commercial news to be extracted from Russia unless Kremlin leaders themselves released it. "Truth" behind the Iron Curtain, was found only in the official state-run paper, *Pravda,* and not even a reporter of Cronkite's caliber could change the way the Soviets manipulated the news.

*   *   *

The Cronkites returned to the States, touching down in Kansas City. He asked the UP for a raise and was told—so the rumor goes—in a rather back-handed way, he had probably gone as far as he could and was encouraged to move on to a job where he could realize his full potential. He took the hint and quit the UP for good.

While looking around for employment, he hit the lecture circuit, speaking to audiences primarily in the Midwest.

He remained prejudiced against radio, going so far as pronouncing, "News is a newspaper's business and it isn't radio's business." He steadfastly believed it was primarily a medium for entertainment. He reluctantly took a position with radio station KMBD in Washington, D.C., where he would cover the capital for a group of Midwestern stations.

In 1948, the same year he and his wife left Russia, the Cronkites took a house in Chevy Chase, Maryland. Their first child, Nancy Elizabeth, was born on November 4, her father's birthday. On September 15, 1950, their family would grow again with the birth of a second daughter, Mary Kathleen.

It was at this time in Cronkite's journalistic career he was truly "in the right place at the right time," as he has often explained his steady climb up the ladder to CBS in New York. It might be an oversimplification of a series of events to say his ascent was meteoric, but from that point on he moved steadily upward, not because of chance or happenstance, but because of his unrelenting professionalism and absolute competence.

* * *

Edward Murrow, who had not given up on getting Cronkite into CBS's stable, tried again in 1950. The Korean War had just broken out, and CBS promised, as a recruiting enticement, to send the seasoned correspondent to Korea to cover the action. Cronkite signed on with CBS, but at the last minute he was assigned to CBS television affiliate WTOP in Washington. The sudden switch didn't please him at all and he angrily complained he had been tricked and he "was madder than hell!" and that he had "been sold down the river to a lousy local TV station!" Despite his disappointment and undisguised fury at not being sent to Korea, his mature journalistic sense prevailed. He was, after all, the first CBS reporter in the nation's capital to be assigned exclusively to television, and he was not going to pass up such a challenge as that. There were stories more important than the social whirl which gossip-happy Washingtonians engaged in and he demonstrated his talents for extracting reports of an otherwise mundane nature by presenting them in a new light. His performing such incredible feats as ad-libbing the day's news without a script, or presenting a clear and concise impromptu chalk-talk on the Korean War, made him an instant hit with his Washington viewers. Cronkite further distinguished himself with skillful and colorful coverage of the Mardi Gras festivities in New Orleans and, with President Truman as his host, was the first reporter to televise a tour of the White House.

*   *   *

Television in the early 1950s suffered many of the afflictions ascribed to radio in the 1920s and 1930s. Both media had come into general usage on the heels of world wars, when comedy, music and variety shows were the major offerings. Early television became the playground for such entertainers as Milton Berle, Hopalong Cassidy, Ed Sullivan, Sid Caesar, and Imogene Coca, as well as "live" studio wrestling. People got their news from radio, newspapers, and newsreels, such as *The March of Time*, shown at movie theatres. News was not yet television's forte, but Cronkite was helping change that. He found news in New Orleans and on Pennsylvania Avenue, always with his own brand of dignity. A case in point was what the *Saturday Evening Post* described as "his somber reporting from the stockyards of Chicago [which] came as a revelation to audiences accustomed to thinking of television primarily as a medium of entertainment."

Cronkite did not go unnoticed by CBS executives, either. In 1951, he was made moderator of the weekly televised program *Man of the Week,* CBS's answer to NBC's *Meet the Press. Man of the Week* was nationally televised and the exposure familiarized Cronkite with ever-increasing numbers of viewers. The show permitted him to demonstrate his talent for conducting lively, informative and interesting interviews week after week. He casually stated he succeeded simply by "throwing the meat on the table and letting them fight it out."

CBS News executive and producer Sig Mickelson chose Cronkite to anchor CBS's network coverage of the 1952 Chicago convention. Since these were the first televised national conventions, the future of those political circuses, not to mention politics and politicians themselves, were shaped and molded by the pioneer television commentators.

The bitter and frequent feuding that broke out between the Eisenhower and Taft camps on national television alarmed the American viewers and severely damaged the Republican Party. The public's outcry over the fighting, and complaints against the boring, long-winded and repetitious speeches sent the Democrats scurrying into innumerable conferences. They discussed the errors their political enemies were making and plotted strategies to improve their own party's image when their television debut was made. President Truman, even though not a candidate, made notes regarding his ideas on convention coverage and passed them on to convention leaders in hopes of helping to create the proper impact on a virgin audience.

The Democrats took great pains to avoid even what smacked of bickering and kept speeches short and to the point. Too, where the Republicans had used long, impersonal camera shots from the sides, the Democrats had the cameras move in for personal close-ups as if to demonstrate to its audience a political philosophy of "come closer, we care," as opposed to a "keep your distance from us," as the Republicans had unwittingly done. The Democrats, in effect, had watched and learned from the Republicans how not to conduct a political convention; they then held their own, capitalizing on their opponents' mistakes. Fortunately for the Republicans, their candidate, war hero Eisenhower, more than compensated for the short-comings of his party at the convention, as he went on to win the election that year.

Cronkite's coverage of the conventions was well received by his American television audience, described variously by enthusiastic critics as memorable and superb. His incredible ability to extemporize smoothly and almost endlessly amazed his audiences. The *Reader's Digest* declared that he was "utterly unflappable even under the most frantic conditions." Co-workers marveled at the ease which characterized his commentary, because only they knew the behind-the-scenes way he brought order out of chaos: he wore earphones with different conversations on either channel, followed the activities on the floor, yet could calmly talk into the camera, ignoring totally the confusion at the production level. Four small television monitors gave him minute-by-minute balloting, according to geographic regions. He received additional information from six broadcast monitors, a multi-feed monitor, and a writer who handed him notes from beneath his desk .

Generally, the press had nothing but praise and the laudatory letters from viewers convinced Mickelson that his choice of anchorman was a good one. Following the successful venture, Mickelson denied any speculating or high-risk gambling in placing Cronkite in the anchor spot: "Walter has an instinctive feeling of when to talk and when not to . . . he is so thorough, it's fantastic . . . he has a big, bearish quality that is appealing and he is colorful. Too, he likes to ad-lib around."

Despite the high praise from Mickelson, the press and a dedicated audience, some high-ranking CBS executives who had compared CBS's coverage with NBC's Bill Henry, had concluded that, among other complaints, Cronkite had talked too much. The criticism reached Cronkite by way of newspaper articles and he was prompt to defend his rationale by the same medium. He felt talk was necessary because, as he told one newspaper interviewer, "The big problem in television is that you don't know your audience. Is it intelligent, or is it made up of people who know nothing about political procedures?"

Because television was a new medium and this was a convention's first coverage by that medium, discussions and debates of the phenomenon were cropping up everywhere. Val Adams of the *New York Times* asked in his column, "Will the more lasting effect of television in 1952 be to impress on the national mind that the political convention *per se* is often a chaotic and far from from democratic machinery for choosing candidates? What is the viewer's reaction to the whole procedure?"

As if responding to Adams's rhetorical questions, Cronkite wrote his opinions concerning the potential of television in influencing politics at the request of *Theatre Arts* magazine. The piece, entitled "Government by Hooper Rating?" prophesied, somewhat naïvely, perhaps:

"Television will force a middle ground between personality and politics and that is a good thing.

"Democracy cannot work unless people participate in it. The people cannot participate intelligently unless they are informed. The people cannot be informed no matter how hard the experts try if they do not listen. The people will not listen unless listening is painless, even enjoyable, as well as instructive.

"The conclusion is that the politician who can command the highest Hooper rating is likely to achieve office and the power that goes with it. And, once in office, he stands the best chance of being able to keep the public informed, since the public, presumably, will listen to him because it likes to listen to him.

"It also could engender as much evil as good. We had spellbinders in politics long before television. Dictators rose abroad and some incipient ones rose at home on their ability to arouse the emotions of their audiences. They did it from the platform or on the air waves.

"With television, there still will be spellbinders, and some of them might perhaps succeed with the new medium. But it seems to me that their chances of success are diminished by television, not increased by it."

Whether knowingly influenced by Aristotle's beliefs that "a good man will speak well" or not, Cronkite continued his remarks by suggesting that "television has an X-ray quality. Television can detect insincerity as a more orthodox X-ray can detect a broken bone. Television can X-ray the soul, therefore, the future breed of politicians is going to be a much higher, not lower type than we have known in the past."

Cronkite concluded the article by evaluating the four political contestants of that 1952 race as they had emerged as television candidates, declaring, "In this first election year of the era of television, the nation, by some happy cooperation, was presented an excellent casting file." General Eisenhower, he wrote, "was a great man who could not hide from the searching eye of television the fact that he was greater than the people who wrote his speeches." Governor Adlai Stevenson, the Democratic presidential nominee, was "the closest approach to the born television actor on the television stage." He felt Richard Nixon was "actually handicapped by his youthful good looks," but was an "aggressive . . . executive type . . . no-nonsense person . . . who was too punchy." He dismissed

Alabama Senator John Sparkman, on the other hand, as simply having "not enough punch."

The Westinghouse Electric Company had sponsored all of CBS's convention programming and many viewers believed Betty Furness, Westinghouse's attractive spokeswoman, might have been the real star. The cameras cut back and forth from the convention to Furness as she sold stoves and refrigerators. By the end of the convention, she had been on camera more than any of the nominees. When *Newsweek* reflected on the television event and Cronkite's debut, it declared: "The affable six-foot, 200-pound anchor man in CBS's Chicago coverage in July became almost as famous as Betty Furness."

                    *   *   *

The premiere of televised conventions in the United States was primitive and resembled the rowdiness and crudeness of Jacksonian Democracy when compared to today's standards, but it was an important landmark in American history. By exposing the face of politics at its gut-level, television forced the rough, frontiers-style campaigning that had become part of this country's folklore to reinvent itself. The television camera inaugurated the beginning of a public and open forum which permitted the entire nation the privilege of vicarious participation. Mistakes were made and precedents were established. The thorns as well as the roses of the political flower garden were exposed to the viewing public.

Cronkite continued receiving rave reviews for his coverage of the conventions as well as for the special reports he filed as he followed Republican presidential candidate Eisenhower about the country. Because of these particularly insightful and informative telecasts, Cronkite, the *Current Biography Yearbook* reported, "suddenly was a star."

The CBS executives who had fretted that Cronkite "had talked too much" were reeling at the notoriety he received. He was quickly transferred to New York, where he was given two news programs to host: *The Twentieth Century* and *Eyewitness to History.* In addition, he moderated the forum *Pick the Winner,* for which he won critic John Crosby's praise for the "charm and wonderful self-restraint" he demonstrated during the political debates that program frequently sparked.

In February of 1953, Cronkite became the narrator for what was to be one of his most popular programs, *You Are There,* in which he walked in and out of famous moments in history. William Doxier, a CBS executive and the show's producer, explained the simple logic behind his choice of Cronkite as host: "He's good, he's effective, and since the national political conventions, he's a household name."

In 1954, CBS introduced plans for its own morning news show to compete with NBC's popular and top-rated *Today,* hosted by David Garroway. The CBS entry was to be entitled simply *Morning Show,* with Cronkite as host. When the over-ambitious program was inaugurated, it utilized an electronic weather forecaster, newscasts by veteran Charles Collingwood and featured puppets "Humphry the Hound-Dog" and "Charlemane the Lion" to compete with *Today*'s chimpanzee, J. Fredd Muggs. Cronkite's monumental job was to unite this conglomeration into a cohesive whole. In a role that was described as being alternately "master of ceremonies, ringmaster and coordinator," he was, nevertheless, considered "a relaxed, smooth-as-silk salesman operating in the anchor spot as the centrifugal force from which the show's proceedings stem."

Lawrence Laurent, entertainment writer for the *New York Times,* commented, "The show is a break for Walter, an old Washington hand, who has never before had an opportunity to project his warm personality or to utilize his bright, quick wit. Behind that bass-baritone and commentator dignity, Cronkite has hidden the best sense of humor in the CBS news department."

A TelePrompTer supplied Cronkite with his lines, introductions and jokes—written by gag writers—but he was still permitted to ad-lib. Even though the show was planned originally as a news and information program, entertainment crept in as a major ingredient and Cronkite, *Time* wrote, "became a hostage to show biz." The program soon became a burden to him. He enjoyed levity, but he wanted to be known as a newsman and not as a comedian. Ultimately, ratings fell sharply and, even though Cronkite felt he had been "reasonably charming, the whole thing didn't work out." It was with no regret he was replaced by Jack Paar. Shortly after taking over, however, Paar received a letter of pretended sarcasm from an unabashed Cronkite fan: "You won't be as good as Walter Cronkite. I should know, I'm his mother."

As Edward Murrow's *Person to Person* program ended for the 1954 season, Cronkite was chosen to moderate its summer replacement, *It's News to Me*. Among his special reports in 1955, he narrated the explosion of an atomic bomb at Yucca Flats, Nevada, and the dedication of the Air Force Academy. In 1956, he asked his producers to let him host a new quiz show, *Nothing But the Truth*. Fearing another *Morning Show* fiasco, permission was denied and a ruling was quickly issued that forbade using CBS newsmen on any other programs of light entertainment or in commercial announcements.

When the political conventions met to choose candidates in 1956 and again in 1960, Cronkite was CBS's anchorman. He was, by then, a permanent fixture at the conventions, as much a part of the political scene as the red-white-and-blue bunting and billboard-sized likenesses of the candidates. Additionally, the term "anchorman," which had been used to describe the last man in a relay race, was so identified with Cronkite that Swedish television adopted the verb *Cronkiter*, which means "to anchor."

In the 1960 conventions, electric adding machines were used by CBS to tabulate national voting. By 1966, CBS utilized its own polls and those of the Louis Harris Company along with calculators and computers from IBM to project winners. Once, when Cronkite was demonstrating to reporters from the *New Yorker* the sophisticated equipment CBS would use in election coverage, he playfully typed up onto the display screen, "Now is the time for all men to come to the aid of their country." Then, for good measure, "The quick brown fox jumps over the lazy dog."

Cronkite continued his regular news commentaries on *The Twentieth Century*, covering such diverse topics as movie history, future lifestyles, outer space, underseas exploration and rocket research. He traveled widely, reporting royal coronations, the 1959 Kruschev visit, World's Fairs, and the 1960 Winter Olympics. As he had covered the Nuremberg war trials, he reported the preparations for the 1960 Israeli trial of former Nazi Adolph Eichmann, as well as every space flight from 1961 until his retirement. In 1963, he anchored the first live transatlantic TelStar satellite transmission, "Town Meeting of the World," in which former President Eisenhower, former British Prime Minister Anthony Eden, Jean

Monnet of France and Germany's Heinrich von Brentano were the participants.

Along the way, Cronkite's diligence and perseverance were earning him a record number of honors and awards. In addition to his two Emmys, he was named 1961 "Broadcaster of the Year" by the International Radio and Television Society. In 1962, he became the first television newsman to receive the coveted George Foster Peabody Television award. He received the George Polk Memorial Award and was named the recipient of the American Civil Liberties Union Award for "distinguished public service in the defense and practice of the First Amendment," and the list of awards seemed to continue *ad infinitum.*

The honors and outstanding work for which Cronkite had been singled out were working forcefully in his favor. CBS executives were ecstatic over their "Golden Boy," and discussions at the highest level were being held to discuss his future with the network.

It was in 1962, while filming a segment of *The Twentieth Century* at the Seattle World's Fair, Cronkite first heard rumors through the usually reliable network grapevine that a massive shake-up in the news staff in New York was underway. Suddenly and without warning, Douglas Edwards, who had anchored the evening news show for fourteen years, was informed of his replacement by Cronkite. Edwards was understandably hurt and disappointed with the change and threatened to resign. He was reminded his contract had four more years to run and he would be held to it. After he had sufficient time to adjust to the situation, the disgruntled newsman accepted the corporate decision, but felt the affair "could have been handled with a little more dexterity." Cronkite, meanwhile, had received official word of his promotion. With the new position went a new title, managing editor. He began laying plans at once for making improvements. At the press conference he called, he told reporters he believed greater use could be made of the existing staff and correspondents and he intended to write as much of his own material as he would have time for, hoping "somehow to justify my salary," which was reported to be in excess of $100,000.

Richard Gehman reacted to Cronkite's elevation in *TV Guide*: "Cronkite may have been picked because he had more 'character' than any of the other CeeBeeEssers. He is like an amiable, relaxed professor of Etruscan civilization, wrinkled in voice and costume. He is as folksy as Arthur Godfrey. His only concession to slickness is a regular trip to the barber."

Cronkite's NBC competitors, Chet Huntley and David Brinkley, had wide-reaching appeal—the former with his droll "trump of doom" voice and the latter, known as the "boyish sarcaster"—providing their audience with news within an entertainment context. The two were virtually unchallenged in the television network news field. Despite the fact they were the giants CBS was out to slay, they welcomed Cronkite to his new post as part of their news coverage and as a tribute to the camaraderie that existed within the coterie of network newscasters.

There is no doubt the ratings game played a significant role in the selection of Cronkite to replace Edwards. NBC had led the three major networks since network news began and CBS wanted to be first. "Hell, yes, there is a battle," Cronkite said, declaring war on NBC. "I don't feel at a disadvantage with two against one. Let 'em put four in there if they want to. I've taken on two. I can take on four!"

Within only two months after assuming his new position as anchorman and giant killer in April 1962, Cronkite's news program began to show definite signs of growth, both in depth of news presentation and in audience size. CBS executives noted with delight the gains being made on NBC, but they would not be satisfied until CBS surpassed NBC in ratings. Brainstorming sessions were held in which company executives presented various game plans for the unseating of their rival. A strategy was developed to force NBC to alter its format radically, thereby losing its momentum. When the giant stumbled, CBS felt it could close in and take the lead.

In those days, network news was an incredibly brief fifteen minutes in length, generally sharing a half-hour news slot with local stations. On September 2, 1963, CBS sprang its battle plan: the *Evening News* was doubled in length to thirty minutes.

The response from the critics and television viewers for the longer format was swift and positive. The concensus was reflected in the review presented in the *New York Times* the next morning: "Last night was refreshingly different. Mr. Cronkite's interview with President Kennedy was leisurely and covered a variety of subjects.

Eric Sevareid, broadcasting's foremost essayist, had a niche for commentary of sufficient length to say something."

The corporate move had worked. The following week, NBC, likewise, expanded its evening program to a half-hour, David Brinkley wryly hoping they would have enough to say to fill the time. In the transition, NBC fell behind CBS, where it remained until the next year.

By 1964, Cronkite's star had risen rapidly with CBS. He drew a handsome salary, enjoyed a compatible family, owned houses, a sailboat, and sports cars, worked with a dedicated news staff, and watched his Nielsen ratings steadily climb. His reputation as an honest and objective newsman was earning him the highest accolades and respect throughout the country and around the world. He was riding a crest that few would ever know.

In an effort to maintain the momentum he had generated with his network, Cronkite and CBS put the finishing touches on their presidential convention coverage in San Francisco and Atlantic City. A full-page advertisement in leading newspapers pictured a photograph of Cronkite thoughtfully puffing on his pipe and promised: "Tonight in New Hampshire— and for the next 238 days— television's most astute and experienced political reporter will cover the developing drama of the 1964 Presidential Elections."

Even though CBS promised drama at the conventions, no one suspected the turn of events which were about to unfold. The drama would not be played out on the convention floor of the Republicans' San Francisco Cow Palace, but in the caverns which are the offices of CBS executives in New York City.

"Not a Choice
but an Echo"

The 1964 Conventions

*As the lights went on at the Democratic Convention
in Atlantic City this week, Walter Cronkite, that grand
old party televised conventioneer, was no longer presiding over the CBS aquarium high over Convention
Hall. It's hard to believe, as the very name Cronkite
has acquired a sound of granite quality. [He] practically invented the system of reporting conventions.*
                                          —Richard Oulahan

THE DRAMATIC impact of network television on national
political conventions in 1952 changed forever conventions, politics
and politicians. By 1960, the broadcast industry's television had developed into a force to be reckoned with. Politicians had immediately taken note of television's power and had assumed a "positive
mode" whenever "on camera." Suddenly, image-makers, make-up
artists, public relations advisers, toupees and photogenic angles
were topics of conversation at cocktail parties, within the confines
of the traditional "smoke-filled rooms" or any place office-seekers
hunkered. As significant or, possibly, as trifling as the above subjects may seem to non-aspirants, the ever egocentric candidates
were dead serious about them.

Handsome and graceful Senator John Kennedy took to the medium of television with a special *élan* that made him not only an important political force and mass media personality, but, in the parlance of our often-superficial culture, a Star. Better yet, he was not just a Star, but a Superstar; one with sex-appeal and, more importantly, one with voter appeal. Kennedy respected the mystical forces television obviously could generate within its audience and planned his television appearances carefully, following to the letter the advice of his knowledgeable and sizable staff of friends—the "Irish Mafia"—and professional consultants.

In what has become recognized as a phenomenon and a political classic, the New England senator challenged his opponent, incumbent Vice-President Richard Nixon, to a series of debates to be carried live on radio and television. Kennedy was considered by many conservative and Protestant Americans and political experts to be too young, too rich, too Catholic and too inexperienced to be president of the United States. Richard Nixon was far and away the favored candidate prior to what Senator Kennedy facetiously termed the "Great Debates."

Richard Nixon had never been totally at ease with television. His heavy beard and swarthy complexion on 1960s black-and-white sets gave him a sinister look. When he arrived at the studio for the first of the much-publicized debates, Nixon had just been released from a hospital where he had been treated for the flu, exhaustion, and a dangerously infected knee. He had lost fifteen pounds during his hospitalization and his clothes did not fit. Further, as he had left his car that morning at the studio, he banged his tender knee against the car door, causing him considerable pain. His television make-up could not hide his pain or gaunt face; his gray suit blended with the neutral backdrop. Compared with his tanned, energetic and Hollywood-handsome opponent, Nixon was a sad sight to behold.

Nixon chose to debate formally and collegiate-style, addressing himself to his opponent. Kennedy, on the other hand, virtually ignored the vice-president and the newsmen who asked the questions for discussion, and aimed his confident comments directly at the cameras and to the television audience. Visually, Nixon was no match for Kennedy. Gail Cameron, in her book *Rose,* reported that Nixon performed so poorly and looked so dreadful when he met

Kennedy for the first debate, Rose Kennedy remarked, "I feel so sorry for Nixon's mother tonight."

The results of the debates were remarkable and are still discussed: Nixon, unseen by his radio audience, "won" in surveys made by that medium, while Kennedy "won" on television. Audiences estimated at from 65,000,000 to 120,000,000 viewers per debate were allowed to compare the two primary contenders for the presidency, side by side and under nearly identical conditions. Many political analysts felt it was this brief series of public encounters which edged Kennedy ahead of Nixon, resulting, ultimately, in the senator's election by a margin of only 112,000 votes. Even President-elect Kennedy admitted, "It was TV more than anything else that turned the tide."

Four years later, when the 1964 political conventions were being planned, the world had undergone radical shocks and sudden tragic changes: Camelot, the fairy-tale world that idealized the Kennedy White House, was shattered with his assassination in the streets of his vice-president's home state; Lyndon Johnson, who had seized Kennedy's banner before it touched the ground, held it high before the world and the U.S. Congress for successful passage of milestone civil rights and other social legislation; resistance to Johnson's "Great Society" by many Americans was swift, violent and nationwide; police dogs and fire hoses characterized "Bull" Conner's Birmingham; riots, looting and killing were daily fare in Harlem; the savage murders of civil rights activists Michael Schwerner, James Chaney and Andrew Goodman in Mississippi reflected the repulsive and ugly face of racism in the extreme; and increasing fears from Russia continued to grow as an aftermath of the sensitive and nearly explosive Cuban missile showdown between Kruschev and Kennedy. The Cuban situation had brought the world literally to the brink of war as the two leaders rattled atomic swords over the expansion of the Soviet's arsenal in America's back yard. Viet-Nam was a term being used more and more by newsmen, politicians, and militarists.

Lyndon Johnson rapidly put his stamp on his own presidency, becoming somewhat a symbol of stability and sanity to dazed Americans, who saw the world they knew flying to pieces before their eyes. He provided a visible display of continuity from the Kennedy years to the convention of 1964. Johnson was eager to be Every

Man's President. He wanted mightily to be loved by all, to win a mandate that would leave no doubt in any mind that he was, indeed, The President, elected by the greatest margin of voters in America's history.

The badly splintered Republican Party searched assiduously for a leader who could convince the electorate he could salvage the mess that was the United States and defeat the confident incumbent Democratic president. Open hostilities, reminiscent of the 1952 campaign, broke out among the camps of Nixon, Rockefeller, Goldwater, and Scranton. Nixon was branded a loser and dumped early: his squeaking loss to Kennedy in 1960 grated on Republican nerves, prompting the old political game of "If." "If" Nixon had made this speech, "If" he had gone to that city or shaken that hand or kissed that baby, he might have achieved a Republican victory. Political analysts were able to show, with considerable empirical support, that Nelson Rockefeller might have been the best GOP candidate in 1964. In more normal times, he probably would have been chosen, but, as previously noted, the 1960s were far from normal.

Rockefeller's divorce and remarriage to "Happy" Murphy infuriated conservatives and provided gossips with more to wag their tongues over than scandal tabloids ever could. Adding to Rockefeller's political troubles, Happy had been compelled by complicated and unpleasant circumstances to leave her own children with their father when she married Rockefeller. The affair split the Republicans and probably forever ruined his chances for a nomination.

Barry Goldwater, in his campaign speeches, promised he would employ whatever means were required to quell riots, dissent and violence and to eliminate what he regarded as the Communist menace. He further pledged to reduce government spending drastically, beginning with the possible sale of the Tennessee Valley Authority, followed by cutting educational loans and even reducing Social Security benefits. In effect, his conservative social platform succeeded in offending everyone—everyone, that is, except the Republican strategists.

Prior to the conventions, as the Republican hopefuls stumped about the countryside, Cronkite was busily reporting their trials, travels, speeches, and activities on his evening news program. He covered the news concerning each of them with professional and unbiased objectivity, but privately was becoming increasingly more concerned with what he felt were saber-rattling and rabble-rousing by Senator Goldwater. In late May, he could contain his feeling no longer: he continued his impartial network coverage, but privately telephoned his friend General Eisenhower at his Gettysburg farm in hopes of persuading the former Republican president to speak out publicly against Goldwater's extremism. The General had been one of the most popular presidents of all time and, in 1964, was the figurehead of his party. Even though it would have been quite within his power and philosophy to censure Goldwater, he refused to do so. The telephone conversation and Cronkite's terrible disappointment with Eisenhower's reluctance to call down Goldwater quickly became news items.

Whether Cronkite's conversation stirred Eisenhower's conscience or merely reinforced his own beliefs will probably never be known, but he seemed to take a sudden political turn. Only a few days after the Cronkite call, Eisenhower invited William Scranton to a meeting at the General's downtown Gettysburg office. For one and a quarter hours, the two spoke of many topics in general, they later told reporters, but of nothing in particular. Scranton, however, interpreted the dialogue as support, subtle or otherwise, from General Eisenhower for his presidential aspirations.

The following day, Scranton was scheduled to appear on *Face the Nation*. He confidently decided to use that nationally-televised program to announce his candidacy with what he assumed was General Eisenhower's blessing. Scant hours before Scranton left for the television studio and the live broadcast, however, Eisenhower called him on the telephone to say he hoped there hadn't been any misunderstanding in their conversation the afternoon before, stating, "I will not, nor would not, in any way, be a part of a stop-Goldwater campaign." Scranton was stunned and totally confused. His strategy at that point was completely and utterly destroyed. His major purpose for appearing on *Face the Nation* was now moot. He gamely went on the program, but since he had no candidacy to declare, no candidate to support, no issues to discuss, he made a pathetic showing. He joined Nixon in the Republicans' elephant graveyard.

The Nelson Rockefellers' announcement of the birth of their child erected yet another candidate's gravestone. America was not prepared to elect a president who was divorced, especially one who had rushed into remarriage with a divorced woman and produced a child in such a scandalously short period of time.

So, now all the Republican candidates had been eliminated with the exception of Arizona Senator Barry Goldwater. The conservative Republican would be pitted against the liberal incumbent Democrat. Neither party, therefore, would use the 1964 conventions as nominating caucuses, but as televised political hurrahs, full of sound and fury, signifying nothing, save a foregone conclusion— that Lyndon Johnson and Hubert Humphrey would represent the Democratic Party, Barry Goldwater and William Miller the Republican opposition.

Television, in the 1960s, was not exempted from an uncertain period of aimlessness and instability. As that medium searched about for its *raison d'être* during that dark period in America's history, it reflected the nation's mood and, in some cases, even seemed to contribute to the apparent characteristic state of chaos. Unfortunately, for some in television management in those days, in order to be news, a story had to be overly dramatic or even tragic. Another requisite was for the news to be "live." The succession of riots in New York's black ghettos was too much for the television cameras to ignore. Theodore White wrote in *The Making of the President, 1964*: "Protected by the police from the mobs, cameramen could thus catch the police at work in the ugly business of grappling with rioters, subduing them by clubs when necessary. Television, reaching for a distorted dramatic effect, ignored the triumphant achievements of such negro communities as it ignores, generally negro political leadership of good will."

Many Americans had come to the angry decision that television itself was a causative factor in situations similar to the one White described, particularly as the fires of civil unrest were seemingly fanned by reporters and cameras in the 1960s. That resentment for television news would be dramatically demonstrated shortly at the Republican National Convention.

The importance of televised politics in 1964 was indicated by the exorbitant sums of money appropriated by the networks. The three major networks' combined budgets for both parties' conventions exceeded $25,000,000. The Republicans prepared an advertising campaign that would cost nearly $5,000,000, the bulk of which was appropriated exclusively for television. The Democrats allocated a similar sum for television advertising, but only $1,700,000 at the network level. The remainder would be spent at the local level, but on television, nevertheless.

ABC's convention reporters Howard K. Smith and Edward Morgan were joined in San Francisco by General Eisenhower, whom that network had recruited for commentary. NBC's Chet Huntley and David Brinkley were re-enforced by Frank McGee, Sander Vanocur and John Chancellor. CBS's sole newsman, Walter Cronkite, armed with his political savvy and experience gleaned through six previous presidential conventions and three elections, made ready to do battle with his formidable network opposition.

As the festivities began, spokesmen for America's poor and lower middle class leveled considerable criticism at the number of well-heeled delegates seated on the convention floor of the Cow Palace, allegedly to represent the nation's Republican voters. Loudon Wainwright wrote in *Life* that he believed the convention to be nothing more than a "gathering place of the utterly comfortable, coming together to protest that they should be having it better. . . . As a spectacle, the Republican Convention was a handsome affair in which suspense was replaced by inevitability."

Wainwright's assessment appears to have been a fair one. There were, by contemporary records, few surprises in that rather dull and self-laudatory exercise in party politics. The scattered high points during the convention often did the Republicans more harm than good. During Nelson Rockefeller's one futile address, for example, he was outshouted by members of his own party. His speech was reckless crowd-baiting at its inflammatory worst and he seemed to glory in the mob action he evoked. The following is Theodore White's account of the event, which revealed the mood of the country and the Republican convention:

"Chairman Morton with difficulty gaveled the auditorium to silence, and Rockefeller began. His five minutes were allotted to the topic of extremism—and, as with absolute zest in the first minute, he swung into his call, the audience exploded again. It was as if Rockefeller were poking with a long lance and prodding a den of hungry lions—they roared back at him. This was the face of the enemy—more important than columnists or switchblade hoodlums; this was the man who had savaged Barry Goldwater from New

Hampshire to California all through the spring. This was the man who called them kooks and now, like kooks, they responded to prove his point. As Rockefeller progressed and the roars grew, his tone alternated between defiance and mockery; he smiled; the audience yelled and roared, and the bass drum thumped; and Rockefeller taunted them all. In a passion that he had rarely achieved in his entire spring primary campaign, he was reaching emotion—and delighting in it. And as he taunted them, they raged. Nor did they, apparently, know what they were raging at: The East; or New York; or communists; or liberals."

Another dramatic and frightening moment of the convention occurred when General Eisenhower addressed the gathering. In a bombshell passage, thinking, perhaps, of the newsmen who had capitalized on the riots in Harlem and other places, he made a derisive reference to "sensation-seeking columnists and commentators who could care less about the welfare of the Republican Party." The attack was totally unexpected and directed to the wrong people at the wrong time and place. The conservative crowd, already in a nasty mood, became a jeering and angry mob, unleashing the hostilities it felt toward "liberal" television and print media journalists. It came screaming to its feet, shaking its fists at the network's representatives in their glass booths high above the convention floor.

Eisenhower's remark had brought the heads of the commentators up sharply. The former president was a personal friend to many of the very men he had just attacked, Cronkite foremost among them. Throughout the convention, the General had been joking with newsmen from the radio and television networks and had just left the ABC booth, where he was supplying political commentary. His remark, therefore, was felt at a personal rather than a professional level. The reporters believed they had been betrayed and humiliated publicly by an old and trusted friend.

Following the berating, Cronkite acted as a self-appointed spokesman for his colleagues in the former president's hotel room by expressing the ire and consternation they all had felt. Eisenhower, plainly surprised at the furor he had caused, asked Cronkite innocently, "What was all that about, anyway?"

Senator Everett Dirkson's nominating speech for Goldwater was looked forward to as a relief from the alternating boredom, tension, and rudeness which had, up to that point, characterized the convention. The sometime-thespian-playwright-turned-Illinois senator, however, disappointed most of those who heard his nauseating address, in which he made frequent references to Goldwater as "the peddler's grandson," alluding to the candidate's grandfather, who began his successful mercantile career as an itinerant salesman. Loudon Wainwright dismissed it as "more of the same sort of oratorical baloney that is common to all conventions." Theodore White, on the other hand, flatly stated it was "the most tasteless nominating speech ever made."

When the nominating speeches were completed, Goldwater and Miller and their wives stepped forward to receive the praise of the Republican faithful. A "gold-water shower" of 10,000,000 pieces of gold foil was released from the ceiling as a glittering conclusion to an otherwise lackluster convention.

The news media personnel packed up their equipment and headed east, where the Democrats were readying their Atlantic City convention site. San Francisco was written off as an utter waste of time in the annals of American political conventions.

The networks and independent pollsters, meanwhile, were analyzing the effects of the convention. Three days after the convention ended, the television surveys told the story CBS did not want to hear: NBC had run away with the television audience. Not only had the Huntley-Brinkley team outdrawn CBS statistically—it had amassed a following larger than the combined audiences of ABC and CBS. In New York, CBS executives flew into a panic when the results came in. They had in front of them an April survey assuring them that Cronkite's news program was leading the *Huntley-Brinkley Report*, but executive consternation and frustration were openly displayed because CBS finished so far down the Nielsen scale from NBC in convention coverage.

It should be noted here that in 1964 the public overwhelmingly preferred paired teams of newsmen like Huntley and Brinkley over CBS's singular Cronkite. "Uncle Walter" apparently lacked the pizazz and show-biz appeal of NBC's "glamour boys." Huntley and Brinkley's light banter and showmanship simply out-entertained and outdrew Cronkite's straight reporting.

Closed doors and high-level conferences were the order of the day and night at CBS headquarters as board chairman William S.

Paley, CBS president Dr. Frank Stanton and other executives probed and inquired into the humiliating debacle. Citing "pressure from upstairs," CBS News president Fred Friendly telephoned Cronkite, who was vacationing in San Diego, for suggestions and ideas for improving the statistics for the upcoming Democratic convention. A week later, on Monday, July 27, Friendly flew to California to deliver the decision Paley and Stanton had made: Cronkite would not cover the Democratic convention. Friendly later told reporters the decision had been reached because "we have concluded that a dual anchor arrangement provided more flexibility, mobility and diversity of coverage"; therefore, Robert Trout and Roger Mudd would be the CBS pair to replace Cronkite.

A memo tacked to a bulletin board informed CBS employees of the abrupt change.

Robert Trout, then fifty-four, was a thirty-year veteran of broadcasting who had been called "The Iron Man of Radio" for once broadcasting fifteen hours straight without a script. He told newsmen he was stunned at the news, and that he couldn't believe such a thing could happen between conventions. Recognizing the change as another power play in corporate politics and that he and Cronkite were merely pawns, Trout wired his condolences to Cronkite. Roger Mudd, then thirty-six, who had just spent sixty-seven days covering the civil rights debates in the Senate, also admitted his surprise at the sudden switch, and with his new assignment.

Cronkite, deeply embarrassed and humiliated, became the center of attraction as his colleagues of the print, radio and television media reeled with disbelief at the CBS move. In his initial attempt to remain philosophical, he told a *Newsweek* reporter, "I'm not bitter yet, but I may be." He recognized the problem for what it was: he was simply unable to compete with NBC during the difficult Republican convention. He confessed, "Great credit must be paid to Huntley and Brinkley. And I don't mean to be derogatory when I say they have entertainment quality. I wish I could be as wry and witty as Brinkley or that I could arch my eyebrows like Huntley," to which Richard Oulahan responded, "Those who wanted information chose Cronkite, while those who wanted entertainment chose Huntley-Brinkley."

As the network rumor mills whispered that he would resign, Cronkite said he was concerned about staying on in any capacity.

"Oh, they gave me all kind of assurances," he told *Life* magazine, "but assurances aren't worth the price of a phone call at a time like that."

At one of his many conferences, Cronkite, who felt he was being made the scapegoat, commented, "One trouble with this business is that it's like Hollywood. You can change all the news executives and it wouldn't mean a thing. It has to be dramatic, so the star has to go. If I were a news executive faced with the same situation, I would have probably done the same thing." Sardonically twisting Goldwater's theme for the Republican convention, he remarked, "Critics may say that CBS is giving them not a choice but an echo."

Cronkite's colleagues and champions in the various media in 1964 began piecing together what they thought caused the dramatic shifts in personnel. One factor that had to be considered was the organizational structure of CBS. The news department is a separate entity from entertainment. The rivalry between news president Friendly and James T. Aubrey's entertainment division may have been such that an attempt was made to balance the ratings in each of those areas. Another speculation was based on Friendly's refusal to pair Cronkite with either Trout or Mudd. It was suggested that Friendly, who had collaborated with Edward Murrow and later, Cronkite, on the landmark *I Can Hear It Now* recordings and other CBS ventures, had never cared for Cronkite and had viciously taken the opportunity to unseat him. Friendly denied both charges by explaining, "That experiment has been done," referring to the Murrow-Cronkite teaming in 1960. "Cronkite is a take-charge guy. He just doesn't mesh with another guy. The chemistry is no good." *Newsweek* immediately took issue with Friendly's statement by writing, "Underlying the matter of Cronkite's 'chemistry' is the whole problem of television's schizophrenia about its news coverage. Perhaps this is the real significance of the Cronkite demotion. CBS News has become an offshoot of show business."

Richard Oulahan realistically suggested that part of Cronkite's troubles, as well as his network's, lay in the cut-and-dried nature of the convention itself. What he termed "ugly tribal rites" were papered over decisions already made. Merely because Huntley and Brinkley together were more capable of relieving the tedium of the event, they beat Cronkite with their higher ratings.

Cronkite's outraged journalistic friends refused to let the issue die. *Newsweek*'s account of the removal sarcastically snipped that the panic occurred because "CBS stock dropped a point," while *Time* echoed the recurrent theme of other journalists by adding that "The story is purely and simply the Madison Avenue ratings game." Jack Gould wrote in the *New York Times*: "As the attractively realistic Mr. Cronkite observed after the announcement of his unseating, everyone in television lives by courtesy of the interest audience figures, and CBS took a statistical drubbing in its coverage of the Republican convention in San Francisco." A *Life* article summed up the feelings of the majority of sympathetic journalists by stating succinctly, "His crime was playing it straight."

John Chancellor, a long-time friend of Cronkite's—present in San Francisco and bodily removed from the floor at that gathering—was indignant over the cavalier treatment his colleague received. In a 1974 interview, he reflected that "There was a certain amount of jubilation at NBC and a certain amount of anger among those of us at a junior level because we didn't think you should pitch a guy out because of that. I thought it was CBS management at its worst and I think CBS acknowledged that when they put him back. It was just one of those ghastly moments when they lost their nerve.

"I don't think it was anything Walter did that resulted in his being taken off the air. It was what Huntley and Brinkley and the four of us on the floor were doing. We were just creaming them in terms of ratings and, I think, in terms of coverage. I think our coverage was a hell of a lot better. They were taking a bath at our hands and it had nothing to do with him, which made us say, 'Damn it! You're not supposed to do it that way!' "*

Harry Reasoner was sitting in for Cronkite in New York when the announcement of the change was made. He remembered well the amazement he felt at the time and believes the decisions the executives at CBS made were "in response to a problem they were having at that time. They didn't have it all together at the San Francisco convention, and I think Walter, at the time, said he didn't particularly greet the news with joy. I don't think any of us did, because whatever our feelings were about what we were doing, we

* The complete text of Mr. Chancellor's interview is found in the chapter entitled "I'm Really a Big Fan."

didn't think that was the right way to handle it. And it turned out not go be. The whole thing had an emergency, panicky, un–CBS feeling to it."

A few days after Cronkite's removal, the CBS management reminded its detractors that Cronkite would retain his *Evening News* program, that he still had nine years to go on his contract and was drawing an annual salary of $100,000. Cronkite, while still disappointed, gratefully admitted, "There was no evidence of a deep-dyed plot against me, but an honest effort by the network to try something dramatic to enliven a pretty dull convention."

Many in the industry in 1964 believed there was a good possibility if the Trout-Mudd team succeeded in Atlantic City, the pair would take over the *Evening News* spot as well. Any who placed bets on success lost, because the Cronkite replacement was a dismal failure. The network's ratings dropped even further than at San Francisco.

When asked how he felt when NBC beat out CBS in the ratings, even after his removal, Cronkite replied, "I was delighted. No, I was vindicated."

The lesson CBS learned concerning the ratings game was a powerful one. Whenever the subject was mentioned to a post–1964 Fred Friendly, he bristled: "It may be important in selling the program to advertisers, but it's not important to us." Watching the ratings, after all, Cronkite agreed, was playing NBC's game: "Ratings are an artificial measurement of the true status of the competition between network news departments. This constant effort to associate the criteria for entertainment with those for television news . . . is untenable."

Symbolically thumbing his nose at CBS, Cronkite moved his *Evening News* program from New York City to Atlantic City for the duration of the Democratic convention, and remained pretty well at the center of things. One evening during that time, he happened to share an elevator with NBC president Robert Kintner. As the two rode down to the main floor, Cronkite impishly said, "Bob, we've been presented with a great moment." When they reached the lobby, filled with people who knew them both, they exited arm in arm and, as Cronkite gleefully stated, "We started a hundred rumors."

The reaction to the great humiliation of Walter Cronkite was overwhelming. The game of corporate politics had wounded a folk hero and, apart from the solid support of his colleagues, the viewing public expressed its resentment: the network was flooded with mail at the rate of 11,000 pieces a week protesting Cronkite's removal. Cronkite survived and emerged stronger than ever. The effects were astounding. No changes were made in his format, nor were any public relation cosmeticians called in to alter his image, but he began to show an immediate and considerable increase in his following. By 1967, he had edged ahead of NBC, and CBS boasted that Cronkite had 16,000,000 nightly viewers.

In a 1966 *TV Guide* article, Richard Schickel reflected on the renaissance of Cronkite:

"It is now clear that square, sober Walter Cronkite, with his muted sing-song delivery and his kindly Old-Uncle-Fred-from-Iowa expression must be doing something right. But what? In an industry where the notion that you gotta have a gimmick is reverenced as if it were the Sermon on the Mount and the Pledge of Allegiance combined, he remains something of a mystery. After years of being No. 2 and trying harder and all that jazz, how has he finally succeeded in succeeding? Can it be, Charlie, that there is something in those slogans after all?"

In 1967, Fred Friendly, by then with the Ford Foundation, broke his silence on the affair. In his memoirs he reflected on the episode:

My worst blunder as president of CBS News was not due to an error of judgement but to a lack of will power and stamina. The Republican Convention in San Francisco in July of 1964 was held during my first few months as president of the news division, and although the newly formed election unit had done well in the 1962 off-year elections and in most of the primaries, this was its first national convention, and NBC did a superior job. It had been argued by many observers that no network adequately covered the Goldwater takeover of the G.O.P. apparatus; in any case we lagged far behind in content and audience.

Paley, who was in San Francisco throughout the convention, agreed that the final two days showed definite improvement. I remember saying to him as we left the Cow Palace for the last time that this was a new team and that if we didn't panic but allowed the election unit to gain experience, we would eventually have a seasoned organization, a luxury that the news division had not had for some time. Back in New York I found that Stanton agreed with me, and Bill Leonard and the election unit immediately set about correcting the mistakes made in San Francisco.

I believe that what aggravated the situation was a full-page story in *Variety* which heralded NBC's overwhelming victory and predicted that nothing could stop Kintner until after 1968. I was summoned to a meeting with Paley and Stanton, and after an exhausting post-mortem the suggestion was made by the chairman that perhaps the problem was Cronkite. It was true that Walter had not been at his best in San Francisco; he had been uncomfortable about sharing his anchor booth with Sevareid, who did his analysis there, and occasionally had been unresponsive to the producers' instructions to switch to other correspondents on the floor. But the decisive difference had been the sprightly staying power of Huntley and Brinkley, and some aggressive reporting from the floor of the convention hall by NBC's John Chancellor, [Sander] Vanocur and [Frank] McGee.

When my superiors suggested that we replace Cronkite with a new team, Roger Mudd and Bob Trout, it struck me as a debatable solution, but I agreed to think about it.

At subsequent meetings, I realized that it was not so much a suggestion as a command. Two of the other executives in the news division with whom I discussed the proposal were violently opposed to it. My own reaction, which I expressed to Paley and Stanton, was that the proposed change resembled CBS's panic in 1960, which had resulted in the unsuccessful Cronkite-Murrow partnership. Furthermore, the shift would upset the morale of the election unit and the news division, where Walter was much respected, and might humiliate him so that he would feel impelled to resign. Lastly, and most important, change merely for the sake of change was not likely to work. Mudd and Trout were two correspondents in whom I had unlimited faith, but nothing was going to stop Huntley and Brinkley at the Democratic Convention in August, and it would be better to stay with the combination we had, gain experience and rely on the lessons learned in San Francisco.

After it became obvious to me that I was expected to replace Walter, I spent the entire afternoon walking around in New York. It seemed to me that I had little choice; I was convinced that if I resisted this drastic step, the future of the news division would be jeopardized. I now believe that if I had stood firm and refused to substitute anyone for Cronkite I could have prevailed.

At the time, Cronkite was in California with his family. Because it was unthinkable not to let him hear the news face to face, Bill Leonard and I flew out to meet him at the Los Angeles airport. By the time we got there I had his demotion all couched in euphemisms and had conceived a play by which Walter would play a dominant role from the convention floor. But he knew exactly what was happening, and in the way he took the demotion, he turned my worst moment into his finest.

There were so many stories in the press about the change that Walter was finally forced to hold a news conference in New York in which he said that the decision was strictly a matter of ratings and that he understood the company's position. Our announcement of the shift employed some fancy language about the uniqueness of the Democratic Convention requiring a new kind of coverage because its presidential candidate had in effect already been selected, but we did not fool anybody, and it hurt our credibility as a news organization; as many people pointed out, if CBS had won the ratings in San Francisco, Cronkite would still have been there.

The cruelest blow came from Hal Humphrey of the *Los Angeles Times.* Under the caption 'There's No Business Like TV Show Business,' he wrote: 'Last week's scuttling of Walter Cronkite . . . put him on the same level as a comic whose jokes weren't registering high enough on the laugh meter.'

In point of fact, Mudd and Trout did a remarkable job at Atlantic City in August. The entire unit had spirit, and the notoriety of the sudden midcourse maneuver almost brought us even with NBC in the ratings some of the time.

Cronkite came out of the affair a bigger man than before, and I learned how to apply the courage of my convictions at least enough to insist that he be the national editor at the November elections.

"Go, Baby, Go!"

The "Other" Astronaut

In the early stages of the long day's coverage, CBS News showed a clear initiative in spot pickups, both around the United States and by satellite relay from abroad, before and after the landing [on the moon]. The sustained coherence of Walter Cronkite, CBS anchor man, attested again to his remarkable human endurance.

—Jack Gould

WHEN the modern Space Age began with the launching of Russia's *Sputnik* on October 4, 1957, America's pitiful attempts to compete with the Soviet Union were not only frustrating and self-defeating but a source of national humiliation. In 1960, President Kennedy, smarting from the numerous failures on American launch pads in the late 1950s, vowed before the U.S. Congress and the world that the United States would have a man on the moon and safely returned to earth before 1970.

The aerospace community, under the direction of NASA, was blessed and generously funded by Congress. Vice-President Johnson took on his role as presidential representative with relish and great energy. The Air Force's Florida wilderness near Cape Canaveral was bulldozed and surfaced, and structures went up as America prepared to make its first tottering steps into space. The area grew into a gigantic launch-site of the first order and tracking stations were constructed at sixteen strategic locations encircling the globe. America geared its mentality and its industrial complex for the space race, determined to be the first nation to place a man on the moon.

There had been neither broadcaster nor photographer to cover Henry Ford's first historic drive through the streets of Detroit; only photographers were present to record for posterity the flight of the Wright Brothers' airplane at Kitty Hawk. Flight and broadcasting matured and expanded together—both in sophistication and distance. The solo flight of Charles A. Lindbergh across the Atlantic in 1927 was covered by motion pictures, radio, and the press as the "Lone Eagle" departed from New York in his single-engine aircraft, the *Spirit of St. Louis,* and as he landed in Paris. Many historians agree that Herb Morrison's live and compassionate account of the 1937 explosion and conflagration of the German dirigible *Hindenberg* at Lakehurst, New Jersey, was probably the greatest disaster coverage in radio's history. Both of these dramatic events were positive proof of radio's ability to provide a news-hungry world with historic moments as they transpired.

By the time the United States entered the race for the moon, radio and television were technically prepared to flash the happenings around the world with the speed of sound and light, in high-fidelity sound and color. Space age coverage, ironically, was made globally possible by means of communication satellites previously launched by rockets to accommodate the progress each of the other—rather like Eric Sevareid's assessment of how Americans used to assume the Chinese made a living by taking in each others' laundry.

NASA initially had kept its space exploration plans secret, fearful that if it received negative coverage, public opinion against the entire program could cause it to be scrubbed. Criticism of the secrecy, however, forced NASA officials to debate the pros and cons of permitting access—limited or total—by the press. Favorable coverage, it was argued, might ensure the success of the program's goals of travel to the moon and beyond. After much discussion, NASA relented and opened its gates to the world's press corps, despite the fact that space program, at that time, was uncertain, expensive, and to a large degree unsuccessful.

Four hundred and eighty newsmen and photographers, Cronkite among them, attended the May 5, 1961, launch of Alan B. Shepard, America's first astronaut. Throughout the busy week of delays in the launch before the first successful lift-off and flight, the Western Union's wires fairly hummed with activity, moving some 83,000 words each day from central Florida. Now press-conscious and overtly cooperative, NASA distributed 12,000-word information packets which included data describing virtually every minuscule aspect of the astronaut's program, including exercise, prelaunch diet (seven-ounce filet mignon wrapped in bacon, poached eggs, toast with jelly and orange juice), and the names of the Naval vessels assigned for recovery.

Despite NASA's assistance, television coverage *per se* for the space program would in effect have to invent itself. As Cronkite explained it, "In the early days of space reporting, I had to learn for myself. Even after the unmanned flights, I remember the Shepard flight on a Redstone that was one-fifth the size of the escape rocket carried on the nose of the great Apollo 11. Then, there was only a producer, a cameraman, and me, standing in a snake-ridden marsh that was called Cape Canaveral, and which is today known as the Kennedy Space Center." (Cronkite's assessment of the space program is found at the end of this chapter.)

The launch of Shepard and a concomitant favorable press gave NASA breathing room. America had been vindicated and the space program was "Go."

In retrospect, Cronkite recalled for Arthur Unger of the *Christian Science Monitor* that Shepard's "little minute poop-down into the Atlantic was, next to the Apollo moon landing," his most exciting moment in his years of space coverage because "Rocketry was so uncertain then. We had been watching failure after failure—rockets blowing up on the pad, tumbling from the air a few hundred feet up. And now, suddenly, a man was going to sit on top of all that fireworks. I just didn't know whether or not I was going to be able to watch, I was so caught up in it. The launch was the thing, though—once the rocket cut out, we knew he could land safely."

The tracts of land the Air Force assigned each of the three commercial networks early in the space program eventually became the sites for fully self-contained remote television studios. By 1965, some four years after the Shepard flight and during the Gemini program, larger plots measuring thirty feet by one hundred feet were provided. Millions of dollars were invested by the networks to construct temporary facilities to improve space coverage. CBS television's facilities were somewhat typical of the three major networks: four trailers were used (CBS radio had only one), two laid with their long sides together as a first level and the same configuration on top. Walls and partitions were removed to make two twenty-foot-square rooms. The lower level was used as a control room while the upper level became the studio, accessible only by an outside wooden stairway. A large picture window behind Cronkite's desk permitted an unobstructed view of the launch pad in the distance and it was from this glass-enclosed aerie he broadcast his space coverage.

Each of the networks employed full staffs of about fifty engineering and production personnel at Shepard's flight. Additional millions of dollars were spent in covering each individual flight, $500,000 being pooled by all three networks for microwave circuits to New York for the John Glenn flight. Because of limited space and access at Glenn's launch, the networks also pooled on key camera positions. NBC extended its coverage of the Glenn flight considerably by arranging use of General Dynamics' tracking facilities in San Diego.

The lead that NBC's Huntley and Brinkley had achieved at the 1960 and 1964 presidential conventions was still a bone of contention with many CBS executives. It was feared that the televiewing audience would remain with NBC for its space coverage as well, but CBS's fears were unfounded. Cronkite's characteristically thorough, clear, logical and cool style of researching, writing, and reporting established him early on as the foremost space newsman in the business.

In preparing background for his coverage, Cronkite searched tirelessly in his quest for information. As anchorman, he was responsible for maintaining a continuous flow of material to his audience. Since he knew little about the space program at its outset, he undertook the task of learning through total immersion.

Cronkite's interest in rocketry actually began during his World War II correspondent years. The daily buzz-bombing of London had introduced him to the destructive capabilities of modern weaponry when the V-1 bombed him out of his flat. After he crash-landed by glider in the Netherlands, he was one of a handful of Westerners to see rockets being launched by the Germans: "A night or two after we landed I happened to be looking west. About 100 miles away I saw that contrail which was a V-2 being launched. This was back in 1944."

Cronkite began collecting relevant information at his disposal: he received thick, mimeographed news releases containing extensive technical material about the individual launches as well as detailed data on the astronauts. The Martin Company contributed reams on the Titan vehicle; McDonell Aircraft, the Gemini capsule; and the Department of Defense provided data concerning recovery of the vehicles after splashdown. Full-scale mock-ups and samples of the food the astronauts would eat on the flights were made available by the manufacturers. He talked with engineers, astronauts, NASA personnel, visited the construction and assembly sites of the rocket components and made trips to every tracking station between Florida and Ascension Island—keeping notes and handouts in a binder which grew with each visit and each flight.

Arrangements for the trip to the British-owned Ascension Island in the South Atlantic took Cronkite several weeks. When permission was finally granted to visit the tracking station there, he was told he would have to leave immediately. As he dashed from his office, he asked a CBS executive to telephone his wife Betsy. Later that day, when she was told her husband was "in Ascension," she couldn't resist punning, "Oh, my goodness! How many times has he been around?"

Prior to Shepard's sub-orbital flight, Cronkite arrived a week early to begin interviewing, studying and planning the logistics and background of the mission. He spent an average of from fourteen to sixteen hours each day in preparation. Assistant producer Sanford (Sandy) Socolow was so impressed he remarked, "Walter's read everything he can put his hands on."

In 1968, Cronkite flew to Langley Field, Virginia, where he was fitted with a special harness which permitted him to experience moon gravity, which he demonstrated later on his *Twenty-First Century* television series. While in the moon-gravity rig, he demonstrated the walk for his television audience and even performed a few somersaults. He enthusiastically explained to *TV Guide* that his purpose for such unusual experiments was two-fold: "Ever since the space program began I've tried to go through simulators. They have a special fascination for me. Also, I was interested in doing this because I have a desire to report on the sensation.

"What the thing does is come close to the feeling of walking on the moon—not precisely, because gravity is still there. The feet, however, experience one-sixth the earth's gravity. Everything seems in slow motion; steps are longer and slower; the more momentum, the longer the step.

"Doing the flips is easy. Holding your head up is hard."

On another occasion, he experienced total weightlessness in a parabolic flight high above Patterson Air Force Base in a specially-equipped and crewed airplane. He admitted to *Life's* Paul O'Neil,"they didn't run it very fast, but I did feel my eyes sinking into my head."

The reference material and diary of his personal experiences continued to accumulate. He had the information typed—over 200 pages—with extra-large letters and arranged under specific headings for quick, on-camera reference. Titles such as "Holds: Built-in," or "Delays: Why," afforded him quick referral to any section during a launch.

Cronkite's intrigue with the space program was so intense and personal that he covered every manned flight but one from 1961 until his retirement in 1981. He was on vacation when the Skylab was launched and, he said, "it just didn't seem worth breaking into that holiday. But it felt awfully strange, sitting up there at the Vineyard watching it happen on TV."

Through tragedies, interminable holds, scrubs and letter-perfect launches, the "fourth" or "other" astronaut—as he has been called at various times because of his popular recognition with the space program—kept millions of viewers glued to their television screens. He captured the imagination of the American public with his skillful narration of the live launches and his enhancing, animated, in-depth commentaries. He never assumed anything, never stopped being a perpetual student of the space program. A case in point was the forty hours he spent acquainting himself with the newer concepts and developments in the Apollo 14 program. Richard Gehman summed up the Cronkite magic by succinctly declaring, "He does his homework."

All that knowledge, fortunately, is not left permanently spinning around inside his head. He claims once he uses the material he gathers for a particular program, "my mind goes blank. If you ask me three or four weeks later who won the downhill in the Olympics, I probably couldn't tell you what the downhill was."

From the hours of preparation came the security and poise that won him the honors. An example of his self-confidence and determination was vividly illustrated during the Glenn flight and told by Isabella Taves in *Look*. Sandy Socolow, whose job was to stay out of camera range and in touch with New York by telephone, was unexpectedly instructed to tell Cronkite of a change in plans in the middle of his live coverage. Theoretically, New York has the final say on what a production will contain, but in this particular case, Cronkite, Socolow, and New York had already reached consensus on the best procedure to cover the flight (which had been postponed four times at a cost of $27,000 a day to the network). Socolow slipped a red-pencilled note to Cronkite to tell him of the modification. Cronkite glanced at the note, laid it aside and continued his reporting; he had no intention of changing anything on the air on such short notice. A second note was likewise set aside and ignored. When Socolow attempted to pass a third note, without batting an eye or dropping a syllable, Cronkite pressed the assistant producer's wrist to the desk with such fierceness that the poor man winced in pain. The New York staff, having witnessed the scene via closed-circuit television monitors, returned to the original plan. No more notes were passed and Cronkite won the day.

As he did his work, Cronkite expected the same from his staff. Once, when he arrived at the Cape the night before a space shot, he found his advance crew had not finished its ground work. He called a meeting and shook the table before him in anger, demanding to know, "What have you guys been doing here? Spending all your time in the pool?" The men quickly excused themselves and completed the assignments. As he could be severe, he could praise the same personnel when they did their work. He readily admitted he couldn't do his job "without our crew and planning staff and their determination to report the news as it happens."

The CBS coverage of the John Glenn three-orbit flight around the earth in 1962 was unanimously declared by the press and the public superior to the other two major networks'. Cronkite emerged as the leading lay U.S. expert on rocketry, trajectory and orbital flight. His detailed commentaries on various phases of the flight successfully translated into lay terms the intricacies and some of the mysteries of weightlessness, inertia, apogee, perigee, and reentry. Of his masterful handling of that historic flight, Alistair Cooke, then writing for Britain's *Manchester Guardian,* wrote, "Mr. Cronkite made engrossing sense of the miracle otherwise beyond the comprehension of the hundred million Americans who were watching." (Cooke's statistics were a bit exaggerated. The combined networks' own audience estimate for radio and television was only 60,000,000.)

Cronkite's personal acquaintance with each of the astronauts permitted him to capitalize on their individual and collective expertise. Their first-hand knowledge and experience further enhanced his own interest in the program, enabling him to discuss the launches with increasing authority and insight. His friendship with Navy Captain Walter Schirra preceded the latter's six-orbit flight in 1963 and inspired Cronkite to write an intimate and insightful article entitled "Walter Schirra: Our Next Man in Space" for *Look* magazine. Six years later, Captain Schirra took a position with CBS News as its guest space analyst. Beginning with 1969's Apollo 11 moon flight, the team of the two Walters met with overwhelming approval from viewers following the space program. Alluding to his own "gee-whiz," wide-eyed amazement of the U.S. space adventures, Cronkite confessed that Schirra had "a subtle and gently firm way of bringing broadcasters back to earth whenever they tend to become over-dramatic or boyishly breathless."

Cronkite's unabashed fascination has caused many good-natured winks from his colleagues. More than once he openly exhibited his vicarious pleasure with the launches. As the Apollo 11 crew lifted off the pad at the Kennedy Space Center, he encouraged the flight's progress with "Go, baby, go!" After Neil Armstrong stepped onto the moon's surface on July 20, Cronkite declared, "There's a foot on the moon! Look at those pictures! Wow!" Witnessing the blast-off from the moon's surface to rendezvous with Charles Collins in the command module, the excited, grinning, hand-rubbing Cronkite exclaimed on the air, "Oh, boy! Hot diggity dog!"

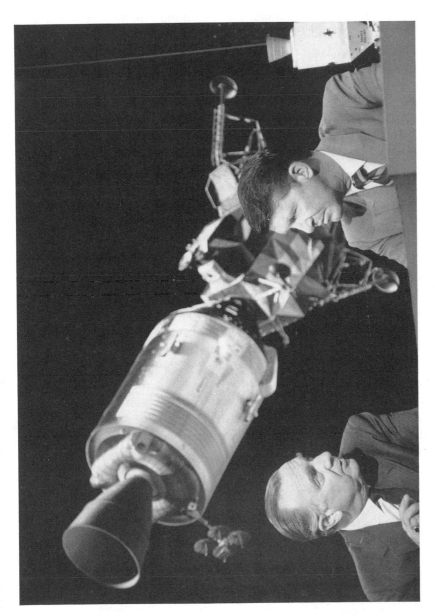

"Walter-to-Walter" coverage of the space program.

The Apollo moon landing was probably the high point in his space coverage, but Cronkite was by no means alone in his enthusiasm for that historic moment in mankind's history. Former President and Mrs. Lyndon Johnson were at the Cape for the event. The usually reserved *New York Times* ran banner headlines, the size usually reserved for announcing the ends of wars, heralding the occasion: MEN WALK ON MOON. Prominently featured on the front page of that issue was Archibald MacLeish's commemorative poem "Voyage to the Moon." The first 18 pages of that issue of the *Times,* even the advertising, were devoted exclusively to the lunar landing of the Eagle. President Nixon was so taken by the moon landing, he, perhaps overenthusiastically, declared that it rivaled the Creation.

Cronkite was so fearful of missing some important phase of the space shots he often wouldn't leave his desk, even to eat, preferring to have his meals brought to him. During one of the moon landings, J. O. Conner of the *Times* reported that he ate sandwiches, taking "a bite every time one of those three-minute film pieces was on. I don't eat very much. I drank a lot of tea and soft drinks. They kept me up. I almost got caught once. I had just taken a bite of a sandwich when the camera came back to me. I got the cud over to my left cheek just in time."

Cronkite's durability was so well known and highly regarded by viewers and critics that he earned the title "Old Ironpants," as much a tribute to his remarkable bladder as to his own enthusiasm. During Scott Carpenter's 1962 Mercury 7 flight, the seemingly indefatigable newsman was on the air for ten and a half hours. When the historic Apollo 11 crew landed on the moon in July 1969, Cronkite broke his endurance record by staying at his desk for an incredible thirty-one hours straight. He signed on at 9:45 Sunday morning and didn't leave until 3:15 Monday afternoon. (While covering the 1968 presidential election returns, he remained on camera for seventeen hours without a break; sixty-nine hours the weekend President Kennedy was killed.) Following the thirty-one hour Apollo 11 marathon, when he was asked why he didn't show signs of fatigue, he replied, "You don't think of that. This was something we've been aiming at for all these years." It wasn't coffee that kept him going, but "Adrenalin. Actually, I'm so interested and excited that I don't get tired—I get too emotionally involved."

In a *New York Times* review of television's handling of Apollo 11, Jack Gould hailed the CBS coverage in general and the Cronkite-Schirra team in particular with glowing praise:

> On the domestic front, there was not the slightest doubt about the superior coverage. It came from the tireless Walter Cronkite and his colleagues. In alertness, diversity and know-how, CBS was ahead by a wide margin.
>
> Mr. Cronkite for many years has been something of a one-man phenomenon in space coverage. If late yesterday afternoon his face began to show a few lines of strain, his constitution apparently is immune to fatigue. He was on the air far more hours than any other commentator, or so it seemed, and showed the greatest intimate knowledge and excitement over his assignment. He is a rare mixture, a reporter who keeps atop of developments and still reflects intensely human reactions to an unbelievable drama.
>
> A major CBS coup was the engagement of Walter M. Schirra, former astronaut, at Mr. Cronkite's side, as an expert adviser. On any number of occasions, Mr. Schirra calmly explained details of space technology, putting inconveniences in the flight into a reassuring perspective based on his own experience.
>
> Television news does appear to be undergoing subtle shifts of the limitless implications to the moon landing. Its seminars on the flight, and the reactions of militant youth were much the best. Harry Reasoner of CBS had a diverting essay on the disappointment of the moon landing— with the loss of mankind's most treasured sources of lore, and the discovery of forbidding dust and rocks.
>
> . . . In the long hours of sampling the networks, CBS— at least, in this instance—emerged with a quality of style to go along with an alert journalistic instinct second to none on the home scene.

The erudite yet easy rhetoric which characterizes Cronkite's delivery has been achieved by over-preparation. Typical of his style, which reflects his exhaustive research, is the following excerpt from his extemporaneous pre-flight narration of Gemini 3 in a story entitled "Pad 19," from the *New Yorker* magazine:

> Good morning from Cape Kennedy. This is Walter Cronkite, reporting from our CBS News building for GT-3—the flight of Gemini 3 into outer space—a flight scheduled for just two hours from now.
>
> Out there on pad 19 stands the great 90-foot Titan missile on its erector stand, and on top of that is the Gemini capsule, ready to receive Gus Grissom and John Young, the astronauts who, this morning, have a date with destiny out there 150 miles above the earth.
>
> It's T-minus 55 seconds and counting. Let me tell you quickly of some of the critical points to be watching for in this flight."
>
> (A hold is called by NASA, interrupting him.)
>
> We must explain about this oxidation hold . . ."
>
> (The hold is lifted before he can explain it.)
>
> They're on their way, then, for those 3 orbits—4 hours and 50 minutes in space. If they had not got that Go in that 20-second decision there, if they had missed that little keyhole in the sky by just a comparative few miles per hour in their speed, they would have been given the signal to abort their mission.
>
> And this mission of GT-3 is Go—a beautiful launch in an almost cloudless sky here at Cape Kennedy.

The narrative was not always so breezy or knowledgeable, however. Because of frequent and sometimes long holds, he often ran out of pertinent information and found himself thrashing about, simply trying to kill time. More than once he had to call on his colleagues to help him fill air time. During the delay-ridden Glenn launch, Cronkite called on Douglas Edwards in New York to make a contribution. Edwards, unfortunately, had nothing to offer, save a report on New York's weather.

His love of space is not just vicarious. When asked in 1974 if he would go on a space flight, he responded, "You're darn right I would go. I'd go on any flight they offered me— especially one to the moon. Only nobody is asking me. I've suggested it many times, but nobody takes me seriously. I do think that with the space shuttle there will be a chance. Newsmen ought to be going by 1980 or 1981. And I certainly hope I'll be one of the first."

In 1969, *TV Guide* invited him to share his love and knowledge of space travel and the space program with its readers—his viewers. That article is presented here in its entirety:

We Are Children of the Space Age

> *The Yankees, the first mechanicians in the world, are engineers, just as the Italians are musicians and the Germans metaphysicians, by right of birth.*
>
> *—Jules Verne, 1865*

That comment of the French author, more than a century ago, was coupled with his prediction that Americans would be the first men to land on the moon, that there would be three men in the spacecraft and that it would return to a splashdown in the Pacific Ocean. Not bad, I'd say, as a 100-year old prediction.

Verne also envisioned television. I don't think he would have doubted that the age of electronic broadcasting and the age of Apollo would coincide. They grew up together. Each is necessary to the other as man is to woman.

If all goes as planned, that period of Midday, July 20, to Midday, July 21, when Apollo 11 is on the moon, will be the most expensive and extensive televison coverage in history.

And I believe it will be the most exciting and historic event that I will have reported in 37 years as a journalist. (I'm not really that old—I started while in high school.)

The space program seems to be to demonstrate—at about two and a half billion dollars—that particular combination which represents America at its best: pragmatism with the dogmatic objective, hard-headedness with a soft heart.

When the Russians first orbited Sputnik in 1957, you'll recall the official reaction of our government—it was not important, we were "not interested in an outer-space basketball game."

The initial shock wore off quickly and we got into space, first with unmanned flight and then with our original suborbital flight, that of Alan Shepard. Parenthetically, Verne in his predictions that we would be first on the moon, said that it would be so expensive a project that we would seek foreign aid and receive the bulk of it from the Russians. And in a sense we did get aid from the Russians, but it was in psychological prodding, which can't be measured in rubles.

It remained for that most romantic and tough-minded of our recent Presidents, John F. Kennedy, to spell it out to Congress, May 25, 1961:

"I believe this Nation should commit itself to achieving the goal, before this decade is out, of landing a man on the moon and returning him safely to earth."

It is as though he had given marching orders to television.

In the early days of space reporting I had to learn for myself. Even after the unmanned flights, I remember the Shepard flight on a Redstone that was one-fifth the size of the escape rocket carried on the nose of the great Saturn that will launch Apollo 11.

Then, there was only a producer, a cameraman and me, standing in the snake-ridden marsh that was called Cape Canaveral, and which is today known as the Kennedy Space Center.

For the flight of Apollo, more than 100 cameras will be employed and virtually every member of CBS News will be involved in around-the-world coverage. We have all come a long way from 1961.

And so, in an encouraging manner, has the National Aeronautics and Space Administration. In those early days, its attitude toward reporters was to ignore us.

Today, as in the flight of Apollo 10, when the Lunar Module seemed dangerously out of control thirteen miles from the moon, we were given absolute freedom to report the story, and a great flow of information from NASA. I would suggest that this freedom and the comparative reluctance of the Soviet Union to tell the facts until after the fact is an indication of the difference between an open and a closed society.

This combination of the television camera, which does not lie, and the Age of Apollo seems to be the most dramatic coupling of events in man's history. It has sophisticated and educated our children to a world we thought existed only on the pulp pages of science fiction.

Along with millions of other Americans a decade ago, I flattered myself that I was familiar with our language. Today, my 12-year-old son, along with millions of other 12-year-olds, knows words I did not know then and new meanings for words I did. "Mylar," "retrofire," and "drogue" on the one hand; and "dock" and "Snoopy" on the other.

That's true of all of us, in or out of the space program. No matter how old we are, we are children of the space age. The executive producer of CBS News coverage of the Apollo flights is Robert Wussler; he made an interesting comment recently on this link-up of television and outer space—executive producers always make interesting comments, by the way, or it's back to a career as mining engineer.

"For years," Wussler said, "We've had a problem picking up [space] terminology. Now, in one flight, they've picked up ours! There was one point when an [Apollo 10] astronaut said 'Hold on and I'll zoom in on California.' That kind of sums it up."

There are those cynical enough—and I'm one of them—to suggest that increased television from outer space is a kind of NASA ploy to see the flight program continues beyond its scheduled flights. But there is more to it than that. I think that the astronauts understand now, as they did not always understand, an obligation to share their view of the universe with those of us who are earth-bound. I think they want to show us tomorrow.

And as a commentator and taxpayer, I believe we are getting as close to 100 cents on the dollar as the nature of governing ourselves will allow. Those of us who covered the early flights grew accustomed to the failures that paved the way to success.

At that time, much of the difficulty was finding out what was going on. In those days—so close, so far away—it seemed NASA's policy to say our men in space were choir singers. Religious pre-pilots. They are among the most dedicated men I've ever known. And they are in the business of selling a program to a country that feels the economic pinch.

Each space flight proves something, but it does not assure the future. I remember when Wally Schirra found himself in a near disaster on the Gemini 6 launching pad. He did not panic and the moment passed quickly. But for those of us who were there, the heart stopped. I remember the tumbling of Gemini 8 and the wild gyrations of Apollo 10 and, most of all the words of Gus Grissom to CBS's Nelson Benton:

There's always a possibility that you can have a catastrophic failure. . . . This can happen on any flight. It can happen on the last one as well as the first one. So you can just plan as best you can to take care of all these eventualities.

"Stringing Up the Western Union Boy"

Agnew and the First Amendment

*Congress shall make no law respecting an establish-
ment of religion, or prohibiting the free exercise there-
of; or abridging the freedom of speech, or of the press;
or the right of the people to assemble, and to petition
the Government for a redress of grievances.*

*—First Amendment to the
Constitution of the United States*

*The trouble is that the broadcast media are not free;
they are government licensed. The power to make us
conform is too great to lie forever dormant. The ax
lies there temptingly for use by any enraged administration, Republican, Democrat, or Walleceite. We are
at the mercy of the whim of politicians and bureaucrats, and whether they choose to chop us down or
not, the mere existence of their power is an intimidating and constraining threat.*

—Walter Cronkite

AS EARLY AS 1932, when H. V. Kaltenborn inaugurated the
reading of editorialized news over the radio, the audience's response was curiously mixed. Even though Kaltenborn read essen-

tially the same editorials over the air that he wrote for the *Brooklyn Eagle,* the two media met with divergent reactions. It became immediately apparent that the differences between the reception of the spoken word and the written word—as intangible and elusive in definition and understanding then as now—were going to present problems. Kaltenborn was eventually ordered by his station's owners to refrain from editorializing on the radio, but no changes were dictated for his newspaper editorials. The written word was deemed acceptable; the spoken word was anathema, a situation not unlike the one that exists today.

The study of how radio and newspapers affect people has long been one of curiosity and even frustration. The debate has been going on for years and will likely continue. The following CBS policy statement regarding radio editorials was reported in the *Atlantic Monthly* in 1943:

The printed press and the radio as joint guardians of freedom of speech have a lot in common but at one point they differ widely. Rare indeed is the newspaper or magazine that has no editorial page, for the flat-footed out-speaking of the editor or publisher. Rarer far is the radio station or network with an 'editorial page.' There are many reasons why, but they all add up to to the conviction in radio that its greatest service to the whole of the American people can be performed if folks are given the facts and allowed to form their own opinions. Radio sometimes envies the press its freedom to wade in and pitch hot bricks, especially on an issue involving its own interest. The press, on the other hand, often envies the inherent power of radio to make words come so much more alive than they do lying flat on a page. Both systems of communication are human, and both like to grumble, but the seasoned people in press and radio realize increasingly that their great inherent powers of communication are not to be abused without paying that most disagreeable of all penalties—popularity.

In the same year the above article appeared, Federal Communication Commission chairman James L. Fly castigated unnamed newsmen and news programs "for peddling ideas from company headquarters [in an effort] to get away from the news of the day to the philosophies of the particular sponsor." The unidentified culprit was, in all probability, none other than Mr. Kaltenborn, at that time primarily a radio commentator and one especially fond of expressing his opinions on the air. Kaltenborn obviously felt the attack was addressed to him and he responded to Fly's charge by stating "no news analyst worth his salt could or would be completely neutral."

The networks continued walking their tightrope of restraint and self-censorship as dictated by their own National Association of Broadcasters—the NAB—which networks or individual stations join of their own volition. Radio, for the most part, "knew its place" and there was rarely any serious friction with the presidentially appointed seven-member FCC.

Franklin Roosevelt was the first U.S. president to grasp the effects radio could have on the people and he took to it frequently and quite successfully, it might be added, to help implement his various social and political programs. The "Nothing to Fear" address made at his inauguration helped build confidence in a nation undergoing the worst economic conditions of the century. His "fireside chats" were eagerly listened to during the long, dark days of World War II. His masterful use of radio for the thirteen years he was president established a precedent all later chief executives would follow.

Because radio generally withheld its editorial comments during his administration, President Roosevelt never had any serious problems with it. Print journalism was another thing, however. During his years as governor of New York, Roosevelt adored and courted members of the press, frequently having them in his home in Albany, where his wife Eleanor served them cheese, crackers, and beer during press conferences. When he was president, the same happy conditions continued with the White House press corps. David Brinkley charged in his book *Washington Goes to War,* however, that there was a long-standing love-hate relationship between Roosevelt and newsmen from newspapers and magazines outside the White House. FDR seemed to enjoy playing "cat-and-mouse" games with them—at times, Brinkley suggested, bordering on rudeness and arrogance.

Harry Truman endeared himself to members of the press. His famous "constitutionals" through the streets of Washington were always accompanied by a group of reporters. They liked his "give 'em hell" candor and there was a strong bond between them.

The Eisenhower, Kennedy, and Johnson administrations saw a widening schism develop between members of the press and the White House that would grow alarmingly during the Nixon years. A charge frequently leveled at the White House, beginning with the Kennedy administration, was "news management"—a charge likewise denied by the administrations in question.

As early as 1966, Walter Cronkite was speaking out, off-camera, to friends or in speeches to various groups around the country, against what he felt was a steadily enlarging credibility gap between the press and the Johnson White House. In a speech he delivered that year at Johns Hopkins University, Cronkite openly denounced the secrecy and lies he believed were becoming characteristic not just of the White House but of the entire governmental complex:

"Today, truth and honesty are surrounded by untruth and dishonesty, by dissembling and distortion, by cynicism and disbelief. In the areas of government, this is a matter for which we all bear responsibility in a democracy and which should be a matter of direct concern and immediate action."

He continued his attack, referring to the war in Vietnam, agonizing over the proper balance which should be maintained between the government and the press in a democracy when that government is at war. "This administration and preceding ones did not level [with] the American people on the scope of the commitment, which, I submit, they themselves must have known was one of the ultimates of our policy.

"Our problem is how the nation can be kept informed and how it can be given all the information that is necessary for the viable function of a democracy while denying to the potential enemy the information which is capital to his cause."

The speech was dismissed by many critics as mere rhetoric, but Cronkite was honest and earnest in his analysis of the dilemmas and frustration existing between the government and the press since World War II. Basic to the problem, as he saw it, was the redefinition of the term "war" by the U.S. government. Since the conclusion of World War II, the government had begun extending the meaning of the word to include "total war," "undeclared war," "hot war," "cold war," and "potential war." The Reagan administration, influenced, perhaps, by astrologers and/or Hollywood, would introduce yet another concept—"star wars." Within such a multitude of definitions of perpetual war and terror, "potential enemies" are ever present and, therefore, free access to information theoretically could forever remain unobtainable. It cannot be denied, when viewed after the fact, that Cronkite's observations were correct.

The irritation Cronkite was expressing against the Johnson White House, specifically, was for withholding news and even lying on occasions. Though both the Kennedy and Johnson administrations were known for playing their cards close to their chests and misrepresenting the truth—bad enough in themselves—neither administration, it might be lamely argued, had reputations for hardcore vengeance or vindictiveness in their dealings with the press. It was for the Nixon White House to compound the sins of the Oval Office by later attempting to subvert and destroy the reputation of that segment of the American press which disagreed with the policies of that administration.

It should be noted here that there had been instances in which pressure or rumors of pressure for the purpose of manipulation of the news were exerted by presidential administrations other than Nixon's. In 1966, for example, CBS News had scheduled a broadcast of a controversial Senate Foreign Relations Committee hearing in which George Kennan testified against President Johnson's Vietnam policies; instead, the network ran a fifth repeat of *I Love Lucy*. There was much speculation among members of the press and politicians that President Johnson had exerted sufficient influence on his old friend, CBS president Frank Stanton, to kill such contrary televised debates on Vietnam. Even though the charges were never publicly confirmed, CBS News president Fred Friendly, nevertheless, resigned over the affair.

As was noted earlier, Richard Nixon was never able to grasp the basics of proper use of the mass media, nor did he indicate he had learned to take criticism from the press, constructive or otherwise. That he was photographed roughing up his own press secretary, Ron Zieigler, in public didn't contribute to his endearment to newsmen, either. A long history of altercations had characterized his dealings with newspeople during the years he had been a public figure. In 1962, when he denounced all newsmen as biased, many believed the Californian had sung his political swan song. He had tearfully vowed that day the press corps would "not have Nixon to kick around any more." Only six years later, when he was elected to the presidency, he—wittingly or not—made himself fair game for the press again.

There were some who felt there was one instance in which Nixon used television effectively, however. During his 1968 presidential campaign, he appeared briefly on TV's popular *Laugh-In*, daring the zany cast to "Sock it to *me*?" The phrase usually resulted in a bucket of water in the face, but did not, of course, in this instance. His appearance, which his campaign directors said demonstrated his human qualities and a sense of humor, probably was a plus in his election bid.

Much has been written about Nixon's paranoia toward the press, of the wall of isolation which rose solidly around the White House. Nixon even proposed "Student Prince" costumes for the guards who protected the White House, which would have certainly completed the image of the fortress the executive mansion had become. The plan failed, however, because of unrestrained guffawing from all quarters. The more the press or other White House critics pushed, pulled, probed, or otherwise inquired about presidential goings-on, the more the White House resisted. The mood deteriorated from what Ron Ziegler dismissed as "an adversary relationship between press and government" to one of belligerence and open hostility. As the White House persisted in its war with the media, various newsmen stiffened their resolve, speaking out privately or publicly against what they identified as carefully planned and concentrated attempts by the White House to suppress news and curtail freedom of the press.

Of the many nationally-known newsmen to travel the lecture circuit, speaking out against the repressive Nixon White House, none was considered more abrasive than Walter Cronkite. Cronkite further exacerbated the rift by admitting the veiled White House denunciations had a reverse effect on him: "When intimidated, I react the other way."

In an effort to understand the war that existed between the Nixon administration and the press, it might be of some value at this point to examine the cast of characters who made up the infamous White House staff, all of whom later served time in federal prisons for their role in what Cronkite first broke on the *Evening News* as "the Watergate caper."

Even though it is generally agreed that H. R. (Bob) Haldeman was the person, other than President Nixon, who was most responsible for the ongoing conflict with the press, he was closely followed by Attorney General John Mitchell and White House aides John Erlichman and Charles Colson.

During Nixon's first term as president, the news media began to feel the pressures the White House could exert. Then–CBS White House correspondent Dan Rather lay the bulk of Nixon's long-standing anti-press feelings squarely at Haldeman's feet. In his book *The Palace Guard,* Rather explained that Haldeman and Erlichman had been influential students together at UCLA in the late 1940s, a period in America's history when many patriots believed a communist lurked behind every tree and under every bed. Senator Joseph McCarthy was conducting his ruthless congressional witch hunt and Congressman Richard Nixon was making headlines with his pursuit of Alger Hiss, an alleged communist sympathizer. Haldeman and Erlichman were likewise infected with the scarlet fever which gripped the country. Even as college students, they were so fearful their school newspaper had been infiltrated by communists that Haldeman organized a campaign to have student editors elected rather than appointed by "communist sympathizers," as they believed had been the procedure.

Following graduation, Haldeman took a job in New York with the advertising firm of J. Walter Thompson. On an assignment in Washington, Haldeman met his long-time hero Richard Nixon and the two became fast friends. According to Rather, when Nixon lost to Kennedy in 1960, Haldeman told Nixon the villains responsible for his loss were members of the "hostile, liberal press [who] had tipped the balance to Kennedy." As Haldeman fed Nixon's hatred and mistrust of the news media, he surrounded Nixon with likeminded assistants on their symbiotic road to the White House.

John Mitchell, Nixon's first attorney general, was allegedly not above trying to subvert the very law he was sworn to uphold—the Constitution—in this case, specifically, the First Amendment. He obviously did not restrain members of the Nixon staff in their illegal tactics against the press. His suit against the *New York Times* over publication of the so-called "Pentagon Papers," resulting in a judgment against him upheld by a Supreme Court ruling, repudiated Mitchell's efforts to control what could be printed.

The fourth White House zealot—who hated the press as vehemently as he hated the Kennedys—was Charles Colson, who has since become a "born-again Christian," working as a prison chaplain-at-large. A former marine, Colson's three heroes at the time were blood-and-guts Marine general "Chesty" Puller, John Wayne, and, of course, Richard Nixon. He was fond of boasting that he considered himself a "flag-waving, kick-'em-in-the-nuts, anti-press, anti-liberal Nixon fanatic." He was even dubiously credited with stating in 1972, "I would walk over my grandmother to get Nixon re-elected." Even though a 1976 *Time* article reported Colson denied ever making the grandmother pledge, he did not deny his unabashed fascination with and devotion to Richard Nixon.

The article depicted Richard Nixon as a "man incapable of savoring his triumphs, for beyond them his enemies were still lurking. While his finger circled the rim of a wine glass, Nixon told his aides, 'One day we'll get them on the ground where we want them. And we'll stick our heels in, step on them, crush them, show them no mercy.' "

The feelings of most Americans during all but the final tragic months of Nixon's second term in office were generally antipodal: one either believed and trusted the White House and abhorred the press or risked the label of being considered "liberal" by mistrusting the administration and believing the press. Ambivalence was a rare commodity in those days and, according to polls taken following Vice-President Spiro Agnew's 1969 attacks on the press, most Americans believed their president. Even super-patriot Bob Hope got in his licks, frequently supplying the vice-president with anti-press jokes.

In *The Palace Guard*, Dan Rather summarized the events leading up to the open attacks by the White House on the press and other "enemies." First, he wrote, came "an era of good feeling," as campus unrest and street riots, which had typified the Johnson years, abated. More "good news" for the White House came on the same weekend in June 1969; the spectacular Apollo 11 moon landing was made and the Ted Kennedy/Mary Jo Kopechne Chappaquiddick tragedy occurred (the news of Kopechne's death was met with jubilation at the White House since it removed yet another Kennedy from the list of potential challengers for the presidency). Finally, Nixon's triumphant trip to Romania was praised at home and abroad. All of these events contributed to dizzying euphoria at the White House.

By mid-autumn, however, the high spirits gave way to a mood of stress and turmoil as the White House became embroiled in a series of intrigues and hostile acts against its growing number of foes—any and all who disagreed with White House policies immediately went on a literal list of the administration's enemies.

There was, for instance, the dispute over Nixon's nomination of Clement Haynsworth to the Supreme Court. Haynsworth's rejection led to a far more venomous fight the following spring over the subsequent nomination and rejection of a second candidate, G. Harrold Carswell. The Haynsworth-Carswell controversy did more than just end the honeymoon with Congress—it created an atmosphere of abomination and enmity which, from that time forward, would define the administration's corroding relations with Capitol Hill.

The unceasing vendetta by the executive branch against many in Congress, the press, and even some cabinet members, began in 1969. Nixon and Haldeman began to mobilize their plan by first openly attacking the "liberal press" (the adjective was nearly always used). Vice-President Agnew was selected as the spokesman for the all-out assault, even though some in the White House joked privately about Agnew's intellect and suggested he might need a remedial reading course before beginning his new assignment.

A former public relations woman, Cynthia Rosenwald, and White House aides Bill Safire and Patrick Buchanan were to be Agnew's speech writers, although most of the work was attributed to Buchanan.

In the first of his two major addresses attacking the television networks, the vice-president spoke before the Mid-West Regional Republican Committee in Des Moines, Iowa, November 13, 1969, ironically being carried live over the very networks he was attacking. One week later, he flew to Montgomery, Alabama, where he extended his criticism of news coverage to newspapers.* In Des Moines, Agnew complained about the coverage of Nixon's address on Vietnam one week earlier.

"The audience of 70 million Americans gathered to hear the president of the United States was inherited by a small band of network commentators and self-appointed analysts, the majority of whom expressed in one way or another their hostility to what he had to say. It was obvious their minds were made up in advance. . . .

"Now every American has a right to disagree with the president . . . and to express publicly that disagreement. But the people who elected him, and the people of this country have the right to make up their own minds and form their own opinions about a presidential address without having a president's words and thoughts characterized before they can even be digested. . . .

"The purpose of my remarks tonight is to focus your attention on this little group of men who not only enjoy a right of instant rebuttal to every presidential address, but, more importantly, wield a free hand in selecting, presenting and interpreting the great issues in our nation."

Agnew decried the concept that "a small group of men, perhaps no more than a dozen anchormen, commentators and executive producers," could decide what an audience of up to 50 million Americans would see on the evening news—and thereby raise issues and people to prominence they would not otherwise have had. He accused this group of bias based on geographical proximity and on the fact that they talked to each other:

"We do know that to a man these commentators and producers live and work in the geographical and intellectual confines of Washington, D.C., of New York City, the latter of which James Reston terms the most unrepresentative community in the entire United States. Both communities bask in their own provincialism, their own parochialism. We can deduce that these men read the same newspapers. They draw their political and social views from

---

* To avoid slowing down the gathering storm against Cronkite and the defenders of the First Amendment rights, the speeches were not included here. For a better appreciation of the White House vendetta, turn to the Appendix and read the speeches in their entirety.

the same sources. Worse, they talk constantly to one another, thereby providing artificial reinforcement to their shared viewpoints. . . .

"The American people would rightly not tolerate this concentration of power in Government. Is it not fair and relevant to question its concentration in the hands of a tiny, enclosed fraternity of privileged men elected by no one and enjoying a monopoly sanctioned and licensed by Government?"

The vice-president accused the networks of pursuing controversy—"more action, more excitement, more drama"—for the sake of profit, and of ignoring what Nixon would later call the "silent majority" of Americans. He maintained alliteratively — one of his trademarks — that "Normality has become the nemesis of the network news."

Agnew insisted that he was not advocating any form of censorship, but merely wanted the networks "made more responsive to the views of the nation and more responsive to the people they serve." First Amendment issues did not apply, he claimed, because of the vast audience television reached compared to newspapers, because of the "tremendous impact of seeing television film and hearing commentary . . . compared to the printed page," and because of the small number of competing stations compared with the number of available newspapers.

That the Des Moines speech raised many hackles was evident from the Montgomery speech a week later. Agnew claimed that the address "produced enough rugged dissent in the last week to wear out a whole covey of commentators and columnists."

In Montgomery, Agnew raised the question of a "trend toward the monopolization of the great public information vehicles and the concentration of more and more power in fewer and fewer hands."

"Should a conglomerate be formed that tied together a shoe company with a shirt company, some voice will rise up righteously to say that this is a great danger to the economy and that the conglomerate ought to be broken up. But a single company, in the nation's capital, holds control of the largest newspaper in Washington, D.C., and one of the four major television stations, and an all-news radio station, and one of the three major national news magazines— all grinding out the same editorial line—and this is not a subject that you've seen debated on the editorial pages of the *Washington Post* or the *New York Times*.

"For the purpose of clarity, before my thoughts are obliterated in the smoking typewriters of my friends in Washington and New York, let me emphasize that I'm not recommending the dismemberment of the *Washington Post* Company, I'm merely pointing out that the public should be aware that these four powerful voices hearken to the same master. I'm raising these questions so that the American people will become aware of—and think of the implications of—the growing monopoly that involves the voices of public opinion, on which we all depend for our knowledge and for the basis of our views."

He continued to defend the war in Vietnam and the superiority of his generation over the current generation of young people. The main point of the Montgomery speech, however, was a defense of his earlier address and a pledge to continue his attacks on the media:

> One magazine this week said that I'll go down as the 'great polarizer' in American politics. Yet, when that large group of young Americans marched up Pennsylvania Avenue and Constitution Avenue last week, they sought to polarize the American people against the president's policy in Vietnam. And that was their right. And so it is my right, and my duty, to stand up and speak out for the values in which I believe. . . .
>
> But my political and journalistic adversaries sometimes seem to be asking something more—that I circumscribe my rhetorical freedom while they place no restriction on theirs. As President Kennedy observed in a far more serious situation: this is like offering an apple for an orchard.
>
> We do not accept those terms for continuing the national dialogue. The day when the network commentators and even the gentlemen of the *New York Times* enjoyed a form of diplomatic immunity from comment and criticism of what they said is over. Yes, gentlemen, the day is passed.
>
> Just as a politician's words—wise and foolish—are dutifully recorded by press and television to be thrown up at him at the appropriate time, so their words should be likewise

recorded and likewise recalled. When they go beyond fair comment and criticism they will be called upon to defend their stalemates and their positions just as we must defend ours. And when their criticism becomes excessive or unjust, we shall invite them down from their ivory towers to enjoy the rough and tumble of public debate.

I don't seek to intimidate the press, or the networks or anyone else speaking out. But the time for blind acceptance of their opinions is past. And the time for naive belief in their neutrality is gone.

*   *   *

The unleashing of Spiro Agnew to attack the news media forced the press into a defensive posture. The vice-president's assaults on the television networks were, Dan Rather wrote:

> . . . The opening round in the administration's holy war against the press, which two years later would be carried to the Supreme Court in the Pentagon Papers Case, and would continue on afterward with ever-deepening hostility. The president himself added to the turmoil. It was in a television speech that fall, given in an effort to blunt the resurgence of the anti-war movement . . . that Nixon made his famous appeal to the 'silent majority,' thus driving a wedge that much deeper between Americans who sympathized with Vietnam protesters and those who regarded them as traitors.
>
> All this commotion was a far cry from the low-key centrist approach, reminiscent of Ike. No longer was there any pretense that the Nixon White House might serve as a forum of conciliation, a temple of togetherness. By the fall of 1969, it had become an embattled fortress, complete with invisible moat and drawbridge. Within its walls, hidden from public view, there festered a poisoned climate of fear and suspicion, of brooding rancor—the 'us-versus-them' mentality that would affect many future decisions, up to and including Watergate and related crimes. As it took shape that first autumn, it reflected the new power structure that had formed like a shield in and around the Oval Office.

*   *   *

The attacks on the news media from the White House had, up until the Agnew speeches, been discharged in a scatter-gun fashion. Now the White House zeroed in on those who were considered its greatest enemies: the *Washington Post* and three CBS television newsmen—Daniel Schorr, Dan Rather, and Walter Cronkite. Schorr had been referred to as a "clown" by White House speech-writer Patrick Buchanan; Haldeman personally ordered an FBI investigation of him in 1971. Dan Rather, the cocky Texan and White House press corps *persona non grata,* was treated with utter contempt by White House staff members. In 1972, he routed noisy but unseen burglars from the basement office of his Washington home with a shotgun. (He opened the door to the stairs, let the invaders hear him drop two shells into the barrels and then threatened to "blow your ass away.") He told an *Esquire* writer he believed the intruders had been dispatched by the White House. Cronkite long suspected his home and office phones were bugged, as did Marvin Kalb and other newsmen. *Time* magazine alleged the FBI tapped newsmen's telephones over a two-year period. Chet Huntley was cut off completely from all White House communication after he made unkind statements about the Nixon administration in a *Life* article.

In May, 1969, Cronkite was the recipient of a special presentation from the New York Chapter of the Association of Industrial Advertisers. In his remarks at the awards luncheon, he denounced the White House's attempts to control broadcast news by proclaiming "a threat against newsmen was an attack against us all. . . . As long as local broadcasting can be regulated by the Government it cannot be free. We must get out from under this outmoded concept that because we use the people's air the government can say what goes over it. This is no longer valid, it is clearly a restriction of free speech."

The controversy stirred up by the vice-president's unprecedented attacks on the press had left virtually no corner of the nation untouched. A survey conducted by the University of Missouri School of Journalism indicated that the majority of Congressmen interviewed agreed with Agnew's criticism of television network's reporting. (The same poll showed that those questioned, including

Republicans, believed Walter Cronkite was the most fair national newsman and David Brinkley was the least fair.) Overall, however, the majority of Americans seemed to concur with the vice-president's remarks, according to an article in the February 1970 *New Republic*, Agnew received a veritable avalanche of nearly 150,000 letters and telegrams in less than four months after the speeches, all but about 10,000 of which approved of his stand against the press. A Gallup Poll in May 1970 reported that forty-nine percent of Americans questioned were favorably impressed by the two speeches, which were delivered with passion and great professionalism. Agnew became the most sought-after speaker in the country, receiving an average of fifty speaking requests daily.

In a *Senior Scholarship* interview with Peggy Hudson in 1970, Cronkite responded to the increasing criticism of network news programs and commentators:

> We welcome criticism as long as we get it from all sides. It's proof to me that we're doing a good job.
>
> Some people are even questioning whether a free press is feasible at a time of turmoil and strife. I personally feel there is no such thing as a 'little' freedom or a 'little' control. You either have it or don't.
>
> We know 95 percent of the charges [of bias] are false. Most are probably made out of ignorance. We get it from the left. They feel we don't pay enough attention to their causes. We get it from the right, who feel the same way. We get it from Mr. Agnew and those who seem to believe government shouldn't be criticized—certainly the most unbelievable doctrine of modern times. We get it from the center, from people who ask why we pay attention to those long-haired kids.

In an eloquent and prophetic speech delivered March 2, 1970, before the Economic Club of Detroit, Cronkite released the frustration he and his colleagues felt as a result of the vice-president's attacks, a challenge to the Nixon administration and future generations of Americans. The entire text of his speech follows:

Rebel or Die — The Call for Revolution

You probably thought we were through reviewing the past decade and looking blearily ahead at the next. But then you perhaps hadn't counted on this appearance.

Actually, I'm not running a couple of months behind. I'm about 10 months ahead. The first year A.D. was not the year zero, but the year one. The first decade was over at the end of year ten. Thus, this decade will be over, properly, at the end of this year, so, before I start talking about Vice-President Agnew—perhaps inadvertently—let's take a quick look at the Sixties.

It has been some decade—but you haven't seen anything yet.

We in this country have come to a state in the last 10 years that even the most pessimistic sociologist would not have dared predict.

Our cities have been racked by riots.

Our political leaders have been assassinated.

Our youth have been accused of war atrocities that we'd always thought were reserved to our enemies.

Ghastly crimes have been committed by the drugged dregs of society.

Our streets are so crime-ridden that our city dwellers cringe in fear behind bolted doors.

We have millions of undernourished, hundreds of thousands actually hungry, in the midst of plenty.

Our land has been gouged, our air and water befouled by unplanned, thoughtless, selfish use.

And yet, perhaps the worst thing that has happened to us in this last 10 years is a loss of self-confidence.

This proud nation of ours has begun to doubt, to wonder about that pride.

It is conceivable that our doubts began gnawing at us as the horror of Hiroshima began sinking into our consciences. Our certainty about our own superiority was shaken with the beeps from the Soviet Sputnik. Racial strife, a generation that we begot but that in large part turned its back on us, a distant war that has shaken our foundations of patriotism and national service—they have deflated our national ego.

And they have left us, in our frustration, fighting mad. Nations as well as individuals can be blind with rage, and we are so mad with ourselves right now that we seem incapable of rational action. We are striking out in all directions to find the enemy—when all the time I suspect we really know that the enemy is within ourselves.

We know we have so much riches—and are doing so little sharing. We know taxes already are burdensome, and yet we permit our money to be squandered in false schemes and maladministration. We cannot find an escape to spending on nonproductive arms while people live in slums, their bellies painfully empty.

By misdirection, misconception or a lack of vigilance, we built our own trap in Vietnam and watched in perplexed horror as it drained our natural resources, bankrupted our economy, and alienated that portion of youth it didn't kill.

Vietnam disenchanted the nation over its international commitments and caused this president to renounce an American role as policeman for the democracies. That may have been the grand plot of the communists for it would seem that by weakening our resolve to play Galahad, Vietnam has effectively disarmed the United States at a minimum cost to the Soviet Union.

It is frustrating. And we are fighting mad—in a blind rage.

Even for those who voted against him, the quiet, boardroom voice that Mr. Nixon brought to Washington seemed a welcome relief. The hope sprang forth that the United States was not in such bad shape that a little business-like administration could not fix it up.

But I sense that our people are now growing again impatient—concerned by recession in the midst of inflation, by vacillation on the school integration issue, by conflicting stories on the success of Vietnamization, now by the specter of another Vietnam in neighboring Laos. And, yes, instead of wildly applauding I sense that the thoughtful are concerned about non-constructive demagogy by appointed spokesmen of the administration.

Yet, despite our concern, at a time of great need of a dynamic society, we find those who we normally count on as the backbone of our American enterprise, furiously running on a treadmill of regression. Instead of applying ourselves to the problem of social order in a rapidly changing society, we are turning off, seeking solace in divisive recriminations, and, uncharacteristically for Americans, seeking scapegoats for the failures of the society we built.

Our attention focuses on our new revolutionaries and somehow, rather than seeing them as the sad end-product of our society's failures, we view these militantly disaffected as the causes of our problems.

A nation disgusted with its revolutionaries—perhaps because of a guilt complex involving its own inadequacies—could easily turn to simple solutions—to a leader and an ideology promising to bring order out of the chaos—with just a little trimming here and there of traditional American freedoms.

Already we see a concerted attempt by a bruised establishment to muzzle the powerful voice of the free broadcasting industry, and some members of the public cheer— failing to understand that anything which blinds and mutes the free press blinds and deafens them.

Some who attack us are merely misguided and sincerely believe that a nation could guarantee a free press and free speech by regulating them.

I am not certain that Vice-President Agnew fits into this category, although there were few of us who doubted that the intent of his unprecedented Des Moines speech was intimidation.

There have been suggestions, even sometimes from within our industry, that we in the news end have reacted too strongly to the criticism of radio and television news. If we had been reacting solely to criticism, the suggestion would be valid.

This has not been our intent, however. We have rushed to the barricades not to uphold some freedom from criticism— far from it—but to protect the very right of criticism.

For isn't that what freedom of speech is all about? The right to say what we feel it is necessary to say about our government, our politicians, our neighbors, our schools, our TV programs?

We in television news are not immune from that criticism and, indeed, we should be fostering more of it. What this country desperately needs, in this day of increasing monopoly in publishing and time limitations in broadcasting, is a better informed public that will demand a better product of us.

There should be courses in every high school in the land to teach how to read a newspaper, how to listen to radio and how to watch television news. This would create a far more discerning and selective audience than we now have. It would teach our limitations so that the public would not expect more than we can possibly deliver. It would broaden the public's horizon so that it would seek supplemental sources of information which would in turn foster a healthy communications industry encompassing all media.

This approach is vastly different from that of those on the left who believe that, because access to the news media is a right, a committee of self-servers could do a better job of editing our media than the professionals now on the job. And it is a vastly different approach from that of those politicians who believe they are above analysis, instant or otherwise, and who prefer to do the public's business behind a screen of secrecy to be erected by a subservient regulatory agency.

The arsenal of both of these groups is wide-ranging and varied. The former would challenge station licenses. The latter have turned to harassment by subpoena.

Those who simply do not like today's programming for whatever reason and would like to try running the business themselves and those who would hobble TV news for more sinister reasons believe they have the instrument at hand in the licensing of radio and television stations. Their rationale is that we who broadcast are using the people's air and that the people have the right to say what goes on it.

I think we might take a moment to examine that doctrine to see if it is not archaic, dictated by circumstances that no longer pertain.

In the early days of television, as in radio, there were only a few channels available for commercial broadcasting. It was necessary for somebody, and it logically was the government, to allocate those channels.

The law that gave the government that authority said only that the stations so licensed would operate in the "public interest, convenience and necessity." That law specifically forbade government censorship by the regulating agency, but the Federal Communications Commission has assumed the right to examine a station's programming and to require a certain portion of time to be allotted to so-called public affairs programming in fulfillment, presumably, of the "public interest" stipulation in the law. And now, it would seem they would go further than that.

But since that law's inception, thanks to the opening of the ultra-high frequencies in television and the FM band in radio, scores of additional channels have become available.

Already there are more radio and television stations than there are newspapers. It is the rare city today that is not served by more television stations than by newspapers, and by infinitely more radio stations.

There are more one-newspaper cities that there are one-television cities.

There are more television networks serving radio and television stations than there are major news agencies serving the newspapers.

And yet there are still more channels available for the bidding on UHF and FM.

In many situations it would be cheaper to start a television than a newspaper. It would be easier, economically, for a group with a cause—public education, art, political propaganda, or simply profit—to get into broadcasting than into publishing.

Thus it would seem possible that the government's reason for being in the business of controlling what goes onto the people's air is no longer valid.

It clearly is a restriction on free speech for the government to retain that control after the necessity for it has passed. Control over what is said on the people's air should be vested in the people's good sense to accept or reject what is said, the ultimate freedom of choice.

Ideally we would have a system of totally free broadcasting stations—free from commercial control, free from foundation control, free from all political, social and economic pressures.

Such an ideal station would be an electronic Union Square or Hyde Park Corner, providing a soap box for anyone who could make it to the studio.

But this is utopia. Somebody would have to pay the upkeep; some one would have to allocate the available air time, and we would be right back to control, by one establishment, one group, one political philosophy, or another. After all, even the town meeting needs a moderator.

No; far better than that imperfect stretch for the ideal is the freedom of competition that has served us reasonably well so far in preserving our freedom of information.

Mr. Agnew was right when he said that a small group of men determine what will go on the network news. I know of no way to beat this problem. A fast-breaking evening newscast could hardly be edited by plebiscite.

The only question is who does the selecting? Would Mr. Agnew prefer a committee of, say, politicians, or bureaucrats, or sociologists, or teachers or ministers—people whose motives might be good but who would measure the news by that which they consider good for us, and least harmful to themselves?

Rather, I feel the public would prefer to leave the function of news judgment in the hands of journalists, who, in a life-long pursuit of the facts, have learned to be on guard as nearly as one can against their own bias and prejudice, who have adopted a professional ethic even as has the doctor or lawyer in putting aside personal feelings in the interest of the patient, or the client, or the reader, watcher and listener.

We really should be judged only on how successful we are in telling it as it is. If our democracy is to live, we journalists must not be deterred from pursuing that objective without fear or favor. And, for the public's part, it must not be afraid of hearing it like it is.

We all know how bad our situation is. We aren't going to improve it by faith healing. By shutting our eyes we can't make it go away.

For telling it as it is, it isn't going to do any good to shoot me, or even turn me off, which is worse. It won't change the text of the telegram to string up the Western Union boy. It won't change events at the other end of the line to tear out the telephone.

Far better than grasping for easy solutions, it seems to me it is time, hopefully not past time, for America to take the harder but more rewarding road of critical self-examination.

The mere fact that the species has survived so far seems hardly adequate cause for self-applause, nor can we indulge in self-congratulations for our civilization's considerable material and cultural development that has failed to guarantee survival or nurture the bodies and the spirit of all mankind.

If we are to survive and wipe out not only the symptoms but the causes of injustice and decay, there must be change.

There is going to be change. This is inevitable. The question that the future asks is: what kind of change—for the good or the bad, coming rapidly or more slowly, by radical excisement of the old, by amputation and transplant, or by mutation?

Some of our institutions have served us well; others have served us less than adequately, because we have served them poorly.

We can believe that we can improve our use of them, and thus, bring about a more perfect society. Or, we can believe that we must replace them with something new.

To determine what we keep, what we change, and what we discard, we must pursue full and open inquiry, which may require throwing off old concepts and shibboleths in the spirit of basic research—for in political action research must precede advocacy.

In doing so we should recognize that suggested solutions will come from both the classic right and left of the political-economic spectrum, and there will be radical suggestions from both.

Because it is customary to consider radicalism only on the left, let us look dispassionately at a radical question from the right.

It concerns the comparative rights of the majority and a minority. Worthy albeit minority groups—the colored, the impoverished, the dissident students—have chosen as their tools for change civil disobedience and, on occasion, violence and have interfered with the normal commerce of the majority.

The more complex a society, the greater the power of a smaller minority for disruption of that society.

Which has led to the question, asked by serious scholars, as to whether it is possible that in the crowded condition of the late 20th century man's civil liberties are going to have to be curtailed for the greater good of the greater number.

Is it possible that that freedom of individual action that was permissible when this nation was young and underpopulated no longer can be permitted as we enter middle age and overpopulation?

These are radical, shocking thoughts, but listen to some others: someday, and the dawn of that day cannot long be held back, we must take a new look at the doctrine of national sovereignty—not because we believe any less in the principle on which the doctrine was conceived but because we realize that the nature of our world is changing. The possession of ever more fearful means of warfare will not long permit the nations to live in anarchy, and yet any system of world order will require a surrender of some national freedom for the greater good of all.

On the federal level, the whole question of states' rights may need reexamination.

Our fiscal policy is in a shambles, partly because of unnecessary duplication of government. Taxes are duplicated and, what is worse, hidden in an attempt to deceive the people. Efficiency of government is impaired and the machinery overwhelmed by proliferation of government agencies, on both the federal and local levels.

Nor is this tendency restricted to government. Big business itself sometimes becomes burdensomely top-heavy as it expands, and the people pay a tax for inefficiency in the form of higher prices.

If reform takes top-to-bottom restructuring of the American system, then we should not be afraid of such rebuilding. That which is sacred in our past does not require lip service to obsolescence.

A very keen observer of the scientific scene and a philosopher, Lord Ritchie Calder, notes that scientific revolution is the "replacement of one set of propositions that have served practitioners satisfactorily (even in spite of anomalies) with a new set." A set of propositions, called a paradigm, provides model problems and solutions, the framework in which science works. He notes that to reject a paradigm—to foment scientific revolution—is to commit a "breach of accepted scientific tradition."

Yet the great scientific discoverers have been revolutionaries. They have rejected an important paradigm of their discipline.

In political thought, in the discipline of the political sciences, we must be willing to escape our paradigm, we must listen to those who would escape, we must hear out the dissenter.

We must seek out, and make use of, the original thinkers.

We are now in a scientific revolution. In the life span of the youngest member of this audience we have sped through three eras—the atomic age, the computer age, the space age—and now we stand on the threshold of the most revolutionary of them all, the DNA age, the discovery of the genetic key which unlocks the very secret of life, of what makes us what we are. We soon will have the frightening knowledge of how to make man any way we want him—smart or stupid, tall or short, black or white.

In the next 30 years the transplant of human organs will be commonplace, the birthrate must be controlled, we will be exploring and perhaps colonizing the ocean floor.

Can anyone deny that a political revolution will accompany that scientific revolution? We have the future in our power. The 21st century will not burst upon us in full flower. We can mold it to be what man wants it to be.

But to do that we must know what we want, and we must examine each of our institutions to determine whether they stand up to the challenges of the century ahead.

We of our generation may have to look no further than our own failure to plan for this future to find the seeds of youth's discontent.

Convinced that we are not doing the job, many of them are turning their backs on us.

And lest they reject that which is good of our institutions and that accumulated wisdom which we possess solely by reason of age, we must not reject those among them who dissent. In youth's rebellion against any unsatisfactory status quo we must assist, not resist.

This does not mean we can tolerate lawlessness, for the law is the foundation of our freedoms.

It does mean that we must not let our revulsion to the transactions of the militants blind us to the future.

Society is going to change. The only question is whether youth is going to help and, indeed, if we are going to help.

Not short of death can any of us avoid being a part of the human parade. The question is: where will we be in it? Up toward the front, carrying the banner? Swept along somewhere in the middle? Or perhaps trampled underfoot as it marches over us en route to the future?

Our help is needed. While our way of life will change, we need to communicate by word and deed to those coming behind us the values we know are constants—right or wrong, truth or falsehood, generosity or selfishness, dedication or cynicism, self-discipline or license.

The ferment abroad today in the land borders on anarchy, and there are frightened calls for law and order.

But as surely as a boiling kettle will not stop generating steam just because a lid is clamped on it, our ferment cannot be suppressed by tanks and guns.

Far better than suppressing ferment, how about handling it the American way; how about channeling it toward a betterment and modernization of this society for the good of all? Why not use that steam to turn the lathes on which we can burnish away our self-doubts, polish our patriotism to a new brilliance and fashion a new American spirit.

A great historian of our earliest days noted of the Virginia gentlemen who met at Williamsburg to lay the foundations of this nation: "Their equality and status questioned, even threatened, the now united gentry became radicals, gentlemen revolutionists. They revolted to preserve what they had."

May I suggest that to preserve what we have we must lead, or at least join, the revolution against that which is evil in our society. Let our new gentry—the gentry of the educated and the wise—become radicals and seek bold new solutions to our problems.

Indeed, to refuse to recognize the need for revolution is the ultimate denial of the principals for which our forefathers risked so much, offering even to lay down their lives.

Ladies and gentlemen, history beckons, ready to bestow its accolade on those who turn today's dissent to tomorrow's victory.

This country has not lost its ability to respond to challenge, and while the challenges of today seem frightening in their complexity, there is no reason for despair. The more and the greater the challenges, the greater the heroism of thought, deed and courage to surmount them—and the more exciting the prospect of the combat and the sweeter the taste of victory."

Following Cronkite's speech, Lawrence M. Carino, vice-president and general manager of WJBK-TV, read questions from the audience for Cronkite to answer:

Q. "Won't you agree that TV has the power to elect or defeat a man?"

A. "Well, it depends on what you mean by TV. If you mean that man's use of TV, it might very well. If you mean the news broadcasts' treatment of the man, I wouldn't think so at all, because there are so many other means of communications which he has. He has his own access to television, which I think is going to be far the more important weapon in his campaign. I do think that television has a certain X-ray quality to it. I think that it does have a way of ferreting out the insincere and I think that very possibly in that sense a candidate is up against it when he faces the television cameras. People are going to be, I think, able to see through any insincerity.

"But as far as the news departments, the newsmen, the correspondents making or breaking a candidate, we see no evidence of that and I don't think they're likely to try. We are professional journalists, we're not propagandists."

Q. "Which do you consider in worse shape—the railroads or television?" [Laughter]

A. "Well, I'm spending a little time daily with each. I think the railroads are in far worse shape than TV. We haven't abandoned any channels yet. We're not trying to get rid of our passengers, as far as I know. Our premises are kept a little cleaner. Our conductors are a little politer. And as far as I know, so far most of the stations are running on time."

Q. "How can CBS object to Agnew's attempts at censorship when CBS censored and canceled The Smothers Brothers Show?"

A. "Well, I think there is quite a difference here in the two things. We're talking about, in one case, of course, government censorship; in the other we're talking about the programming practices of an individual network. I don't consider that censorship. Except for good taste in the programming area; that is, in comedy, songs, dance and funny sayings. I would consider it censorship if CBS told me what to say on the air in the news area and in that case I probably wouldn't be there.

"I think that's true of my friends at NBC or ABC. One of the remarkable things about the growth of this industry is that some very far-sighted men like Bill Paley and Dr. Frank Stanton of CBS and the Sarnoffs at NBC—who did not come out of the news business at all—turned out to be the greatest defenders of free speech and a free press. And although it is very hard for a lot of our friends to understand, in the news areas of the major networks there is absolutely no advertising pressure even. There is no form of censorship that is operating upon our daily news broadcasts.

"To decide on our own programming in the entertainment field is only, it seems to me, to exercise that right and duty that the network has to choose that which is most appealing, most acceptable to the American public. I don't consider that a form of censorship.

"The government is not going to step in and force us to do these things and there still are other channels to go to. Mr. Agnew is talking about a form of censorship that would apply to all the channels, in his intimidation. He denies, of course, there is censorship involved in what he's suggesting, but it would apply to all channels and it would be government controlled. That I think is a major difference."

Q. *"Most of the polls show the American people approving of a large part of what Vice-President Agnew said. Are the American people wrong?"*

A. "No. As a matter of fact, I approve of a great deal of what he said. But on the things I don't approve of, he's so wrong! [Laughter] You know, we're a little bit like the fellow who takes his car to the used car lot. And the fellow, in trying to get the price down that he's going to offer the man for the used car, is telling him what's wrong with it. Well, I dare say that used car salesman isn't going to find out nearly as much what's wrong with that car as the fellow who drove it in to see him.

"I think we in our business know far more what's wrong with television than Mr. Agnew is ever going to find out. There are a lot of things wrong. We aren't perfect by a whale of a long shot. There are a lot of things that we could improve and are trying to improve. That's the point: we are working on it. We are professionals. We're working on it. And I can understand a public discontent these days. When I was stricken with the flu around Christmas time and I spent some time at home watching my own evening news program with Harry Reasoner and without me, I can tell you that after three days at home, I was getting pretty sick of what I was watching on the television. [Laughter] And Harry's a more personable fellow than I am. He smiles more than I do—which isn't hard.

"But the news isn't pleasant. It's not nice. It's not good. It's very disconcerting night after night to hear what's going on in this country and in this world of ours. We are in a period of ferment, of revolution.

"But these are the trends. These are the things we have to know about. The people out there who applaud—I think rather blindly—Mr. Agnew's criticism and answer the pollsters that they agree with him, I think would be the first to be concerned if they suddenly heard from a traveler from New York that there had been a riot in Newark the night before and they hadn't heard it on the air. I think they would be very suspicious, very concerned, very worried about why they hadn't heard about it.

"No, we have to have a free flow of information in this country. Democracy is built on that. If we don't know what our problems are, how are we ever going to do anything about them? This is our function and I don't blame people for being upset about it. As I say, I was myself when I had to watch it three nights in a row and hadn't felt the problem of putting it on the air that day. These things are going to continue, I'm afraid, and as I was saying in the speech, it's a question of just learning to hear it as it is, to accept it as it is.

"Let me just say one thing about the current problem—Laos. A friend of mine came up to me yesterday and said, 'Tell me. Are we really in Laos?'

"And I got a little upset. I said, 'Well, of course we're in Laos. Why do you doubt it? The United Press has reported it, the Associated Press has reported it, Reuters has reported it, *Agence France* has reported it, CBS has reported it, NBC has reported it, ABC has reported it, the *Chicago Tribune* has reported it, the *New York Times* has reported it, the *Washington Post* has reported it.'

"You can go right down the line; there are a couple of hundred correspondents in Vientiane who have reported it. Now does anybody seriously think that they're sitting in a back room in Vientiane somewhere—in a country that's not at war; where there are no Americans—saying, 'Listen, let's put Americans in Laos this week. That'll be a whale of a story. Let's do that. Let's see. Let's figure out that all of these airplanes are really being flown by Americans. Let's figure out that all those aircraft carrier-borne fighter planes are coming from American aircraft carriers instead of those Laotian aircraft carriers that we know are really out there. These B-52s—let's pretend those are American and not really Cambodian.'

"Does anybody believe that the press can sit there and dream that up? And yet people can say, 'Are we really in Laos? I mean, because the administration hasn't said we're there.' Well, I think we'd better start believing the press for a change." [Applause]

Mr. Carino. "There have been many questions concerning the following topic, but perhaps we can get all of them in these two."

Q. "Is there any way to get better balance of news reporting between the sensational and the significant?"

"What steps are being taken to assure fair and honest reporting of news events?"

A. "Well, all I can say to both of those questions is that—and I know it's difficult for those who choose to be critical to believe it—we're all professional journalists. We have all been through college, or most of us have, studying journalism, studying an ethic, believing in an ethic, believing in freedom of information and a free press. Well, we make mistakes. We're constantly studying the means of getting significance across to the American people.

"Sensationalism? Yes, there's a little. I admit to that. Some are more guilty than others. I would admit that we occasionally dip our toe, perhaps, into it, in maybe using a few feet more of the footage of a riot than we absolutely have to, to get the story across.

"That might happen occasionally. But don't think we work on it. Every day we're worrying about this problem of balance. Every day we're worrying about, are we going to be too sensational? Every day we worry and weigh each of the stories as to whether this story is really needed to further the truth. This is a constant examination.

"Self-reappraisal is not something that began with Mr. Agnew, nor is it going to end with Mr. Agnew. I have a hope and a feeling that the free press of this country is going to be seriously weighing its obligations long after Mr. Agnew is there to chide us about it. There are men who I think are doing a far better job, certainly, than I at that, and who I look up to. And I hope that there are some younger ones coming along who are looking up to me because all of us are carrying on a tradition of fighting until our last breath for this right of the people to know; not the right for us to do anything, but the right of you to know. That's all that freedom of speech and press means and if you don't know, you're never going to be able to exercise your franchise to keep this democracy strong and healthy." [Applause]

Q. "Does a news broadcaster write his own news broadcast, or does a staff accumulate and write his news items?"

A. "Well, a little bit of both. Speaking only for my own shop, each topic is, first, assigned to one of three writers. Their product is carefully read and frequently rewritten and certainly edited by me. No word that I speak goes out without my full approval. And I have never—with maybe one or two exceptions in the early days— said anything on the air to which I could not personally subscribe. I have said some stupid things through ignorance but I have not said anything to which I could not personally subscribe.

"And my evening newscast I can tell you, except on a day when I have the privilege of coming before you here in Detroit, is a 9:30 a.m. start for a 7:30 p.m. finish, without time for lunch. And it's true of the rest of our staff. It's a long 10-hour day. At 9:30 we begin reading the newswires and talking to our correspondents around the world and getting the stories together. By 3:30 we know something about our film that we're going to have that day and we make our first lineup and begin writing. And at that time I'm at the typewriter and I write part of it, and three writers are writing part of it, and between the four of us, we put a program together.

"But I do not believe that in any of the major networks are the news correspondents you see on the air news 'readers.' They all participate actively in the preparation of their own broadcasts."

Q. "How do you justify making a national hero out of 'Rap' Brown or Eldridge Cleaver by giving them so much air time? Is that really news?"

A. "I don't see how you can deny that it's really news. That would be a strange judgment, it would seem to me, if you thought that you could suppress the ferment in this country today of which these people are representative and are leaders by putting our heads in the sand and pretending they're not here and that they'll go away. That would be the greatest way to foster their revolution—to let them build it under the rug, so to speak.

"I think exposure is the way to get these things out in the open and the only way so that Americans can react and take whatever action they feel necessary and can recognize the danger when they see it.

"As far as over-exposure, I doubt that that has happened. When these leaders appear, it is true that they gain national prominence perhaps faster than they would otherwise, but also the nation is alerted to the danger far faster than it would be otherwise. I think you balance off the two and I believe that you would come to an answer that it is better to know than not to know." [Applause]

Mr. Carino. "Just one more question so that he can make an airplane in time to be in your living room tonight by 6:30."

Q. "Would you agree that the female on Mission Impossible *last night was the best this year so far, and that CBS should try to sign her on a permanent basis?"*

A. "If we can't get her for *Mission Impossible,* I'm going to get her for the *Evening News.* [Laughter] I would agree, yes. Quite a girl, whoever she was. She was wonderful.

"This has been great being with you. I wish I had a lot more time because I do feel, really, as the kids say, that 'rapping' like this is a help in talking through some of the misunderstandings between media and our viewers, readers, listeners. It's all terribly important that we do understand one another. And I'd like to say that for our part we do understand the criticism. And, as I said in this little speech, I would like to see courses in school and I wish you would all go out and spread the word. We need it. We want to hear from you. We need to know what's bugging the American people and we need a demand from you for a better product because we in the news departments of the networks and local stations aren't the only arbiters of the fate of how much time we have on the air to operate, what we do with that time while we are on the air, and you can help. Demand a better product and you'll get one. Thank you."

*   *   *

The sharp reactions to Vice-President Agnew's speeches persisted. The charges by the White House, now in the open, triggered what amounted to a formal declaration of war against the press. Cronkite and his network colleagues took special pains not to respond on the air to the vice-president, but their speeches before private groups were quite specific and pointed. As tribute to the newsmen's sense of fairness, overt attempts were initiated by the major networks to label opinions and commentaries carefully as such. A decision was reached by CBS to temporarily curtail analysis of President Nixon's speeches. Mr. Agnew's charge that "instant analysis"—a term of his own making—was unfair to the president was quickly dismissed by Dr. Frank Stanton, who revealed commentators usually had more than two hours notice on a speech's content and, in some cases, had a copy of the speech itself.

On January 30, 1970, Agnew suddenly announced he was calling off his war on television broadcasters and networks. In his remarks, however, he nonetheless continued the attack by recalling how pleased he had been, when he was in Baltimore, and the *Sun* was on strike. He said on that occasion, "You know how they get rid of garbage—they print it."

Harry Reasoner, responding to the way Cronkite had addressed the vice-president's attacks, wryly suggested, "Partly as a result of Cronkite's objectivity, I think it was quite natural that he sort of fell into being the spokesman for American broadcast journalism at the time that we were under attack by, uh, whatever-his-name-was."

Reasoner further expanded the philosophy he feels underlies American journalism: "We have to go through a continual process of self-examination, as any profession does. And we have some faults, but I think they're not of collusion or conspiracy.

"In a way, it was unfortunate that Mr. Agnew turned out to be a crook, because that meant the argument got settled without ever having reached a conclusion—just that he was discredited. I would have just as soon that we had kept talking about it and gotten a clear defense through. In other words, I think that the press was sort of let off the hook, not only because of Mr. Agnew, but because of the whole Watergate thing. The press turned out not to be criers of doom, but just right. But it doesn't change whatever basic points Agnew or anyone else might have had, which is: Is there too much power, or are we doing our job properly? This deserves not only our self-examination—I believe it's perfectly proper for public officials and any other concerned citizen to comment on or inquire into."

John Chancellor denied Agnew's claim that an Eastern Elitist movement conspired to control the news during the Nixon years or at any time. He felt the assemblage of newsmen, bankers and other professionals on the East Coast is a national elite, made up of people from all over the United States.

Cronkite echoed Chancellor's views: "One of the myths that Agnew tried to perpetuate or implant, really—I guess [Agnew] was the first who started it—is that there is some kind of network conspiracy, or something like that. It is certainly true that a handful of us make news decisions—I don't know any other way to do it. It can't be done by a committee of disinterested citizens. For one thing, there aren't many disinterested citizens when we get down to the news. Everybody has some kind of hod to carry on almost every issue. Some people see the same piece of news differently. It's good news to some and it's bad news to others.

"The networks do not get together. There is no connivance between us. The proof of that is—while Agnew and others would like us to believe that—you'll notice the pieces we take to lead with each night are usually the ones that the newspapers have led with and nobody accuses those newspapers of being part of the Eastern liberal establishment. The same is true of local television broadcasts—and we certainly don't tell the local stations what to lead with, or how to handle it. And yet, the local newscasts at ten or eleven o'clock at night have more viewers than we do.

"If any one person tried to manage the news—if an anchorman tried to do it—he surely would be brought up by his own writers and editors and so forth. That sort of power does not exist.

"I'm not saying that one man or another could not get on the air once and make a blast, and maybe for a few days he could start insinuating the material in his broadcast, but he couldn't last very long. For one thing, it's going to be immediately perceived by the people as such. The people aren't stupid. That's a great mistake some politicians make. And, furthermore, the management of the stations and the networks are not stupid. You couldn't get by with that."

"You Must Be Pleased"

The Fall of Nixon

[Edmund] Burke said there were Three Estates in Parliament, but in the Reporters' Gallery yonder, there sat a Fourth Estate, more important [by] far than they all.

—Thomas Carlyle

JUST AS the agitation over Agnew's speeches began to lose steam, CBS telecast a documentary and three news stories which rekindled the fire between the network and the White House. The four irritants, in the order they occurred, were the CBS news film of a Vietnam atrocity; the documentary, *The Selling of the Pentagon*; the airing of Dr. Daniel Ellsburg's disclosure of the Pentagon Papers; and the initial television coverage which broke the Watergate incident.

The first story concerned CBS's filmed coverage of the stabbing murder of a Viet Cong prisoner in a South Vietnamese prison camp at Bau Me, at a vulnerable time in America's consciousness: world attention was focused on Lieutenant William Calley's trial at Fort Benning, Georgia, for the My Lai massacre of Vietnamese villagers. The White House contended that the film had been faked. CBS reran the film a few nights later on the *Evening News,* first as originally shown and then in stop action. Further documentation was provided by an interview with a South Vietnamese sergeant who had witnessed the murder and stated that the incident was accurate as presented by CBS News. Following the repeat showing of the film, Cronkite explained to a *New York Times* reporter:

"We broadcast the original story in the belief it told something about the nature of the war in Vietnam. What has happened since then tells something about the government and its relations with news media which carry stories the government finds disagreeable."

In February 1971, as testimonial to Cronkite's veracity and courage, the outspoken newsman received the George Polk Memorial Award for Outstanding Achievement in Journalism for 1970. The award, named for a CBS correspondent killed in Greece after World War II, is given annually by CBS. In making the presentation, CBS cited Cronkite's strong stand against the repeated attempts by the White House to discredit CBS News for disclosing the stabbing.

In the same month Cronkite received the Polk Award, CBS News presented a special filmed report entitled *The Selling of the Pentagon.* The documentary, when viewed long after the furor erupted, appears to be so objective and fair one wonders how any rational person could find serious fault with it. The documentary's major thesis was simple: the Pentagon was too public-relations conscious and spent too much of the taxpayer's money—$30,000,000 to $90,000,000 each year—to hard-sell the American people on the importance of maintaining a strong military.

In introducing the Pentagon documentary he hosted, Roger Mudd assured his television audience that CBS News had not tapped secret files or classified documents in researching the program.

Basing its figures on 1971 expenditures, CBS revealed the following additional statistics: sham battles of only two days' duration to demonstrate U.S. firepower cost $190,000,000; the Caterpillar Tractor Company had received $39,000,000 in defense funds; 3,000 influential civilians—including industrialists, retired military personnel, bankers, and college administrators—were fêted each year by the Pentagon at the taxpayer's expense; the 300 films produced by the Pentagon cost $12,000,000; and the daily news conferences at the Pentagon disseminated prejudicial, hard-core Department of Defense propaganda. In essence, CBS stated that it believed too much money was being spent by the Pentagon to make violence look glamorous; the traveling colonels, shopping center displays, parachutists, jet air shows, and judo exhibitions were extravagant trifles being paid for by tax dollars.

It was at this time Vice-President Agnew ignored his self-proclaimed "non-aggression pact" and, from Boston, attacked the documentary in this newest confrontation between the press and the Oval Office. He questioned CBS's credibility and indifference to earlier criticisms of networks by an executive and a Congressional subcommittee. He found fault with the production as a whole, but felt the editing of Marine Colonel John MacNeil's comments was particularly misleading. Colonel MacNeil's interview had been cut into several segments that were shown at intervals; therefore, the charge was made, the destruction of the continuity took his statements out of context. (Even Cronkite admitted later that he objected to that particular editing technique.) Agnew, while denying he was trying to intimidate journalists or restrict journalism, declared the CBS documentary was "a subtle but vicious broadside against the nation's defenses." CBS president Frank Stanton was pressed by Agnew to answer his charges, but initially declined.

Later, back in Washington, the vice-president called for CBS to admit or deny his Boston charges of "error and propagandistic manipulation." Dr. Stanton maintained his silence, but Senator Mike Mansfield spoke out in defense of all coverage of the increasingly unpopular war in South Vietnam. He urged American journalists to resist the Republican charges of bias, adding, "All the networks are doing a good job, as has the press, and I hope that this constant criticism will not have the effect of intimidating the networks."

Dr. Stanton declared that Agnew's objections were clearly an issue of freedom of the press. Agnew insisted on an opportunity to videotape an official criticism to precede a repeat showing of the controversial documentary. On March 24, 1971, *The Selling of the Pentagon* was re-run with the Agnew statement (edited by CBS), as well as an interview with CBS News president Richard Salant, who insisted "no one has refuted the essential accuracy of the documentary. We can refute every charge. We are proud of *Pentagon* and CBS News stands behind it. We are confident that when passions die down, it will be recognized as a vital contribution to the people's right to know."

F. Edward Hébert, Nixon supporter and head of the House Armed Services Committee, didn't agree with CBS or Salant, charging that the documentary was "one of the most un-American things I've ever seen on the tube." Secretary of Defense Melvin Laird, in an attitude totally uncharacteristic of a Nixon cabinet member, correctly dismissed the whole episode as a tempest in a teapot. Referring to the editing of Colonel MacNeil's remarks, however, he suggested off-handedly that perhaps CBS could have used a little more professionalism in putting the show together.

Not willing to let sleeping dogs lie, the vice-president renewed his dissatisfaction with the documentary after the second broadcast. In St. Louis, he complained that CBS had dared edit his rebuttal. CBS ignored the charges, never explaining why it edited Agnew, perhaps giving credence to Republican Senator Robert Doyle's accusation that the Nixon administration was having a difficult time getting its views across on network television because of the networks' prejudices. Further ignoring protests from the White House and its allies, CBS permitted the U.S. Army television network in Saigon to air *Pentagon* twice—on March 20 and 26. Both were shown without Vice-President Agnew's comments.

Robert Manning, editor-in-chief of the *Atlantic Monthly*, found the episode ludicrous. Referring to the vice-president's notorious golfing hooks and slices and lethal tennis balls, Manning contributed the following letter to the editors of the *New York Times*:

Agnew is playing with the facts again. I refer to his attack on the CBS documentary, 'The Selling of the Pentagon.' Without offering a significant example of misrepresentation or inaccuracy, he castigated the documentary as a severe example of bias and distortion.

I beg to suggest that Mr. Agnew has hit the wrong ball. To one who has enjoyed with more than a passing acquaintance the way Washington works, the documentary rings true more from start to finish; and if it were to be faulted, it should be for the reason that in the time at hand CBS could throw the light on only a part of the story of the Department of Defense's mighty propaganda engine.

For those who might care to assay the vice-president's charges I suggest a reading of Chapters 13 and 14 in the recently published book, *The Military Establishment,* a Twentieth Century Fund study by Adam Yarmolinsky and a team of contributors. I hope Mr. Agnew, at least, will read the material.

History has not recorded whether Agnew took Manning's advice, but the National Academy of Television Arts and Sciences believed the documentary to be of such value in keeping Americans apprised of military waste it awarded CBS an Emmy for its efforts. In the presentation ceremonies, the Academy declared *Pentagon* was "an outstanding achievement in news documentary programming."

The Selling of the Pentagon, like a thorn buried deep in sensitive flesh, continued to rankle staunch pro-Nixon Republicans. In the spring of 1971, the White House Special Subcommittee ordered Dr. Stanton to appear before it to testify concerning the documentary. Despite repeated subpoenas to produce the raw materials and research information, Stanton defied the Subcommittee and was declared to be held in contempt of Congress by at least one Subcommittee member. Later, on June 29, the members voted five to zero to seek a contempt of Congress citation against the CBS president, but the measure failed. Stanton maintained throughout the inquiry he was conducting a fight for the freedom of the press and steadfastly held his ground. The Assistant Secretary of Defense testified against the network, while Colonel MacNeil sued CBS News and the *Washington Post* for $6,000,000 for distortion of his remarks.

On March 30, Cronkite, who had been speaking out privately for the right of CBS to show the truth about the ugly side of the Pentagon, was called to testify before the Subcommittee. Before a standing-room only audience (even Senator Edward Kennedy broke away from his activities to attend what had become a major media event), Cronkite said he believed the government clearly had too much power over the press. He joined earlier journalistic witnesses in stating that both radio and television were being threatened by hostile governmental regulations. Capitalizing on his unique position, Cronkite candidly told his audience:

"Broadcast news today is not free. Because it is operated by an industry that is beholden to government for its right to exist, its freedom has been curtailed by fiat, by assumption, and by intimidation and harassment.

"We are at the mercy of the whim of politicians and bureaucrats and whether they choose to chop us down or not, the mere existence of their power is an intimidating constraining threat in being."

Cronkite concluded his remarks by calling for an end to the authority of the Federal Communication Commission in dictating broadcast content. He asked, "How could we be improved by outside monitors without destroying the independence which is so essential to a free press?"

The rebuff was not what the congressmen had expected. Even though the Subcommittee was capable of merely inconveniencing the witnesses and moderately slapping the corporate wrist of CBS, it was unable to force the network to produce the materials it had requested. The controversy over *The Selling of the Pentagon* eventually died, but the incident served as yet another reminder to many influential and interested citizens of the intentions of the Nixon White House to have the press serve up only complimentary news about its policies.

In May, Cronkite dropped his characteristic restraint and broadened his attack on the repression he felt from the White House. Speaking in New York City before the International Radio and Television Society, he said:

"Many of us see a clear indication on the part of this administration of a grand conspiracy to destroy the credibility of the press. . . . Nor is there any way that President Nixon can escape responsibility for this campaign. He could reverse the anti-press policy of his administration. . . . It attacks on many fronts: often reiterated by unsubstantiated charges of distortion or even fakery planted with friendly columnists, the attempts to divide the networks and their affiliates [and] harassment by subpoena."

Four months later, in September, a concerned Senator Sam Ervin addressed his fellow senators regarding White House attempts to curb the press. The North Carolina Democrat warned that "Some government officials appear to believe that the purpose of the press is to present the government's policies and programs to the public in the best possible light. They appear to have lost sight of a free press in a free society."

Speaking for his president, White House Press Secretary Ron Ziegler immediately responded, "In the last two years, people have been suggesting the administration has an intent to intimidate the press. This is not our interest. We respect the free press.

"But as a government should be criticized and should be self-critical, criticism of the press in itself does not suggest intimidation. In my personal view, there has been too much sensitivity by the press."

Ziegler further decried the tension which existed between the government and the press, to which Senator Ervin fired back, "A free press in a free society . . . means that there will be tension and sometimes hostility between the press and the government, which attests to the vitality of the First Amendment."

*　　*　　*

The third move by CBS which further infuriated the Nixon administration was initiated by Cronkite's fraternization with and defense of Daniel Ellsberg, a Pentagon analyst who had disclosed the so-called "Pentagon Papers." The White House had tried in vain to prevent the publication of the documents by the *New York Times.* In any other time, Dr. Ellsberg would probably have been prosecuted for revealing the sensitive information. When it was learned, however, that his office had been broken into by the notorious White House "plumbers," and with the Watergate affair diminishing his crime, Ellsberg never had his day in court. On June 23, 1971, CBS included an eight-minute conversation between Ellsberg and Cronkite on the *Evening News.* (Two to three minutes on the thirty-minute news show was the usual length of time for important stories. Eight minutes—nearly one-third of the actual time spent for news—was extremely rare.) In that interview, Ellsberg placed full responsibility for the Vietnam war on the United States.

In retrospect, it should be noted that during Lyndon Johnson's term as president, Cronkite was the first major newscaster to take a clear-cut editorial stand against the increasingly unpopular war. In that departure from his objective role as a newscaster, Cronkite spoke of his disillusionment with the U.S. policy in Vietnam and predicted "the end could be no more than a draw." Now, in 1971, on his televised news program, he praised Dr. Ellsberg for exposing the diabolical American posture in that war. Even though he admitted later he would never have approved of any theft of secret papers by CBS staff members, Cronkite openly confessed his admiration for Ellsberg's courage, bravery and fortitude in doing what he did.

When the most publicized political crime in American history broke in the fall of 1972, CBS was the first network to present investigative reports on the scandal. (Cronkite, Dan Rather, and Daniel Schorr were honored with Emmys in 1973 for the work they did to expose the Watergate incident.) The disclosure of the burglary—and the unrelenting pressure from the networks and newspapers to uncover specific individuals and their activities in the sordid affair—intensified the antipathy toward the Nixon administration until its eventual shameful divestiture.

In late August 1973, President Nixon called a press conference at his San Clemente home, the first since June 1972. In that meeting, the president announced the resignation of William Rogers as Secretary of State and his replacement by Henry Kissinger. Nixon also used the occasion to defend his vice-president—Agnew's high-profile speeches and comments against the news media and ever-growing charges of misconduct while governor of Maryland were making him a liability—and to make an emotional appeal to the American people to realize that he was a president harassed and abused by the news media and his political enemies.

The American people from whom the president sought support were gradually beginning to realize something of the magnitude of the corruption within the Oval Office. Despite charges to the contrary from Nixon, it was becoming increasingly apparent it was not the president who was being maligned, but the press and enemies of the White House. Following the initial stories of the break-in of Democratic headquarters at the Watergate by the White House plumbers, the enormity of the sins of the administration—as first revealed by Carl Bernstein and Bob Woodward of the *Washington Post,* followed closely by the networks and, finally, the Congressional Watergate hearings—removed the blinders from the eyes of most of the American people. Now, at last, the press was vindicated and no longer held in the low esteem into which the Nixon White House had forced it.

Despite the darkening cloud of guilt which surrounded him and his administration, the president kicked desperately against the goads in futile efforts to rally his supporters about him. At his October 26, 1973, press conference, President Nixon used the last fifteen seconds to attack the press again by making facetious comments about how "precise, exact and accurate" the press was. Then, with pointed sarcasm, he added, "Cronkite's not going to like this tonight, I hope."

Less than two weeks later, at another meeting with members of the press, President Nixon blasted the "outrageous, vicious, distorted reporting" to which he claimed he had been subjected by the media. He declared the real villain was CBS in general and Walter Cronkite in particular. Cronkite calmly reflected on the verbal barbs by remarking, "I suppose that a man under attack as Mr. Nixon is would look for anyone to lash out at."

As if to absolve the press totally and finally of the curse placed on it by the Nixon administration, Senator Lowell Weicker released a secret memo which summarized shocking plans from February 1970 to February 1971. The document spelled out in minute detail the administration's intention to undermine the media, a plan to have begun during Nixon's first term in office. Senator Weicker revealed that the president's top aides had considered using the Internal Revenue Service, the Justice Department's anti-trust division and the Federal Communication Commission to harass news organizations critical of the the administration. Specifically, the paper stated that Haldeman planned to concentrate initially on NBC for what he described as that network's "totally negative approach to everything the administration does." The Nixon White House had also intended to generate humiliating public attacks on Chet Huntley because of the previously-mentioned remarks made in *Life*. The document further related plans for Charles Colson to exert pressure on network senior executives in an effort to deny air time to Democrats.

Senator George McGovern added his disdain for the subversive tactics by charging the administration had amassed "a simply stunning record of actions against critical news organizations." He confirmed what newsmen had been telling their subscribers all along—the White House had actively sought to cut off the flow of news by denying reporters access to information and by threatening jail terms for those who would not serve as government informants.

As late as February 1974, when the dwindling numbers of White House allies congregated in Queens, New York, to stage a pro-Nixon rally, a sizable anti-Nixon group showed up as well. Bruce Herschensohn, Deputy Special Assistant to the president, spoke to the Nixon faithful in what is recognized now as an desperate administration gesture. He insisted that "a non-elected coalition of power groups [had sought] through every avenue open to them to bring pressure upon this country to be done with President Nixon." Before a crowd whose polar feelings were at fever pitch, Herschensohn dumped the White House's enemies into a single bag—Americans for Democratic Action, Common Cause, Ralph Nader, the American Civil Liberties Union, George Meany, the *New York Times,* Jack Anderson, and, of course, Walter Cronkite. Hearing the list of Nixon's enemies read out served as the breaking point for the gathered mob. A melee erupted between the two factions present that had to be broken up by police.

As the unfolding story of Watergate and the Augean stench in high places were revealed, the president and his Palace Guard were ultimately driven out of office in disgrace—while hoisting their own petard. As it had been attempting to control the press, the Nixon administration was foiled by the very group of men and women being threatened with destruction by guile and deception. The nation that had been betrayed by its leader was left to pull the rags of dignity about itself, but a national calamity had been averted and the country limped forward. Even though it was only too evident who the traitors were, a vestigial tag of Nixon followers still harbored ill feelings for what had been labeled the "liberal press" and the man they believed was most responsible for the downfall of the Nixon administration—Walter Cronkite.

For those who believed he was only carrying out a personal vendetta against Nixon, a man they believed the newsman hated, Cronkite was quick to express his feelings about the former president. As early as 1970, when the charges were being made against him, Cronkite told interviewer Oriana Fallaci, "In personal conversations I like [Nixon] very much. Those who succeed as leaders have a personal charisma. Nixon does, too . . . [but he] doesn't come over in public as he does in private."

After Nixon's fall, Cronkite adamantly denied he received any satisfaction from the Watergate affair. In an address delivered May 3, 1973, to the Chicago chapter of the National Association of Television Arts and Sciences, Cronkite spelled out the potentially dangerous and critical period the nation had just undergone. With inspiring prose, he defended the First Amendment rights guaranteed by the Constitution and warned against future leaders who might again attempt to subvert the Bill of Rights or otherwise misuse power.

The State of the Press

A friend said the other day: "You must be very pleased with the developments in Washington."

It was an unfortunate statement. It suggested that the view held by us in the press of the administration was as distorted, biased and prejudiced as the administration's view of us. That, I think, is insulting to an intelligent man—and I told my friend that.

I am not pleased by the Watergate developments, and I do not think most of my colleagues of the press are, either. I am shocked and frightened to learn of the heights to which corruption has reached.

Any normally human reaction to exult in the downfall of an adversary is more than counter-balanced by concern over the debasement of our democratic system and worry over the stagnation of government while this scandal plays itself out.

There are some who write letters to newspapers and radio and television stations complaining of the attention we are giving the unfolding story—they ask what is so wrong about what the Republicans did. "They didn't kill anybody or rape anybody or steal anything," the letters go. "Politicians always have been crooked. What's the big fuss?" And the letters conclude with something like: "You news people are just blowing up the story because you never have liked Nixon."

I hardly think it is necessary to deny that accusation, and while we were getting some letters of that ilk in late April, they do seem to be dropping off with each succeeding revelation from Washington.

While the writers of such letters, the polls indicate, are in the minority, I do wonder if we in the press have succeeded in getting over the real horror of Watergate—if a lot of the public still doesn't believe that this is just a slightly gamier version of politics as usual.

We tried to point out on the *Evening News* the difference between the bugging of Democratic headquarters and the corruption that touched the White House in earlier administrations.

Almost all of those cases of earlier notoriety—in the Grant administration, the Teapot Dome of the Harding administration, the five-percenters of the Truman administration and vicuña coats of the Eisenhower years—all of those involved the use of power to procure profits, usually for friends and, with the exception of Teapot Dome, with minimal payoff for the culpable in the White House.

Teapot Dome did involve the theft of the people's inheritance, the nation's natural resources, and the evil was the greater, therefore.

But none of these previous cases was so potentially far-reaching as the one now being exposed. For the Watergate bugging was an attempt to steal a birthright far more precious than money—the citizen's privilege to choose his president, fair and square.

The stealing of votes, fraud at the polls, is not exactly unknown in our country, but this case goes further than that. It was an attempt, on the national level, to subvert the two-party system, which is right at the roots of our system. It was a naked attempt to use power for the perpetuation of power, and down that road dictatorship thrives and democracy cannot survive.

It was a naked attempt to circumvent the democratic system of law that its perpetrators had sworn to uphold.

But far from casting doubt on the efficacy of the system, it seems to me that the unmasking of the plot proves that our system of checks and balances works.

It was a federal judge—appointed by the Republican administration, by the way, but under our system now sitting for life and untouchable by political considerations—who refused to accept the cover-up; it was a congressional committee that kept the pressure on; and it was the free press that would not let the matter die when others would have interred it.

If there is any silver lining in all this it may be that administration spokesmen—those who remain—will be a little less hasty in charging the press with ideological venality.

It may even be that, in the light of the Watergate revelations, that segment of the public which had bought the administration line will reconsider the value of a free press.

It may well be that President Nixon might have avoided this disgrace to his administration if *he* had put a little more faith in the press. If we assume he did not know about Watergate and its ramifications until March 21, as he reported to us, then we can assume that he was not reading the newspapers or watching television and that his daily news digest, as written by Pat Buchanan, didn't include mention of Watergate.

We might also assume that it was the success of his administration's campaign against the credibility of the press that neutralized the public's reaction to the newspaper and television stories about Watergate last fall. The Republican leaders told them not to believe the press, so they didn't believe, and the president was about to ignore Watergate as a campaign issue. If he had been forced to face the question then, perhaps the White House would not now be tainted with the additional scandal of the cover-up.

It is an interesting but seldom proffered argument as to the advantages of a free press that it has a major function in keeping the government itself informed as to what the government is doing.

The information that must flow freely from the government to the people, also eddies *around* the government itself. Good newspapers and broadcasters, through their diligence, can provide information about one branch of government to officials of another branch that it would take them far too long to get—if, indeed, they ever got—through secret communications and inter-office memos. This is a source of information that is denied to the leaders of dictatorships, and they are far the weaker for that.

This is a fact which must be coming home rather belatedly to some in Washington who have disparaged the attempts of the press to tell the whole story, the bad with the good.

While it would take extraordinary gall for the administration to resume its attacks on the press now, the atmosphere it has created will take some time to dissipate, and it has set in motion a train of events that still present a serious danger to our freedoms of speech and press.

Let me give you just two examples of the seriousness of the problem. In the present atmosphere, the Supreme Court has stripped the press of the privilege to protect its sources, and without such protection a free press cannot survive.

In the Pappas, Branzburg and Caldwell decision last year, the court ruled that reporters do not have a First Amendment right to withhold confidential sources or information from a grand jury.

There may not have been a decision as important to our survival as a democracy in a hundred years, and yet, in the current aura of suspicion that the administration has generated, we of the press seem to have been unable—with all our vaunted power—to communicate the great stake that the people have in this matter.

Government on the local, the county, the state and federal levels will be able to operate with the shades drawn and the doors locked. What evil can be perpetrated in this secrecy that the Supreme Court decision encourages?

While most government servants might be presumed to be honest, our history is replete with examples of those who have sought to dispense favors to their friends at the expense of the public.

It is the honest bureaucrats who expose their dishonest colleagues. It is rare that a newsman can lay bare the facts of malfeasance or nonfeasance without a tip or collaboration from inside.

Yet, this is the information that the Supreme Court's 5-to-4 decision said cannot be held confidential.

The effect? Well, hear what Justice Potter Stewart said in dissent: "An office-holder may fear his superior; a member of the Bureaucracy, his associates; a dissident, the scorn of majority opinion. All may have information valuable to the public discourse, yet each may be willing to relate that information only in confidence to a reporter whom he trusts, either because of excessive caution or because of a reasonable fear of reprisals, or censure for unorthodox views.

"After today's decision," Justice Stewart said, "the potential informant can never be sure that his identity or off-the-record communications will not subsequently be revealed through the compelled testimony of a newsman."

And Justice Douglas, also dissenting, noted that the decision would "impede the wide open and robust dissemination of ideas and counterthought" necessary in a free society. And he went on: "The intrusion of government into this domain is symptomatic of the disease of this society. As the years pass, the power of government becomes more and more pervasive. It is a power to suffocate both people and causes.

"Those in power, whatever their politics, want only to perpetuate it. Now that the fences of the law and the tradition that has protected the press are broken down, the people are the victims. The First Amendment, as I read it, was designed precisely to prevent that tragedy."

The Supreme Court's decision did, indeed, invite legislative action to clarify the privilege of the press under the First Amendment, but this opens up serious questions that sink us deeper into the quagmire of press restrictions.

For this seems to establish that the First Amendment guarantees are not absolute and can be further refined by Congress—a proposition that would, on its face, seem unconstitutional since the First Amendment clearly states that the Congress, "shall make no law abridging the freedom of speech or of the press."

It seems to me that the Constitution would clearly prohibit many of the privileged communications bills now before Congress—all of those, in fact, which place limitations on the privilege of private sources, although with the good intention of defining the privilege.

These limitations are more or less great, depending on the particular bill, but the most favorable ones would set aside the privilege when there is "probable cause" to believe that a newsman has information clearly relevant to a specific probable violation of the law; that the information cannot be obtained by alternative means, and there is a compelling and overriding national interest in the information.

Aside from establishing the dangerous precedent that Congress can legislate press restrictions, these limitations are highly unworkable and create loopholes that would defeat their very purpose.

Who is going to determine that there is "probable cause" to believe that the reporter has relevant or exclusive or nationally important information?

The prosecuting attorney who impaneled the grand jury in the first place, or a judge who may be beholden to the same political machine? Or is each case going to the Supreme Court while the reporter languishes in jail, and, with another contempt case in the spotlight, news sources again dry up?

It seems to many of us that the only remedy is a law that states simply, and therefore eloquently, that the First Amendment means what it says and no reporter can be hauled before any government body and forced to reveal confidential sources of information.

Opponents of any such absolute privilege have drawn up a long list of possible abuses.

One is the lurid suggestion that the Mafia could shield its members by putting them to work on a front newspaper. This is a specious argument. I don't recall that under present circumstances we have seen a parade of Mafiosi spilling all they know before grand juries, and they've got the protection of the Fifth Amendment, anyway, without evoking the First. Furthermore, the courts could be expected to see through such subterfuge.

Then there is the "good citizen" argument—that there are occasions when the life of an individual or the community is so clearly endangered that no citizen can be exempt from giving information.

A strong case can be made for this point—except that there must be a presumption that newsmen *are* good citizens and are not going to withhold such information in a case as clear-cut as this would imply.

As a matter of fact, newsmen generally do cooperate with lawmen in criminal cases. It is a rare reporter who does not tip off the local constabulary to such matters that cross his attention, and there are many prosecuting attorneys who have expressed concern that the Supreme Court decision is going to cut off this source since the reporter himself now will be under the same handicaps as the authorities.

Even so, we must acknowledge that there would be some abuses of the absolute privilege, but by no stretch of the imagination could these abuses be so frequent or so serious as to endanger the survival of the democracy. A press hobbled by the Caldwell decision would.

This Washington atmosphere so repressive to the free press is now further poisoned with the attempt to bring the network news programs to heel by making them responsive to the local stations, where the government has licensing power and thus can bring political and financial pressures to bear.

It would be another serious blow to the free flow of information if the network news broadcasts were emasculated, for, far from being a monopoly as charged, they are the alternative to the provincial approach of the local stations.

Most of us deny that the network news is shot through with bias and prejudice. We acknowledge that all men, not excluding journalists, harbor bias and prejudice, but it is the mark of the professional newsman that he recognize these in himself and guard against their intrusion into his reporting.

But let's assume that there is some justice in the administration's charges. Still there is a serious flaw in its claim to seek only balance in the news by curbing the network broadcasts.

For there is balance now in the daily fare offered the nation's viewers. They get not only the network news but their local news, and if the rest of the country is presumed to be more conservative than us eastern establishment, then presumably the local news reflects this conservative influence.

Thus, since the network news already has been balanced by the local presentation, the only excuse for trying to control the network offering would be to unbalance the total news available, presumably to the administration's advantage.

It is strange that the administration cannot see that the power with which it would invest itself today might have to pass on to another political party tomorrow. Or, perhaps, does it believe that with such power over a cowed and intimidated press that is not a serious possibility? The arrogance of Watergate might lead us to accept that diabolical theory.

Our concern, that of the press, in recent years of course has been concentrated on the attacks from this administration and other parties.

Who can forget, particularly in Chicago, that it was the Democrats who were down on us for daring to report that 1968 convention as we saw it?

Our power, the power of this high-impact new means of communication, *is feared,* and the frightened and the jealous will not cease in their efforts to bridle us.

The establishment—I'm afraid there is no better word— of whatever age, whatever year, has been wary of its critics. In times of stress it has sought to muzzle them.

Since John Milton first pleaded for the freedom to print and America's founding fathers codified it, attempts to reverse this historical progress, although occasionally attempted, have for the most part failed and the written press would appear to be beyond the reach of the politicians.

Scarcely anyone would doubt that television news has expanded to an immeasurable degree the knowledge of a great portion of our peoples who either cannot or do not read.

We have expanded the interests of another, also sizable portion, whose newspaper reading has been confined to the headlines, the sports results and the comics.

We are going into homes of the untutored, underprivileged and disadvantaged—homes that have never known a book. We are exposing them to a world they scarcely knew existed, and while the advertisements and the entertainment programming whet their thirst for a way of life they believed beyond them, we show them that there are people and movements, inside and outside the establishment, that are trying to put these good things of life within their reach.

Without any intent to foster revolution, by simply doing our job as journalists, with ordinary diligence and an extraordinary new medium, we have awakened a sleeping giant. No wonder we have simultaneously aroused the ire of those who are comfortable with the status quo.

The other side of the coin is no brighter as far as our popularity goes. Those citizens who are happily smothered in their easy chairs under picture windows that frame leafy boughs and flowering bushes and green grass might have reason to resent our parading through their neat living rooms the black and bearded, the hungry and unwashed, to remind them that there is another side of our country that demands their attention.

Are these not precisely the same reasons that the press was looked upon with so much alarm and suspicion a couple of centuries ago? And, as it turned out, for the establishment of that era, with good cause. For it was the free press that in large measure exposed the failings of older systems, that brought about reform, that became the people's surrogate in observing the performance of their servants in government—a vital service without which democracy would have been a hollow word.

It is nothing less than a crime against the people that the heavy hand of government should be laid now on the newest communication medium to prevent it from serving this same function in the future.

This nation—the cause of a free press—can be grateful for the farsighted men who founded the networks, coming to the business without journalistic backgrounds. And those who are following in their footsteps are men in the executive suites who have left the news judgment to the professional journalists and have created in our country what I guarantee is, from the internal standpoint, the freest medium of them all. They have strengthened that cornerstone that is our free press. What we have asked of them has not been easy.

For 13 1/2 hours out of the 15-hour network day, their job is to win friends and audience. They and we live on how successfully they do this difficult job.

But then we ask them to turn a deaf ear to the complaints of those dissatisfied with what we present in the remaining minutes of the day.

We newsmen are not jugglers, dancers, ventriloquists, singers or actors seeking applause. We are not in the business of winning popularity contests. It is not our job to entertain, nor indeed, to please anyone except Diogenes.

Unfortunately, we have seen lately the growth of "happy news time" on some stations, promoted by managements willing to sell their journalistic responsibility for a few fickle Nielsen points. They are the dupes of those who urge more "good news" in the hope, subconscious or Machiavelian, that it will blot out the bad news—in other words, suppress the news of aberrant behavior and dissent from establishment norms.

To seek the public's favor by presenting the news it wants to hear is to fail to understand the function of broadcast news in a democracy.

Radio and television journalists and enlightened executives have spent 35 years convincing the public that broadcast news is not a part of the entertainment industry. It is a shame that some would endanger that reputation now.

More responsible managements have not yielded to this pressure, and we can all be grateful for their strength.

The battle is not over—not by far—and there will be more to come. The First Amendment rights of broadcast news are yet to be won and thus the fullest measure of our freedoms of speech and press are yet to be realized.

*   *   *

The Nixon chapter of war on the press is history. The FCC continues to restrict the freedom of the electronic arm of the press, but it is significant to acknowledge that the fight to defend the First Amendment from the unlawful attacks by the Nixon administration was successful and was led by Walter Cronkite. It was Cronkite who, *Playboy's* Stephen Randall believes, was not anchoring just the news, but the nation. It was Cronkite whose calm, steadfast anchoring guided the country through one of its most perilous times. It was Cronkite who risked his reputation to stand up for the Constitution, for his ideals, and for those of his reputable associates. Cronkite's own words of praise for Daniel Ellsberg could well be applied to himself: "Because of his courage and bravery and his fortitude in doing what he did, the Constitution was defended, not by the Law and Order administration that had publicly sworn to uphold it, but by the conscientious man who never took the Oath, but performed the deed."

"What It's Like to Broadcast News"

Lessons from the Nixon Years

We're going through a revolution today which has already had a far greater impact than the Industrial Revolution. In the last 20 years, we've plunged into three eras—any one of which would be revolutionary. The Atomic Era, the Computer Era and the Space Age. We're on the cutting edge now of what could be the most dramatic of them all—the DNA Age—the ability to make man whatever we want him.

And yet, we've not done anything to make our political institutions compatible with these changes. Our government is not working well enough often enough.
—Walter Cronkite

THE MONTHS that followed Vice-President Agnew's fusillade were painful, embarrassing, and difficult for the many Americans who were forced to draw lines between their elected second-in-command and their favorite and most trusted television newscaster. Most Americans, prior to the Nixon years, had such an idealized concept of the Presidency that they felt those in the White House and those who spoke for it were above reproach; that lying, cheating, any misconduct were simply unthinkable. As was previously noted, most Americans who were interviewed unequivocally sided with Agnew's interpretation of who was the culprit in the battle between the Nixon administration and the national television networks.

Walter Cronkite, as the most visible and vocal spokesman for the networks' reporters, was in great demand as a speaker, then as now. His motivation during the Nixon years was to convince fellow journalists and the American public of what he fervently believed were threats to basic First Amendment rights. Further, in presenting the other side of the issue, he hoped to convince those who were convinced the press was an enemy to the Nixon White House that the "growing cancer" was, indeed, in the Oval Office itself.

The following address was given by Cronkite in Chicago at a convention of Sigma Delta Chi, the national journalistic fraternity. In the speech, he alludes to Mr. Agnew's fondness for alliteration and responded to the "law and order" mentality which was beginning to grip the country. His references to conditions in the Soviet Union were based in part on his frustrating years there as a United Press reporter, years before *Perestroika*. Many of the ideas he expressed had been used in other speeches, but his intention was to hammer away at the same themes again and again to get his points over to the broadest audiences possible.

What It's Like to Broadcast News

When Vice-President Agnew, in November 1969, unleashed his attack upon the news media, he was following, albeit with unique linguistic and philosophic departures, a long line of predecessors. Somewhere in the history of our Republic there may have been a high government official who said he had been treated fairly by the press, but for the life of me, however, I can't think of one.

Mr. Agnew's attacks, of course, were particularly alarming because of their sustained virulence and intimidating nature. But the Vice-President was simply joining the chorus (or, seeing political opportunity, attempting to lead it) of those who have appointed themselves critics of the television medium. Well, I don't like everything I see on television either, but I am frank to say I'm somewhat sick and mighty tired of broadcast journalism being constantly dragged into the operating room and dissected, probed, swabbed, and needled to see what makes it tick.

I'm tired of sociologists, psychologists, pathologists, educators, parents, bureaucrats, politicians, and other special interest groups presuming to tell us what is news or where our responsibilities lie.

Or perhaps I'm phrasing this wrong. It is not those who squeeze us between their slides and hold us under their microscopes with whom my patience has grown short. The society *should* understand the impact of television upon it. There are aspects of it that need study so that the people can cope with an entirely revolutionary means of communication. Those who disagree with our news coverage have every right to criticize. We can hardly claim rights to a free press and free speech while begrudging those rights to our critics. Indeed, that would seem to be what some of them would like to do to us. So believing, it clearly cannot be the responsible critics or serious students of the TV phenomenon with whom I quarrel. I am provoked more by those in our craft who, like wide-eyed country yokels before the pitchman, are losing sight of the pea under the shell.

We must expose the demagogues who would undermine this nation's free media for personal or partisan political gain. That is news. And we should not withhold our cooperation from serious studies of the medium. But we must not permit these matters to divert us from our task, or confuse us as to what the task is.

I don't think it is any of our business what the moral, political, social, or economic effect of our reporting is. I say let's get on with the job of reporting the news—and let the chips fall where they may. I suggest we concentrate on doing our job of telling it like it is and not be diverted from that altered task by the apoplectic apostles of alliteration.

Now, a fair portion of what we do is *not* done well. There are things we are not doing that we ought to do. There are challenges that we have not yet fully met. We are a long way from perfection. Our problems are immense, and they are new and unique.

A major problem is imposed by the clock. In an entire half-hour news broadcast we speak only as many words as there are on two-thirds of one page of a standard newspaper. Clearly, the stricture demands tightness of writing and editing, and selection, unknown in any other form of journalism. But look what we do with that time. There are twenty items in an average newscast—some but a paragraph long, true, but all with the essential information to provide at least a guide to our world that day. Film clips that, in a way available to no other daily medium, introduce our viewers to the people and the places that make the news; investigative reports—pocket documentaries—that expose weakness in our democratic fabric (not enough of these, but we're coming along); feature film reports that explore the byways of America and assure us that the whole world hasn't turned topsy-turvy; graphics that in a few seconds communicate a great deal of information; clearly identified analysis, or commentary on the news—I think that is quite a package.

The transient, evanescent quality of our medium—the appearance and disappearance of our words and pictures at almost the same instant—imposes another of our severe problems. Most of us would agree that television's greatest asset is the ability to take the public to the scene—the launch of a spaceship, a Congressional hearing, a political convention, or a disaster (in some cases these are not mutually exclusive). Live coverage of such continuing, developing events presents the radio-television newsman with a challenge unlike any faced by the print reporter. The newspaper legman, rewrite man, and editor must make hard decisions fast and accurately. But multiply their problems and decisions a thousandfold and you scarcely have touched on the problems of the electronic journalist broadcasting live. Even with the most intensive coverage it still is difficult and frequently impossible to get all the facts and get all of them straight as a complex and occasionally violent story is breaking all around. We do have to fill in additional material on subsequent broadcasts, and there is the danger that not all the original audience is there for the fuller explanation.

When a television reporter, in the midst of the riot or the floor demonstration or the disaster, dictates his story, he is not talking to a rewrite man but directly to the audience. There is no editor standing between him and the reader. He will make mistakes, but his quotient for accuracy must be high or he is not long for this world of electronic journalism. We demand a lot of these on-the-scene television reporters. I for one think they are delivering in magnificent fashion.

Directors of an actuality broadcast, like newspaper photo editors, have several pictures displayed on the monitors before them. But they, unlike their print counterparts, do not have ten minutes, or five, or even one minute to select the picture their audience will see. Their decision is made in seconds. Theirs is a totally new craft in journalism, but they have imbued it with all the professionalism and sense of responsibility and integrity of the men of print. Of course we make mistakes, but how few are the errors compared to the fielding chances!

Our profession is encumbered, even as it is liberated, by the tools of our trade. It is a miracle—this transmission of pictures and voices through the air, the ability to take the whole world to the scene of a single event. But our tools still are somewhat gross. Miniaturization and other developments eventually will solve our problem, but for the moment our cameras and our lights and tape trucks and even our microphones are obtrusive. It is probably true that their presence can alter an event, and it probably also is true that they alter it even more than the presence of reporters with pad and pencil, although we try to minimize our visibility. But I think we should not be too hasty in adjudging this as always a bad thing. Is it not salutary that the government servant, the politician, the rioter, the miscreant knows that he is operating in the full glare of publicity, that the whole world is watching?

Consider political conventions. They have been a shambles of democratic malfunction since their inception, and printed reports through the years haven't had much effect in reforming them. But now that the voters have been taken to them by television, have sat through the sessions with the delegates and seen the political establishment operate to suppress rather than develop the democratic dialogue, there is a stronger reform movement than ever before, and the chances of success seem brighter.

I would suggest that the same is true of the race rioters and the student demonstrators, whatever the justice of the point they are trying to make. Of course they use television. Hasn't that always been the point of the demonstrator—to attract attention to his cause? But the excesses of the militants on the ghetto streets and the nation's campuses, shown by television with almost boring repetition, tend to repel rather than enlist support, and this is a lesson I hope and *believe* that rational leaders are learning. . . .

Without any intent to foster revolution, by simply doing our job as journalists with ordinary diligence and an extraordinary new medium, we have awakened a sleeping giant. No wonder we have simultaneously aroused the ire of those who are comfortable with the status quo. Many viewers happily settled in their easy chairs under picture windows that frame leafy boughs and flowering bushes and green grass resent our parading the black and bearded, the hungry and unwashed through their living rooms, reminding them that there is another side of America that demands their attention. It is human nature to avoid confronting the unpleasant. No one *wants* to hear that "our boys" are capable of war crimes, that our elected officials are capable of deceit or worse. I think I can safely say that there are few of us who want to report such things. But as professional journalists we have no more discretion in whether to report when confronted with the facts than does a doctor in deciding to remove a gangrenous limb.

If it *happened*, the people are entitled to know. There is no condition that can be imposed on that dictum without placing a barrier (censorship) between the people and the truth—at once as fallible and corrupt as only self-serving men can make it. The barrier can be built by government—overtly by dictatorship or covertly with propaganda on the political stump, harassment by subpoena, or abuse of the licensing power. Or the barrier can be built by the news media themselves. If we permit our news judgment to be colored by god-like decisions as to what is good for our readers, listeners, or viewers, we are building a barrier—no matter how pure our motives. If we lack courage to face the criticism and consequences of our reporting, we build barriers.

But of all barriers that we might put between the people and the truth, the most ill-considered is the one that some would erect to protect their profits. In all media, under our precious free enterprise system, there are those who believe performance can only be measured by circulation or ratings. The newspaper business had its believers long before we were on the scene. They practiced editing by readership survey. Weak-willed but greedy publishers found out what their readers wanted to read and gave it to them—a clear abdication of their duties as journalists and, I would submit, a nail in the coffin of newspaper believability.

Today, before the drumfire assault of the hysterical Establishment and the painful complaints of a frightened populace, there are many in our business who believe we should tailor our news reports to console our critics. They would have us report more good news and play down the war, revolution, social disturbance. There certainly is nothing wrong with good news. In fact, by some people's lights we report quite a lot of it: an anti-pollution bill through Congress, a report that the cost of living isn't going up as fast as it was last month, settlement of a labor dispute, the announcement of a new medical breakthrough, plans for a new downtown building. There isn't anything wrong either with the stories that tell us what is right about America, that remind us that the virtues that made this nation strong still exist and prosper despite the turmoil of change.

But when "give us the good news" becomes a euphemism for "don't give us so much of that bad news"—and in our business one frequently means the other—danger signals must be hoisted.

It is possible that some news editors have enough time allotted by their managements to cover all the significant news of their areas—much of it, presumably, in the "bad" category—and still have time left over for a "good news" item or two. But for many and certainly those at the network level,

that is not the case. To crowd in the "happy" stories would
mean crowding our material of significance. Some good-news
advocates know this, and it is precisely what they want: to
suppress the story of our changing society in the hope that if
one ignores evil it will go away.

Others simply are tired of the constant strife. They would
like a little relief from the daily budget of trouble that reminds
them of the hard decisions they as citizens must face. But can't
they see that pandering to the innocent seeking relief is to
yield to those who would twist public opinion to control our
destiny?

It is no coincidence that these manipulative methods par-
allel those adopted a half century ago by Russian revolutionaries also seeking the surest means to bend the population to
their will. You will not find bad news in Russian newspapers
or on broadcast media. There are no reports of riots, distur-
bances of public order, muggings or murders, train, plane, or
auto wrecks. There are no manifestations of race prejudice,
disciplinary problems in army ranks. There is no exposure of
malfeasance in public office—other than that which the government chooses to explain for its own political purposes.
There is no dissent over national policy, no argument about
the latest weapons system.

There is a lot of good news—factories making their quo-
tas, happy life on the collective farm, successes of Soviet diplomacy, difficulties in the United States. The system works.
Without free media—acerbic, muckraking, irreverent—the
Soviet people are placid drones and the Soviet Establishment
runs the country the way it wants it run.

Since it is hard to know the real motives in others'
minds—indeed, it is hard sometimes to know our own motives—and since few are likely to admit that they would seek
to suppress dissent from Establishment norms, it would be
wrong to ascribe much Machiavellian connivance to the good-
news advocates. The only trouble is that the other, more likely
motive—profiting from the news by pandering to public
taste—is almost as frightening. To seek the public's favor by
presenting the news it wants to hear is to fail to understand
the function of the media in a democracy. We are not in the

business of winning popularity contests, and we are not in the entertainment business. It is not our job to please anyone except Diogenes.

The newsman's purpose is contrary to the goal of almost everyone else who shares the airwaves with us, and perhaps we should not be too harsh with those executives with the ultimate responsibility for station and network management. We are asking a great deal of them. For seventeen of the eighteen hours during an average broadcast day, their job is to win friends and audience. They and we live on how successfully they do this difficult job.

But then we ask them to turn a deaf ear to the complaints of those dissatisfied with what we present in the remaining minutes of the day. We ask them to be professionally schizoid—and that would seem to be a lot to ask. But is it, really? After all, in another sense, as journalists we live this life of dual personality. There is not a man who can truthfully say that he does not harbor in his breast prejudice, bias, strong sentiments pro and con on some if not all issues of the day.

Yet it is the distinguishing mark of the professional journalist that he can set aside these personal opinions in reporting the day's news. None of us succeeds in this task in all instances, but we know the assignment and the pitfalls, and we succeed far more often than we fail—or than our critics would acknowledge. We have a missionary duty to try to teach this basic precept of our craft to those of our bosses who have not yet learned it. We in broadcasting, at least, cannot survive as a major news medium if we fail.

We were well on before the current wave of politically-inspired criticism. In my twenty years in broadcasting I have seen more and more station owners taking courage from their news editors, tasting the heady fruit of respect that can be won by the fearless conveyer of the truth. Some years ago William Allen White wrote that "nothing fails as miserably as a cowardly newspaper." I suspect he spoke not only of commercial failure but of the greater failure: not winning the confidence of the people. A radio or television station also can fail this test of courage, and when it does its owner wins not a community's respect and gratitude but its contempt.

Broadcast management is going to need a stiff backbone in the days ahead—not only for its own well-being but for the good of us all. We are teetering on the brink of a communications crisis that could undermine the foundation of our democracy—that is, a free and responsible press. We all know the present economic background. We in radio and television with our greater impact and our numerous outlets have forced many of our print competitors out of business. It is a rare American city today that has more than one newspaper. And yet I think most of us will acknowledge that we are not an adequate substitute for the newspapers whose demise we have hastened. We cannot supply the wealth of detail the informed citizen needs to judge the performance of his city, county, or state. If we do our jobs thoroughly, however, we can be a superb monitor over the monopoly newspaper, assuring that it does not by plot, caprice, or inadvertence miss a major story.

We *can* be, that is, if we are left alone to perform that essential journalistic function. The trouble is that broadcast media are not free; they are government licensed. The power to make us conform is too great to lie forever dormant. The ax lies there temptingly for use by any enraged administration, Republican, Democrat, or Wallaceite. We are at the mercy of the whim of politicians and bureaucrats, and whether they choose to chop us down or not, the mere existence of their power is an intimidating and constraining threat.

So, on one side there is a monopoly press that may or may not choose to present views other than those of the domineering majority. On the other side a vigorously competitive but federally regulated broadcast industry, most of whose time is spent currying popular—that is, majority— favor. There is a real danger that the free flow of ideas, the vitality of minority views, even the dissent of recognized authorities could be stifled in such an atmosphere.

We newsmen, dedicated as we are to freedom of press and speech and the presentation of all viewpoints no matter how unpopular, must work together, regardless of our medium, to clear the air while there is still time. We must resist every new attempt at government control, intimidation, or harassment. And we must fight tenaciously to win through

Congress and the courts guarantees that will free us forever from the present restrictions. We must stand together and bring the power of our professional organizations to bear against those publishers and broadcast managers who fail to understand the function of a free press. We must keep our own escutcheons so clean that no one who would challenge our integrity could hope to succeed.

If we do these things, we can preserve, and re-establish where it has faded, the confidence of the people whose freedom is so indivisibly linked with ours."

One of the saddest chapters in American history ended with threatened impeachment for Richard Nixon, who resigned in disgrace—the only U.S. President compelled to do so. Mr. Nixon, although given many opportunities by sympathetic and compassionate friends, never apologized for his wrong-doings. He was, therefore, never again accorded the respect of the trusting Americans who had placed him in office twice and supported him during the long and painful months of the Watergate proceedings. His White House aides received prison sentences for their attempts to subvert the First Amendment to the Constitution. The once great and powerful passed into oblivion, their very names forever synonymous with deceit and disappointment."

*   *   *

There was neither pleasure nor rejoicing from the men and women of the press who had defended and won their Constitutional rights. As the guilty parties received their condemnation from the Congress and sentences from the judiciary, Walter Cronkite, who had risked his reputation and suffered barbs from the White House, conservative newspapers, and countless trusting Americans who couldn't believe their President would ever lie to them, was exonerated. Cronkite demonstrated no malice; rather, he quietly summed up his personal response to the American nightmare by declaring "The System works."

"I'm Really a Big Fan"

The Chancellor Interview

If it hadn't been for Walter, none of us would be around. Walter believes in the "news" more than he believes in the "show." Walter is one of the good guys, not a hot dog.

—John Chancellor

OF THE MANY friends and colleagues of Mr. Cronkite who were interviewed during the research period of the original dissertation, probably the most enthusiastic was John Chancellor, who was anchor man of NBC *Nightly News* at the time. The following interview was recorded December 18, 1974, in his New York City NBC office, high above Rockefeller Plaza. With a view of the famous Rockefeller Center Christmas decorations behind his desk, a totally relaxed Chancellor was in his shirtsleeves, drinking a cup of coffee and trying to keep his pipe lit. From time to time, the sounds of his puffing and banging the pipe are heard on the tape, as well as the soft thud of the cup's being returned to the desk.

Q. You and Mr. Cronkite are good friends, are you not?
A. "He was at my house Sunday night. We see each other a lot."

Q. How long have you known each other?
A. "Oh, I don't know. I suppose we first got to know one another—other than just to say 'Hello,' the way people do in the

business—at one of the fairly early Apollo space shots at Cape Kennedy, which would have been, I guess, it may have been earlier than that. In the Gemini program, so that's about ten or fifteen years."

Q. Do you ever kid each other about ratings?

A. "We really don't, about the ratings. Of course, we're very close, and last week we were ahead. He's ahead, right now, more times than we are, but—statistically, it's almost too close to call. No, we don't banter about the ratings. We really don't have a lot of competitive talk, except that we make little jokes. If he's off the show and I run into him somewhere, I try to press him on who he's been interviewing, and things like that. But it's a very warm and easy relationship that we both have."

Q. How often do you watch the CBS Evening News?

A. "I watch it out of one eye some nights, and out of two eyes other nights. I guess you know we all watch each other's shows. What I do normally is, I come back up here after I do my show, and there are three monitors. We have our program on ABC and CBS at the same time. I find myself watching CBS more often than ABC."

Q. How often does Mr. Cronkite cover a story you wished you had gotten to first?

A. "It doesn't happen, *vis a vis* Walter and me, very often. But they're a highly competitive and very good news organization, and I think there are times they get things out of Washington that we don't that I would have liked to have had.

On Watergate, aside from two long take-outs that they did in 1972, which I thought were extraordinarily valuable and wished we'd done, I thought our coverage was a little better than theirs. But it goes back and forth, and it's hard to say."

Q. Why do you feel Mr. Cronkite has risen to the high position he has?

A. "Well, I hope that it would be years in service and the kind of experience that Walter has—and I say that because my experience is, to some degree, comparable. I'm younger than Walter is, so I didn't land at Arnhem in a glider. I wish I had. But Walter had that experience. He had overseas experience with the UP in Moscow, which means that he understands the basic tenets—I think I would call them the ethics of print journalism—fairly well. I regard that as valuable. I started as a newspaper man, by the way.

"I think, in Fred Friendly's phrase, 'Walter has paid his dues.' He's done an awful lot of jobs in broadcast journalism and in journalism itself, therefore, as one is in the process of paying his dues, I believe in that kind of development.

"The dangers of journalism in broadcasting are that they will start picking up handsome young men with deep voices and hair spray, and no real experience in the field.

"I salute and celebrate Walter Cronkite. I think he's a very good man."

Q. Yes, today, that seems to be the universal opinion of him, but in 1964, some of his own may not have felt entirely that way. What reflections could you share on the failure of CBS to let Mr. Cronkite cover the Democratic convention?

A. "There was a certain amount of jubilation at NBC, of course, and a certain amount of anger among those of us at a junior level, because we didn't think you should pitch a guy out the way CBS did.

"I thought it was CBS management at its worst, and I think CBS acknowledged that when they put him back.

It was just one of those ghastly moments when they lost their nerve.

"I didn't think it was anything Walter did that resulted in his being taken off the air. It was what Huntley and Brinkley and the four of us on the floor were doing. We were just creaming them in terms of ratings, and, I think in terms of coverage. I think our coverage was a hell of a lot better. They were taking a bath at our hands, but it had nothing to do with Walter, which made us say, 'Damn it! You're not supposed to do it that way!'"

Q. Let me read you statement from a Life *article Paul O'Neil wrote about Mr. Cronkite and then you tell me what you think about it: "Cronkite's professional reputation is based on rigorous objectivity—a refusal to inflict his own opinion on the viewing public."*

A. "I would agree with that. Walter comments when he feels it's necessary—on the the air. Neither one of us believes in structured and systematic commentary, because you end up stuck with nothing to write some nights except the GNP.

"We are, both of us, more flexible and both of us are helped by the fact that he has Sevareid doing his commentary and we have Brinkley doing it."

Q. I think most of us who watch Mr. Cronkite agree on his objectivity, but do you think he nonetheless projects his own philosophies on the Evening News?

A. "I think what comes through on Walter's personality is a kind of a—I think he's more aggressive on the air than I am, and you could do another long thesis on the differences and the reasons for them, because some of the things I say or do are calculated. I think Walter's are more instinctive.

"I think Walter likes the idea of hammering out the news at people. I think that he likes very much the idea of being the kind of 'Iron Anchorman' on space and conventions. I get the feeling sometimes, watching him, that he really has a terribly good time doing this. He just loves to be on. He has a different kind of delivery than I do.

"There's a different rhythm in his giving the news and I think that is one of the reasons for his success—you know—he just hammers away at it and gives it to you. It comes out in a way that does not, according to some surveys I have seen, necessarily feed back to his personality.

"He is a representative of the news. I prefer much more to share the news that we gather with the audience, so I approach it from the other side of that. But one of the reasons for Walter's success is that he brings people the news and, in a sense, sort of, is the news. That's worked terribly well for him."

Q. Let ask you about a charge we've been hearing lately. Do you believe newscasters can successfully manage or control the news?

A. "Well, I don't think so, for various reasons. One is that there are alternate sources of information in the American society. There is an avalanche of factual information—I sometimes think too much—in local newspapers, news magazines, local radio and television programs. And then you come to the networks.

"There are three networks themselves, none of which, in my view, has shown a particular bias that in any way differentiated from the others. Now, does that mean that all three of us are doing the same kind of controlling and molding the audience? I don't really think so. The standards that we adhere to here, and that Cronkite adheres to there, are very much the kinds of professional standards in the judgment of news that make up the AP budget each day. To a considerable extent, we take into account the AP budget and the UP budget when we make up our line-up of stories for that night.

"A great deal of what we get comes out of newspapers and magazines and from our own correspondents. It's a mixture and I don't think that the material—I've never seen an example of anybody trying to shape things. During the Nixon years, as you know, we were accused of running certain kinds of stories that were bad for the administration. But, then, when the size of the calamity became apparent, then that criticism pretty much went away."

Q. Do you believe there was any validity to Vice-President Agnew's charge of information control by an Eastern Establishment?

A. "Pat Moynihan wrote an article some years ago, when I was in Washington, in which he talked about the Ivy League/Georgetown influence. Martin Nolan, who is the bureau chief of the *Boston Globe* in Washington, wrote a marvelous rebuttal. He just called everybody up and asked, 'Where did you go to school?' I went to Illinois. Harry [Reasoner], I guess, went to Minnesota. Walter went to Texas, I think. Brinkley—I'm not sure really ever went. Maybe he went to North Carolina for a while. Sevareid is— well, you get the point. None of us was born in the East. We simply have made our way, either to Washington or to New York, because that's where the ladder leads.

"The other question that's raised is: Once we're here, are we in some way subverted by Eastern elitism? I really don't think so. I would rather work in Washington than in New York, because of the diversity of people we get from around the country in Washington.

"The executive producer of our show is from Duluth, Minnesota—went to school out there. We have two producers under him. One is, I think, from Northwestern University in Chicago. The other is from Boston, and I'm not sure where he went to school, but I think he may have gone to school in Boston. We have a considerable diversity of people here and I don't really see us joining up with what, I rightly think, has been called the Eastern Establishment.

"The Eastern Establishment is made up of bankers, of lawyers, of businessmen, as I have observed it here in New York. I haven't been up here that long. These are the least congenial companions for journalists that I know.

"I think Jack McCloy was a great public servant and a dedicated man, but McCloy and I don't sit around swapping stories.

"Mac Bundy, who I think you could easily identify as one of the anchors of the Eastern Establishment—I've known Mac since he was in the White House—but I see him very rarely, and I don't think he has any influence on me or on Walter and most of the fellows who work here have never even met Mac Bundy.

"I, on the one hand, acknowledge the fact that there is a community here, also made up of Americans from everywhere, that is kind of an Eastern Elite. I, personally, think it is a National Elite, and not just an Eastern Elite.

"Nobody's ever come to me and talked to me about a Western Elite. I think there is a National American Elite. I think Mac Bundy, Jack McCloy and people like that are members of it. They have little to do with what Abe Rosenthal at the *New York Times* does, or what I do here, or what Oz Elliot over at *Newsweek,* or Henry Grunwald at *Time*—we make our decisions up, not on the basis of associations with these people. We know them, some of them. I don't know Walter Reston very well. I think he's one of them—at the Citibank. You meet them occasionally, but that's really all."

Q. I don't have any more questions for you. I wish I did, because you have certainly helped me a lot. I do appreciate your sharing this time with me.

A. "Walter is really an extraordinary guy. Anything I can help with in getting a record built on him—I'm really a big fan."

"Bridge to Galley!"

Family Man

*As far as I was concerned, Walter was a celebrity the
first time he got a byline.*

*Living with Walter has been exciting. It's like being in
the process of history.*

—Betsy Cronkite

DURING WALTER Cronkite's 137,000 minutes as CBS anchorman, unknown numbers of pages were written about him as newspapers and magazines fed America's and the world's curiosity about
their favorite newsman. His love of family, friends, and animals is
legendary. His fascination for machines and natural phenomena still
amuses his wife of fifty years. He frequently and openly declares his
love of the American people and his strong belief in the democratic
process and his country.

Over the years, Cronkite has been compared variously to such
real and fictitious American characters as Walt Disney, Captain
Kangaroo, Norman Rockwell, Bing Crosby, Hopalong Cassidy, and
Ike Eisenhower. His mother likens him most to Dagwood Bum-
stead and wife Betsy sees him as Walter Mitty.

By December 1975, he was such a landmark in Americana he
was featured on the cover of *Esquire* as one of several "Great
American Things," where he shared space with such institutions as
Marilyn Monroe, Rose Kennedy, Lassie, Jackie Robinson, Billie
Jean King, Fred Astaire, and Mary Tyler Moore.

Cronkite has been fortunate to have the drive and ability to command a job with a salary that permitted him to send his children to the best schools, live in a restored New York City brownstone, keep a summer home in Edgartown, and pursue his many and varied interests. It is not that Cronkite is a selfish man—on the contrary, he has always been a thoughtful father, considerate husband, and attentive son. That he is a family man is well known among his associates: in fact he was voted 1958's "Radio Father of the Year." When his children were younger, it was not unusual to see the entire family traveling in tourist class, sitting five abreast.

His mother—whom Cronkite still visits often and who, until recently when her advanced aged slowed her travel, was included in family activities—decries the casual manner so many women today approach their maternal roles. "I can't understand them. I would never dream of letting Walter go home to an empty house. If I were playing cards, or whatever I was doing, I would schedule my day to be home when he was there." The Cronkites' attention to their children's well-being was no different. In his capacity as managing editor of *CBS Evening News,* Cronkite was traveling over 300,000 miles some years. Even so, Chip remembers that his father was still "pretty much a presence" at home. When the writer arrived at his CBS office for an interview, Cronkite was on the telephone with his wife, who was preparing to drive to the airport to get Chip. After hanging up, Cronkite explained that his son had an infected throat and was coming home from his college to see their family doctor.

Basic to the success of the Cronkites' family unit has been the relationship between extroverts Walter and Betsy—they genuinely like each other and have shared their love lavishly with each of their three children. Friends say she provides an oasis of calm in his hectic life. Betsy told a *Family Weekly* interviewer Kate White there was no secret for her happy marriage: "I think one thing that has helped is our sense of humor; the fact that we've always had fun together. Even in our early days in New York, when we had no money, we would take the subway to the beach at dawn." Too, the philosophy the family has come to call "putupmanship" has played an important part. Once when the children were in England with their parents and arguing over which room they would sleep in, their father ended the dispute by explaining the Cronkite philosophy: "I put up with Mommy and Mommy puts up with me and you have to put up with each other."

Betsy, who has a wit and intellect to match her husband's, makes certain he doesn't let his frequent rave reviews, awards, or notoriety go to his head. An example of her bringing him down to earth occurred when he was asked to read the Declaration of Independence at a ceremony which launched New York City's observance of the Bicentennial. As the Cronkites rode in the CBS limousine to City Hall, Walter was reading over the famous Jeffersonian prose. Watching him, Betsy suddenly had visions of his trying to improve the copy and warned him, "Walter, don't edit it."

Betsy—often referred to as "Miss Cornpone" by her children, for the Agriculture Queen title she won back in the 1930s when she was a student at the University of Missouri—has lived with Walter so long she says she can pick up his cues. They love wading into crowds of friends at a party, each taking an end and working their way around, where, Betsy confesses, "We frequently get carried away." Daughter Nancy remembers how she, Kathy, and Chip grew up knowing all the punch lines of old burlesque routines as performed by their parents, but never knew the beginnings.

                    *   *   *

In the late 1950s, Cronkite remembers, "People were always asking me what my hobby was, and it was embarrassing to tell them my work was." The more he was asked about hobbies, the more he began looking about for something that would offer him and his family diversion on weekends. He had always liked cars, and it was not surprising that he would be attracted to imported sports cars, which were gaining a wide post-war following then. As is typical of the way he immerses himself in his work, he wasn't satisfied simply being the owner and driver of a sports car; he wanted to race it.

Without Betsy's knowledge, Cronkite began looking around for a sports car. Soon after he began the search, he received a check directly from a group he had just spoken to. Since it had bypassed his agent—who usually received the payment, subtracted his fee and gave Cronkite the remainder—Cronkite decided to let that amount determine the price of the car.

He and Betsy lived outside New York City then and he commuted to work. One morning as she was driving him to catch his train, he casually asked her to let him off near the station, that he had some business to take care of. When she was out of sight, he raced across the street to a sports car lot and asked the first sales-man he saw, "What kind of a car do you have for $1,721.65?" The surprised dealer showed him an old Austin-Healey, which Cronkite bought on the spot.

After fixing up the car, he raced at Sebring and Little LeMans, where he was on a winning team in 1959. The next year, he drove the pace car for the 1960 Daytona 500, which CBS televised that year. Betsy uncomplainingly went along with his decision, even though she admitted she and her pit-crew family spent many anx-ious moments as he raced, frequently reaching speeds of 140 miles per hour.

Twice he narrowly escaped serious injury or possibly death. The first close call took place in 1960, in the Smoky Mountains, when he went off a cliff at night in a new sea-green Triumph. Even though he rolled end-over-end one hundred feet into a river, he was miraculously uninjured. (The car, however, was a different story. He had it fished out and placed back onto the road, but even though it cranked it wouldn't budge.) The second harrowing event took place in Connecticut, when his car went into a spin near the finish line. He disappeared from the track in a cloud of dust as Betsy and the girls waited anxiously nearby. At last he emerged, unhurt but shaken. Ironically, he had just prematurely been declared the winner by the track announcer, who had shouted over the public address system, "Cronkite is in the money!" As his car limped across the finish line, disappointed Kathy said to her mother and sister, "Well, I guess Daddy isn't in the money anymore."

Racing served as an emotional release from his work and as a personal challenge for Cronkite, who has enjoyed living on the edge of danger throughout his career. By getting behind the wheel of a sports car on weekends, he could pursue the adventure and risk-taking he enjoys. "Not that racing is that dangerous," he rational-ized at the time, "I mean, you seldom get the little minor accidents, like breaking a leg, that you have in skiing." He would then add fatalistically, "You're more likely to be killed than hurt." Some years later, however, in a realistic moment, he confided to a fellow sailing enthusiast, "With race cars, I wanted to die all week, or break my arm—anything but show up at the track. But when the race started, it was two hours of pure adrenaline."

His frightening racing accidents, compounded by the fact that his family was left sitting on the sidelines while he was having all the fun, led him to the decision to sell his share of the Lotus he and two partners owned at the time and give up racing—but not his love for sports cars. Until recently, he continued to keep a Triumph TR-6 or some other high-performance import at the Vineyard.

By his own admission, Cronkite tends "to plunge into things," and sailing was the next hobby he plunged into. He had earlier owned a small Sunfish he sailed on a local pond in 1949, when he was living in Carmel, New York. He was sorry that Betsy and the children didn't share his enthusiasm for sailing, so he reluctantly sold the boat. He was encouraged, however, when he learned shortly afterwards that Betsy was trying to buy back the boat for his birthday. Even though she was unable to purchase the original boat, Cronkite took the effort as her approval to buy another and sail it without guilt.

Cronkite purchased a twenty-two-foot Electra which he soon traded for a twenty-nine-foot Triton. It was at this stage his family (or "the whole famn damily," as Betsy likes to put it) began enjoying sailing and crewing for him. She admitted in the early days, that "Sailing beats standing in the pits at the sports car track and it does keep Walter, myself, and the children together on weekends."

Betsy loved to tease her nautical husband by referring to the bow as "the little pointy end," below deck as "downstairs" and the galley as "the kitchen." Robert Vaughn, in an article for *Motor Boating and Sailing,* told how, once, while sailing the crowded waters of Martha's Vineyard, fellow sailors greeted her famous husband with "H'lo, Walter," so many times she suddenly yelled, "Look out, Walter! They're telling you to look out for the 'low water'!"

Chip, who was eight when the Electra was bought, was ecstatic about sailing, but Kathy and Nancy, teen-agers at the time, were less so. Cronkite laughs that his girls then "would sacrifice a racing lead to continue a conversation across the water." Chip has remained through the years his father's "good racing buddy." In an article she wrote for *McCall's,* Kathy remembers how her brother used to terrify his father by aiming the dinghy at full speed straight for the sailboat. Until Chip would come to a perfect halt next to the boarding ladder, Cronkite would characteristically grab his hairline in panic. When asked about that practice, he says that any sort of scare causes his scalp to tighten, thereby cutting off circulation of air to his hair follicles and causing hair loss. Whether he does it to amuse his family or in seriousness, it has been another private family joke.

In 1965, Cronkite purchased the ultimate in sailboats, a thirty-five–foot Garden-designed ketch, which slept six and was built in Japan of yacal, Philippine mahogany, and oak. Kathy's *McCall* article revealed her father named it in honor of Wyntje de Theumis, of Naarden, who married Herck Siboutzen Krankheyt, the first Cronkite bride in the New Amsterdam colony in 1642. It was chauvinistically "dedicated to all the women who have brought pleasure to Cronkite men in the New World." In 1976, when dry rot made it impractical to keep, it was replaced with a new *Wyntje,* a Westsail 42-foot yawl with teak and mahogany decks, whose construction Cronkite personally supervised. He was at the New England shipyard regularly, fussing over such details as a dust tray in the cabin floor, the amount of space at the galley table or changing the original plans so each bunk had a reading light.

Cronkite's love of sailing goes beyond a mere appreciation for tacking or running before the wind; some say he's a "lunatic sailor." In his best Walter Mitty fashion, he says he often feels like Magellan and dreams of sailing the *Wyntje* around the world some day. At other times, he conjures up memories of C. S. Forester's famous character, Captain Horatio Hornblower. When the *Wyntje* is under sail, and he is lying in a hammock rigged between two stays, he has no difficulty letting his thoughts drift back to those early swashbuckling days. He dreamily reflects on those "strong men doing daring deeds, and a rather simplified moral code—and that makes it rather easy to take. I really enjoy solitude and introspection. That's why I like sailing. I like sitting in the cockpit of my boat at dusk and on into the night, gazing at the stars, thinking of the enormity, the universality of it all. I can get lost in reveries in that regard, both in looking forward to a dream world and in looking back to the pleasant times of my own life." His family agrees; he is more relaxed and more himself on the boat than anywhere else.

The New England winters prevent his sailing there year-round. The *Wyntje* is stored at a marina in Annapolis, Maryland, and Cronkite and his family or friends, like the James Micheners, often charter boats in the Bahamas or the Virgin Islands. When sailing together, either in the clear, blue, warm Caribbean or around the cold, choppy waters of New England, the Cronkites enjoy lying about on deck in the evenings looking for various constellations of stars. The girls could never remember from year to year what the formations were called, but they took great delight making up their own off-color interpretations of what the heavenly bodies resembled, their mother showing her appreciation with what they call her "loud dirty laugh."

Tom Shales, a *Washington Post* writer, recalls that a former NBC News president once jokingly suggested that Cronkite rechristen his boat the *Assignment*; that way, he explained, whenever a CBS announcer said, "Walter Cronkite's on Assignment," the description would be correct.

During the years he was anchor of the *Evening News,* Cronkite felt free to haul anchor and move at will, with no worries in the world, assuming his network could carry on without him. He monitored his radio phone daily, but if he didn't want to be called, a flip of a switch rendered him unreachable. Once, however, when CBS needed him and his radio was off, the Coast Guard was asked to locate the elusive sailor. Cronkite knew something important was breaking when the Coast Guard cruiser hailed him; even so, his first words to the captain of the approaching powered vessel were, "Watch out for my paint!"

*   *   *

The Cronkites' life style is still relatively unaffected by his success and wealth. He enjoys drinking with buddies, dancing with his wife until dawn, snowball fighting with friends on the way home after a party, sailing into Newport or any other harbor he chooses, or dining in public restaurants.

His news staff of some three dozen was devoted to him. He always ended his telecast nearest Christmas with a procession of live shots of the staff and production crew, a tradition which continues. At the Christmas party which followed at his house, he was the heart of the festivities, singing and pumping away at the antique player piano Betsy gave him several anniversaries ago. The highlight of these gatherings was his celebrated parody of a striptease or an athletic reenactment of a sports-car race.

Besides sailing and sports-car racing, Cronkite and Chip have been fond of slot-racing and board games. He has traveled by dog sled, dived to 2500 feet beneath the water's surface in a two-man submarine, and lived under polar ice for a week in a nuclear sub. In one of his *Cronkite at Large* specials for CBS, he floated across the French countryside in one of Malcolm Forbes's unique hot-air balloons.

*   *   *

After moving to New York City from Washington, the Cronkites bought a four-story brownstone on fashionable East 84th Street. They completely remodeled it and, rather than have it professionally decorated, filled it with their own furnishings, doing all the interior design themselves. One first-time visitor, seeing the rather informally and sparsely furnished house, asked if they had just moved in. The Cronkites are more interested in comfort than elegance. There has always been room for their children's friends, Walter's hobbies, the upright piano, a Chinese housekeeper, visits from Walter's mother, and their dogs and cats. Turtles are a particular favorite with Cronkite. He nearly wrecked his car once as he dodged one inching across a highway and he still laments a terrarium specimen who was killed when a dim-witted maid washed it in detergent.

Even though Cronkite is fond of food, he doesn't enjoy cooking as does his friend, gourmet cook John Chancellor. He did share recipes for favorite sandwiches ("Spiedano Romano Buns" and "Rarebitwiches") with the *Ladies' Home Journal,* but he prefers to leave the cooking to his wife or the family cook.

The summer house at Martha's Vineyard often becomes a hotel when family gathers and friends come and go. The workload often becomes burdensome—as linens are changed and rooms made ready—but the Cronkites' gregarious nature overrides any inconvenience they may incur. As a new houseful of guests arrives or visitors descend for a day of sailing, Cronkite tends bar, mixing pitchers of Bloody Marys, and Betsy makes sandwiches. She counts heads, grabs a loaf of bread and deals the slices like cards onto a counter top. She slaps sandwich meat and cheese on one slice and spreads mayonnaise on the other. The food is sent out on paper napkins. "If they want a plate, they can get one," she adds in her casual take-it-or-leave-it manner. When family springer spaniel Buzzy ate a box of chocolates that was to have been dessert, he was punished by not being taken sailing. When a neighbor's dog ran into Walter's mother, knocking her to the ground, it was all part of the active day.

Yuk-Yeh Kui, the housekeeper, called New Yee by Cronkite, quickly fell into the spirit of the household. When notifying Yuk-Yeh he was on the way downstairs for breakfast, Cronkite would frequently communicate over the intercom system announcements like, "Bridge to galley! Bridge to galley! The Captain's proceeding directly to the mess." Yuk-Yeh would chuckle to the children, "Funny Daddy!" When the Cronkites were out of town, Yuk-Yeh was left to house-sit and take care of Buzzy, which she frequently took with her to parties about town.

Craig Claiborne shared the following story in his *New York Times* column about the Cronkites' entertaining on one occasion:

> [The Cronkites] once invited artist Ludwig Bemelmans, a well-established gourmet and connoisseur, to dinner. The question was, of course, what to serve a man who had spent a quarter-century and more dining on the likes of truffles, caviar, *paté de foie gras,* and pheasants' tongues.
>
> Cronkite said to his wife, "Let's serve him family style." Betsy, who considers herself fairly accomplished in Southern-style cooking, agreed to serve Bemelmans her special fried chicken, black-eyed peas and cornbread. Surely, they thought, this would give him gustatory comfort and joy.
>
> The night arrived, and Bemelmans entered the Cronkites' New York home, casting off his sable coat and draping it over a chaise. "Thank God!" he exclaimed. "It's so good to be back in civilization. I've just returned from three awful weeks in the deep South, where all they serve is fried chicken, black-eyed peas and cornbread."

In his capacity as network correspondent, travel is a major part of Cronkite's life. The entire family used to accompany him, but

Betsy wasn't comfortable with the way their hotel suites usually became all-night, smoke-filled offices and meeting places for politicians and correspondents. Too, when the children were small, they were difficult to travel with, and even though they made up their class work she hated for them to miss school. She began keeping them at home, leaving him to go on assignments alone. When the children were grown, however, she began traveling with him again, as she does now, whether to China or to Malcolm Forbes's birthday party in Morocco.

Betsy admits, "The reason I can cope with Walter's strange hours is probably because I'm not very efficient." The entire family seems to share in this characteristic inefficiency. Kathy once described her family's mad running around and taking care of last-minute details as "like a traveling circus." Betsy's adaptability is, in all likelihood, a stronger suit than her efficiency; consequently, the peripatetic nature of Cronkite's work never really upset her or the children. She says the only time she objected to his traveling was "when he went to Vietnam. I used every argument from 'You'll miss boating season,' to 'You can't run that fast anymore.' But, for the most part, I haven't minded."

The entire family adapted early to Cronkite's job, his absences and notoriety: at age three, Chip thought everybody's father was on television on Sunday afternoons. In the early days, however, when things became too hectic for her, Betsy once told friends, "Walter can have the children and go live in the country. I'll take the money and the Austin-Healey and be a girl-about-town."

While Kathy was living in California during the 1970s, she recalls stretching out on a sofa with her boyfriend only to be interrupted by her dad's mood-chilling voice from the television set.

*   *   *

Even when he is off, news-junkie Cronkite can't ignore a story. Betsy remembers how nervous he used to become whenever a fire truck stopped in their neighborhood. He would "run to the living room window . . . and fidget for a while and then invariably say, 'I think I'll take Buzzy for a walk.' That poor dog has been to more fires."

While covering a convention, Cronkite offered to take CBS chief Washington correspondent Bob Schieffer back to his hotel.

When Cronkite heard the wailing of an ambulance going to a traffic accident, he ordered his driver to "Follow that ambulance!" "He heard a siren and was just like an old fire horse," Schieffer said. "He was always like that. He'd get excited every time he covered a story."

Like his family, Cronkite has his own idiosyncrasies. Despite the authority and self-assurance that characterize his televised programs and appearances, he is, ironically, notoriously absent-minded. His forgetfulness has created frequent interesting, if not bizarre, situations in public and at home. A female autograph-seeker once thrust a card at him for his signature. He took out his pen, but was unable to remember his own name—his mind had gone blank. He engaged the woman in light conversation until he could jog his memory and sign his autograph.

His mother recalls seeing him dashing up and down the stairs of his Manhattan home "like Dagwood," as he tried to get everything together before leaving for the studio. He would frequently make as many as four or five trips back into the house to retrieve his watch or briefcase or report. Twelve-year-old Kathy once wrote, produced, and directed a play about her father for a class at school. Entitled "Walter Cronkite," the entire action of the play consisted of a male character's rushing in and out of a house. The dialogue, as Kathy wrote about it later in *McCall's*, ran like this:

"Good-bye, Betsy."
"Good-bye, dear."
"Oh—I forgot my hat . . . Good-bye, dear."
"Good-bye, dear."
"I'm back! I left my briefcase . . . Good-bye, honey."
"Good-bye, dear."
"Betsy! Where's my . . . ?" And on it went.

While living in Moscow, the Cronkites did a bit of what Betsy describes as strictly the "fall-down-home-movie" variety of skiing. In 1960, when Cronkite covered the Winter Olympics at Squaw Valley, he sounded so expert at describing the intricacies of the sport his impressed daughters begged him to let them try it. Soon they were spending winter weekends at nearby ski resorts. While their parents were still struggling with the basics, the girls moved on to the intermediate and advanced slopes.

Despite his obvious love of racing and sailing, Cronkite's real passion is dancing. It has been said that he would dance anywhere with anyone to any kind of music. He confesses to being a frustrated soft-shoe song-and-dance man. He enjoys the Charleston as well as ballroom dancing and counts as one of his all-time thrills waltzing with Broadway and Hollywood dancer Ruby Keeler at a party. At Beverly Sills's televised 1980 farewell from the Metropolitan Opera, a tuxedoed Cronkite delighted the audience—and Miss Sills—with his surprise appearance and skillful waltzing with the guest of honor.

He does an annual jig with the Irishwoman who caters his birthday parties and, when he and Chip get in the mood—if Chip isn't waltzing with his mother around the dining table—the two male Cronkites cakewalk wildly around the house.

Cronkite has never made a secret of his appreciative eye for an attractive woman. He once took a pair of binoculars a group of CBessers was using to ogle some sunbathers on a nearby Manhattan rooftop. "Gentlemen," he announced, handing back the glasses, "there's one hell of a fire over there in Brooklyn!" Since the days of what he calls his misspent youth in Texas, Cronkite has been a devotee of the striptease. He and Betsy turned up in Boston's infamous "Combat Zone" in the fall of 1974 to watch Fanne Fox, "The Argentine Firecracker," unveil herself. In 1981, *People* magazine ran a photo of him dancing in Kansas City with stripper Tempest Storm. When prompted by party guests, he loves to entertain them with a pantomimed striptease using a silk scarf and removing, perhaps, his coat or tie, to the player piano's background music of "A Pretty Girl is Like a Melody"; or with his own improbable version of a Russian Cossack *Kazatski* dance he calls "Desire Under the Elms."

In 1975, Kathy wrote for *McCall's,* the family slipped off to their home at Martha's Vineyard to see in the Bicentennial New Year together. The traditional Guy Lombardo New Year's Eve program was playing on the radio and Cronkite spent the evening dancing first with daughters Kathy and Nancy. When the orchestra played "As Time Goes By," Cronkite and his wife, their eyes closed, slowly circled the room, lost in the moment.

*   *   *

Except for the benign tumor he had removed from his throat in 1972 and occasional pain from his back injury, Cronkite enjoys excellent health. During his junior years as a reporter, however, he frequently developed the symptoms of a sore throat just before going on camera. As soon as he was on the air, however, the symptoms disappeared. He decided the illness was psychosomatic and determined to cure it by mental attitude. The measure seemed to work, but he continued to keep near him an emergency supply of sprays, lozenges, and a lemon-and-honey mixture when he anchored the *Evening News*. On one occasion, after he had suffered several days with what seemed to be a cold, he finally called his doctor about it. The physician, who followed Cronkite's news program, had already diagnosed his ailment as tracheal bronchitis. He informed Cronkite of the diagnosis and then added, "I was wondering when you would call."

*   *   *

At six feet, Cronkite's 190 pounds give him a bearish appearance. He has short, bowed legs and most of his bulk is in his torso. He is forced at times to resort to low-calorie breakfasts and cottage cheese lunches to keep his weight down, because he habitually has milk and cookies before bedtime. Whenever he is at home watching football games on television, he eats popcorn and drinks beer.

As often as he can he plays tennis, at which he is fairly proficient, frankly playing to win, taking lessons as he has time. In his hectic pre-retirement days, he could be seen changing socks in a taxi as he dashed from a match at the Manhattan Club to a meeting. He often participates in charity tournaments, playing friend Ethel Kennedy, Ilie Nastase, or some other celebrity. While still news anchor at CBS, he frequently played commentator Andy Rooney; during his summer vacations, he plays Martha's Vineyard neighbor Art Buchwald nearly every day. He also enjoys swimming in the pool at St. Bartholomew's Episcopal Church in New York City, where he is a member.

Cronkite is often invited to serve on special committees or participate in commemorative festivities in addition to the aforementioned tennis tournaments. In 1974, he served on a planning committee to schedule a series of concerts to assist victims of the African famine, which was unusually widespread and devastating that year. His fellow committee members included the late John Lennon, John Denver, and Eric Sevareid. Later that same year, he was invited to give a dramatic reading from the works of Thomas Jefferson at Washington's Constitution Hall. In a spontaneous burst of appreciation for his reading, the director of the sixty-five piece Air Force band invited Cronkite to take the baton. Cronkite gamely accepted the challenge and conducted John Philip Sousa's rousing "Stars and Stripes Forever."

One of the most popular series on television in the early 1970s was *The Mary Tyler Moore Show,* a comedy centering around a Minneapolis CBS affiliate's news program. In 1974, Cronkite made a cameo appearance on the show as himself (acting being another suppressed facet of his diverse personality). Even though his performance was generally praised by critics and viewers, he received undue criticism from some cynics who felt the appearance was undignified. Cronkite chose to ignore the comments from his detractors, saying he believed the brief fling at acting was both harmless and fun.

Kathy took her father's theatrical interests more seriously. She has had small parts in various films, including one of the *Billy Jack* sequels, as well as the Patty Hearst figure in *Network.* Her grandmother, Helen Cronkite, still enjoys telling about the family's theatre trip to see the *Billy Jack* movie when it was playing in New York. At the last minute, Cronkite had to attend to some business and asked his wife and family to save him a seat. When he arrived at the movie theatre, his request had been amply carried out: his family comprised the entire audience. Mrs. Cronkite said proudly of her granddaughter, "Kathy had a few lines, and I thought she was very good." In a quieter voice she quickly added, "But the movie was awful!"

Betsy once told Marguerite Michaels for a *Parade* feature, "Walter likes to be amused at night. He says there's enough bad news all day. We both love the theatre and all kinds of music— waltzes, dixieland, jazz—anything with a nice tune and no message. It's a life without cocktail parties—fortunately—and without movies—unfortunately. Walter gets embarrassed when he's recognized and brought to the head of a movie line."

Cronkite also hates being taken advantage of. In 1978, without his knowledge or consent, the Sakowitz Christmas catalog offered a dinner with Cronkite for $94,125. It might have been Sakowitz's idea of a joke, but Cronkite was outraged. He demanded that the department store not only cease and desist advertising the bogus meal, but also stop sending out the catalog.

Andy Rooney recently wrote of his famous friend in *Diversion.* Cronkite, he revealed, had lots of shortcomings, but "being late and keeping people waiting isn't one of them. He's always on time. He's easily the busiest person I've known, but if you've agreed to meet someplace at 12:30, don't arrive at 12:35 or he'll have been there waiting for you for five minutes."

As a testimonial to their pragmatic natures, Cronkite and his wife each have "living wills," which specify, in Betsy's words, "if the time comes when [we] can no longer take care part in decisions for [our] own future and there is no reasonable expectation of . . . recovery from extreme medical or physical disability, [we want] to be allowed to die and not be kept alive by medication, artificial means or heroic measures."

The Cronkites have extended their "right to die with dignity" philosophy even to their pets. When 17-year-old Buzzy became blind, arthritic, and incontinent, they could no longer bear seeing him bump into furniture and whine from the pain caused by his arthritis. It was while they were being visited and supported by friend and syndicated columnist Ann Landers that the Cronkites determined to take their beloved Buzzy to their vet to have him euthanized.

Cronkite has vowed he wouldn't let himself get into that heart-breaking predicament again, and dogs are no longer a part of the household. Even their cat, Dancer, is theirs by default: one of their children asked them to keep him "temporarily," and Dancer became a joyful permanent fixture.

*   *   *

When considering his mother's long life, and his reasonably good health and good state of mind, it is quite probable that Walter Cronkite has "miles to go" before he sleeps. When *Life*'s television reviewer, "Cyclops," reviewed Cronkite's *You Are There* series some years ago, he optimistically noted, "One believes that Walter Cronkite probably was there. He is as much a part of our modern consciousness as are parking lots and bewilderment. He will be the

anchorman when Sirius the Dog Star decides to sterilize all earth-
lings as an antiseptic precaution on behalf of the cosmos."

"Thank You, Walter"

The Problem of Succession

The Evening News *has been less and less fun. Walter would never say that out loud. He's such a company man.*

—Betsy Cronkite

Oh, God   what are we going to do without Walter Cronkite?

—Los Angeles T-Shirt, 1981

There'll never be another Walter Cronkite!

—Los Angeles Placard, 1981

A S CRONKITE'S retirement at age 62 approached, newspapers, periodicals, newscasters, and rumor mills, who all knew a good story when they saw one, cranked out endless speculation on when the Mount Everest of newsmen would surrender his anchor desk and to whom. CBS executives talked of waiving its mandatory ruling, allowing him to remain indefinitely; in 1980, however, he made it clear he wanted to retire the next year, while he was on top. CBS executives agreed to replace him as managing editor of the *Evening News* but keep him on as a special correspondent.

Of the sizable stable of contenders to the throne, Roger Mudd and Dan Rather were the two most likely heirs. Neither, CBS executives sighed, was another Walter Cronkite, and they rightfully feared a drastic drop in ratings once the transition was a reality.

Mudd was the steady, reliable low-key newsman who worked hard and always produced a story without a ripple. His expertise, unfortunately, was politics, centered in Washington, where he had excelled in covering the capitol beat.

Rather, on the other hand, had developed his skills over a more wide-ranging set of experiences. He was first noticed by CBS chief of correspondents Ernie Lester in 1961, as he covered hurricane Carla for KHOU-TV in Houston, standing "up to his ass in alligators," another CBS official remembered. He was made head of the Dallas bureau, traveling throughout the South, covering the civil rights struggles.

Rather was in Dallas the day President John Kennedy was assassinated and performed so admirably (he feels his reporting during those sad days was his finest) it was up the ladder from there. He was named White House correspondent, but after one disappointing year in the Johnson White House he was transferred to London for twelve months. He requested to be sent to Vietnam, but that, too, was a disappointment for him. He was reassigned to the Nixon White House, where he spent eight years as a burr under Nixon's saddle. As his coverage of the Kennedy assassination had turned his career around, his infamous 1974 live coverage of Richard Nixon's mid-term election campaign trip to Houston nearly did the same. As Rather stood to ask a question, a mixture of boos and applause erupted. President Nixon, in a friendly, joking manner asked, "Are you running for something?" Rather quickly and irreverently shot back, "No, Mr. President, are you?" That caustic, "Now get this!" attitude that frequently characterized his personality had made "Gunga Dan" unpopular with many; he genuinely feared he might lose his job over that disrespectful exchange with a sitting and popular president.

Rather weathered that storm and in 1980, when CBS executives were trying to choose Cronkite's replacement, Rather's maverick quality was re-evaluated. ABC's Roone Arledge openly courted Rather and waved a checkbook under his nose in an attempt to win him over, as he had with other former CBessers Barry Serafin, Sylvia Chase, John Laurence, and Hughes Rudd. Rather made no secret of the fact that he was talking to NBC as well as

ABC and would sign on with one of them, probably the latter, if he were not chosen as Cronkite's successor. Who, if not selected, could do CBS the greatest harm? It was a similar quandary fellow Texan Lyndon Johnson faced when contemplating the fate of over-age FBI director J. Edgar Hoover, who had accumulated massive and damaging files on every politician in Washington, including the president himself. Johnson let him stay, reasoning, "It would be better to have him inside the tent, pissing out, than outside, pissing in."

Following weeks of futile debate in the CBS higher circles, no decision could be reached. CBS News president Bill Leonard said he had made identical offers to Mudd and Rather, that they could be co-anchors of the news desk. Mudd denied the statement, claiming that he had been offered a doubled salary and an indefinite assignment. Rather was reported as agreeing with the shared anchor position—but, he added, Mudd was unwilling.

Cronkite, who had tried to remain neutral and out of the battle, was asked to name his successor. He eventually selected Rather, he said, "because of his greater experience in news coverage. Roger had never been outside the U.S. on a news assignment." CBS management went along. Rather became known as the "$7,000,000 Man" as he signed a six-year contract as managing editor of the *Evening News*. Mudd resigned from CBS and joined NBC and former CBS newsmen Marvin and Bernard Kalb. Mudd is now with the Public Broadcasting System's *McNeil/Lehrer Report.*

Undaunted, ABC ran an unprecedented full-page ad ostensibly bidding a fond farewell to Cronkite. With the ABC logo prominently displayed, the copy ran, "Thank you, Walter," causing a CBS press relations person to remark, "Those people at ABC will do anything to call attention to the fact that Walter will no longer be anchor on the *CBS Evening News*." CBS countered with full-page announcements "Introducing our newest correspondent . . . Walter Cronkite," who, it was touted, would simply be shifting positions at CBS.

As the March 6 deadline for Cronkite's final newscast approached, Cronkite's face began appearing on virtually every magazine cover in the U.S., and he came near to "being interviewed to death" as America and the world paid tribute to newscasting's premier reporter. (Far too many of the tributes ended with his signature closing "And that's the way it is.") Even the Soviet weekly *Literaturnaya Gazeta* made mention of the event, praising his years of even-handedly covering the news, and lauding his "kind, open face." Some of the articles were so solemn and had such a ring of finality to them that one might have confused the transition with his obituary. Andy Rooney reflected that mood in an uncharacteristically serious vein: "It's a little dramatic for the retirement of a television newsman, but the thought of Walter leaving evokes the same sense of terror I get from the contemplation of death."

Deadpan and serious former Secretary of State Henry Kissinger rasped in his gravely voice, "When I wanted to make a point, Cronkite was one of the first people I would call. I was sure of getting a fair interview—tough, but fair." He then confessed that Cronkite "had that look of a beagle in distress. You went right to the edge of telling him everything because you felt you owed it to the guy."

Judy Flander of the *Washington Star* reported that Av Westin, ABC's executive producer of news, confessed, "Walter is Walter. He almost represents God, mother, the American flag, the four-minute mile, and Mount Everest."

At the 1980 Democratic Convention, his sixteenth—and the last one he would anchor—fellow correspondent Charles Kuralt surprised "Old Ironpants" with an on-the-air tribute. As he presented Cronkite with the microphone he had used at the first televised convention in 1952, Cronkite was nearly overcome. At a party given that night in his honor, he confessed, "I was perfectly capable of blubbering us right off the air."

As he was packing up his personal effects, he was asked, perhaps unnecessarily, in an interview for *Current* magazine if he would miss the post he had held for nineteen years. He responded sincerely and without annoyance, "Sure I'll miss it. It'll be a real trauma . . . with withdrawal symptoms, I'm sure. Whenever there is a major breaking story I will look at the *CBS News* and say to myself, 'I wish I were there.' However, if a big story breaks or I stumble on something of interest, I would hope to offer the *Evening News* a piece, and take some part in it. On major stories I plan to do on-the-spot analysis but not interfere with the coverage at all . . . assuming the *Evening News* feels they've got time for me.

"There's no question—anybody leaving something he has done and loved for such a long time as I have is bound to miss it. It happens everywhere . . . especially in our profession. A guy comes off the police beat and gets a promotion to city editor but he never gets over the feeling that he'd like to be back on the beat. I suffered that when I moved here from being a foreign correspondent."

He hoped he would be asked to "pontificate a bit" during the elections and rocket launches. "But," he said with a sigh, "I certainly won't be in the anchor chair."

On March 6, 1981, Cronkite conducted his last newscast as if it were any other. As he took a few moments at the end to sign off, he coolly and briefly commented on the "transition": that he was not leaving CBS but was simply changing jobs. There was no noticeable emotion on that occasion, for CBS had packaged the move thoroughly—running ads in newspapers and televised spots, reassuring viewers that even though personnel would change, CBS would not. The competition was not idle, either: NBC joined ABC's full-page ads in the *New York Times,* as a reminder that, despite CBS's downplaying of the event, Cronkite was one of a kind and nobody—certainly not Dan Rather—could ever take his place.

At a party that evening, Cronkite cracked up Rather and the gathering of friends when he stood for a short and light-hearted farewell address before handing over the keys to his office.

After his final "And that's the way it is," even as he and his friends were celebrating that night, workers had immediately begun repainting the set. By Monday evening the orangey background that was so complimentary to Cronkite's pink skin was repainted a sterner blue-gray for Rather's ruddy flesh tones. A few days later, CBS News temporarily worked out of its Washington studios while the entire New York set was transformed from Cronkite's slightly worn-looking working newsroom to Captain Kirk's bridge aboard the starship *Enterprise.* The last vestiges of Cronkite's CBS *Evening News* were forever gone.

The shift in assignments did nothing to slow down the deposed managing editor. The intrepid correspondent signed a new seven-year contract with CBS, reported to be for one million dollars a year, and threw himself full-throttle into his new science program, *Universe,* whose topics he was free to choose. At that time, when his future with his network seemed so promising, his mother was pleased to report that "Walter is busier and happier than he's ever been!" Betsy humorously thought he might try to shake off the image of father figure he had acquired and try his hand at being the sex object she claims he would like to be.

Cronkite admitted that he would have liked to have retired on a 60-foot boat with a 20-year-old mistress. Instead, he joked, he wound up with a 20-foot boat and his wife of fifty years.

The *Universe* series began, but was pre-empted so often that it was never really given a fair chance to prove its mettle. Three seasons later, a disappointed Cronkite complained, CBS "elected to let it go down the drain." Never one to give up, he launched into other pursuits: reissuing the 1960s' *I Can Hear It Now* series under the new title, *The Way It Was*; writing the copy for *South by Southeast,* a coffee-table volume of water colors and oil paintings by Ray Ellis; and going on the requisite book-autographing tour. He has since completed *North by Northwest* and *Westwind.*

On one of his rare *Walter Cronkite at Large* programs, he returned to a theme he had promoted in the 1970s — the environment. He confided to his audience, "Next to keeping the peace, I still feel no more important issue [exists] than making our planet habitable for ourselves and our children."

He did the narration of a documentary series on Leonardo da Vinci, the prophetic threat of *1984,* a D-Day special in which he introduced a replaying of an earlier program he had made with President Eisenhower, a return to the news booth as commentator during the 1984 political conventions, a Truman commemorative, and the narration for a *Time-Life* video series on the Vietnam War. In 1986 he shared tacos with Prince Charles and Willie Nelson in Austin and was trotted out a time or two for brief comments at the beginning of the 1991 Gulf War.

He began showing up annually on New Year's Day, introducing the Vienna Philharmonic's special Strauss celebrations in that beautiful Austrian city , and on CBS awards. Traveling widely (by his own reckoning, he has now traveled to every major city in the world except Buenos Aires), he remains a favored personality, whether in Denmark, giving out Hans Christian Andersen Awards at the Royal Danish Ballet Theatre; being interviewed for *Entertainment Tonight* at the opening of the Broadway revival of *Meet*

Me in St. Louis, a musical about a town not far from his birthplace; or yet another chat with Barbara Walters on the front lawn of his new house in Martha's Vineyard. (From the lawn of his first house on the Vineyard, Cronkite could see the infamous Chappaquiddick bridge where Mary Jo Kopechne was drowned. He watched, over the years, as people stopped to whittle a piece of the bridge to take back home with them. Cronkite has difficulty understanding the morbidity of his fellow countrymen sometimes.)

He and Chip are working together on a $30 million project for the Media Access Corporation. He will be the host, narrator, and executive director of a series of videotapes and an encyclopedia on the 20th century, a monumental task to be completed by the year 2000.

His desire to be invited to go on a NASA shuttle flight or be the first correspondent to report from the surface of the moon has not diminished. He is realistic enough to admit he is not likely to be asked, but would certainly go if the invitation were ever extended.

His first experience at serving on a board of directors, at Pan-Am Airways, turned out to be a wrong choice for him. Being the "benign Calvinist" he says he is, he felt a conflict of interest existed and removed himself. He is currently a CBS board member and an active advisor for the journalism program at his alma mater, the University of Texas in Austin.

Many were hopeful Cronkite would consider politics after he stepped down from his anchor position. In 1972, for example, Cronkite had often been mentioned as a possible running mate for presidential candidate George McGovern. It was rumored in 1980 that John Anderson and he discussed the possibility that he might run as a vice-presidential candidate, although Cronkite denied the charge. There are many, his friend Kurt Vonnegut among them, who believe Cronkite could hold any post he wanted, even president. Cronkite had once felt he might enjoy being a senator, but he declares he no longer has a desire for any political post.

*   *   *

As Cronkite tried to settle into his semi-retirement, CBS felt the vacuum of his absence in a most dramatic way. Initially, Rather was able to keep the ratings up, but he began to lose many of the

Cronkite faithful and the audience count continued to slide downhill. Cronkite had forewarned him: "Don't be surprised, don't be disheartened. You may go way up. You may go way down. You may just bounce around, but you're going to make a mistake if you pay much attention to that stuff. What you need to concern yourself with are stories and news."

The rumors began and persisted that Rather would not last and Charles Kuralt or Roger Mudd would replace him. Rather confessed to Lally Weymouth in a *Parade* interview, "I would love to tell you, 'Hey, I don't feel the pressure,' but I do. Some days, some weeks, I feel it more than others. I frankly had no idea that the pressure would be as great as it has turned out to be. I like to think I'm a pressure player. I'd better be."

It was reported that CBS was so concerned about the ratings it called Cronkite in to consult with Rather. Cronkite denied the rumor, dismissing it as nonsense. "I think Dan's had a tough row to hoe because of this hypercritical examination of him. If I'd been put under that pressure, I don't know how I would have fared.

"I think he's doing fine. There was a little bit of tenseness at first, as there was in my case [when Cronkite relieved Douglas Edwards some twenty years earlier]. That's not serious. The main thing about any anchorperson is his news credentials, and Dan's are impeccable."

George Garneauy reported in *Editor and Publisher* in 1988 that Cronkite defended Rather in the charge his successor had been rude to then Vice-President Bush. Cronkite, however, maintained "considerable reservations" about Rather's performance as CBS anchorman.

Rather's trademark suspenders kept a few viewers watching for a short time. When that novelty waned, he switched to a vest and immediately his stock rose. Asked if that might be a gimmick, he answered, "I'll wear them as long as they work." In 1989, as *CBS News* sank below Peter Jennings's ratings at ABC, Rather announced he would no longer sit behind his news desk but stand to deliver the news. Tired of the obvious gimmicks all the networks were attempting to keep their audiences, more and more viewers began switching to Ted Turner's *CNN Headline News* or *CNN Evening News*.

Stephen Randall, in a *Playboy* article, likened Rather to "a tense man with the uneasy smile of a sniper about to open fire on a mall." Brokaw, he said, is "an Eagle Scout with intellectual pretensions."

The charades of the "big three" networks did not go unnoticed by Thomas Hoving, either, in the September 1989 issue of *Connoisseur*. Hoving wrote disparagingly of "Wynken, Blynken, and Nod" (Jennings, Rather, and Brokaw), whom he referred to as "the millionaire automatons of our nightly newscasts." The humorous and insightful article is reproduced here in its entirety:

Anchor Watch

The credibility of network television, we have always been led to assume, lies squarely on the shoulders of the gentlemen anchors of the nightly news. Peter Jennings, Tom Brokaw, and Dan Rather are meant to symbolize the integrity of the corporations—ABC, NBC, and CBS—that they work for. In a world of quavering values, these men should seem like Rocks of Gibraltar forever holding firm against the corrosion of standards.

But do they? Today's anchors appear to be actors who do not have to memorize scripts, entertainers who use all their clever wiles to seduce the viewer into not switching. In an earlier epoch, Walter Cronkite, David Brinkley, and John Chancellor gave the impression that they knew what they were talking about, because they behaved on-screen like real people, with plenty of quirks. Their popularity may have been due, far more than anybody figured in those days, to the solid respect the viewer had for these obviously human and capable men.

Today's anchors are automatons, who, but for very slight variations, are identical. And viewers have lost respect for them—and the networks—because they perform in so predictable a manner.

Try studying Jennings, Brokaw, and Rather with the sound off and a stopwatch in hand. I did, for a dozen evenings, and discovered to my amusement that, no matter what the story on the Telepromter script, each anchor acted the same, night after night.

JENNINGS: In every story his head nods, tips to one side; his eyes blink; head bobs again; he looks down; his head moves right, then left quickly. Every six seconds Jennings goes through the sequence. When he shakes his shoulders, the interval is eight to ten seconds.

You can be sure a commercial is on the way when Jennings makes a furtive look down, abruptly up, and then out to the right (obeisance to the sacred moment). Ten minutes into the program, he settles down, and movements become less mannered. But when he is reporting on an amusing item his head bobs more vigorously, for "energy." Frequently he looks down at notes, existent or nonexistent. In the last five to three minutes, Jenning's chin rises dramatically. A series of fierce winks begins, normally seventeen every thirty seconds. At the end he always looks out, then down.

BROKAW: He is introduced with a close-up, dead center. We see that his shoulders are set at an angle, but his head remains straight. Precisely two minutes into the program, Brokaw's shoulders square off. When he is interviewing, his head cocks to the right and his hands come into view, often shuffling through papers. Eight minutes into the program (in seven out of twelve of my stopwatch tests) Brokaw shifts uneasily into his chair, no matter what the story happens to be. He almost never raises his eyebrows. Winks increase as the program continues. His face becomes animated when he deals with juicy, human-interest news. He almost never looks down.

Three minutes before the end of the broadcast his shoulders move back to the angled position. He grows serious, almost somber. Twenty seconds before the end he bursts into a smile.

RATHER: Compared to his counterparts, he is as frozen as *No* drama. His great, square face always fills the camera. His mouth gapes about a quarter open. The left eye twitches barely perceptibly. The left eyebrow lifts every eight seconds. He looks down every twelve to fourteen seconds. He delivers a "sweet" smile before looking off toward a reporter. Five to three minutes before the end of the program, he stiffens and, in the last ten seconds, breaks into a painted smile.

Day in, day out, all three perform their unreal rituals like clockwork. Try setting your watch by watching their movements, if you don't believe me. Then you won't believe them.

Stephen Randall feels the three are suitable news-readers, but "lousy Walter Cronkites."

*   *   *

Cronkite has seen *CBS News* drop to second place after ABC, even dropping to third on occasion, and is now resigned to the fact that CBS is content to proceed without him. Things were so bad in 1990 that Rather had to broadcast November's election returns without sponsors. It is no secret that Cronkite has bitter feelings toward Rather's failure to keep the *CBS Evening News* afloat. *Time* reported in September 1990 that Cronkite "let slip some frank criticism" of Rather. When the Persian Gulf crisis erupted, Rather telecast an exclusive interview with Saddam Hussein. Cronkite acidly observed that Saddam "saved Rather's skin." Cronkite further feels Rather has "blown it as an anchor. He's stiff and uncomfortable. Look at the ratings. If it weren't for developments in the Gulf, he might be out of a job by now." Some shifting of management personnel is currently going on and rumors persist that Rather's days are limited. Not only has the news division fallen on hard times, unable, Cronkite contends, to adequately cover news events, the overall programming is so bad some now refer to the network as "CBS: Completely Banal Shows."

Despite the hopes he had of playing a more significant role in reporting the news, as his friend John Chancellor has done at NBC, he accepts the CBS corporate decision to let the younger crowd run the show. "I've been disappointed that CBS has made so little use of me in the news department over the last nine years since I stepped down from the nightly news. My attitude has always been that it's their candy store, and they can run it any way they want to. I'll do whatever I'm asked to do. If I don't like it, I'll quit."

Richard Salant, his former CBS News boss, is openly irritated that his network has treated Cronkite in such a shabby manner. It's "a scorn for the old-timers," he accuses. Some of the other "old-timers" believe CBS executives are placating Dan Rather.

Adding insult to injury, Cronkite has watched as CNN has aggressively pushed to the top, inaugurating the one-hour late-night program that he, for years, has steadfastly maintained is the optimum way television news should be presented. Stephen Randall believes CNN, with its "mostly anonymous anchors are not themselves the news. The *news* is the news, something the "stars" of the big three networks failed to recognize.

Cronkite maintains an office at CBS that serves as a base of operations between his many trips. (One of his harried secretaries lamented, "He travels so much. He was in the office today for exactly twenty-two minutes.") Besides the videotape project, he spends busy days answering mail, granting interviews, reviewing scripts, giving speeches, and working on his autobiography, a task he agreed to twenty-five years ago. He has been so busy living his life he has not had time to write about it, but he hopes to have it completed before 1992.

To Cronkite, family is still of paramount importance. Betsy travels with him regularly now, and they spend many of the colder months in New York. Summers are still spent at Martha's Vineyard, where he is surrounded by his children and three grandchildren. Daughter Nancy lives at the Vineyard year-round in her father's original house on Wyntje Road. Betsy, who is married to an Austin attorney, works for a cable TV company and is the mother of two sons. Chip is married, a New York film editor, and the father of Walter Leland Cronkite IV. Like their father, none completed college, but this has apparently not been a burden.

*   *   *

In searching for a proper final salute to such an incredible career and such an incredible, Norman Rockwell life, any number of sources might have been used. One in particular, by Ron Powers, seems to sum up the ingredients that have been basic to Cronkite's success. Powers, who writes for the *Chicago Sun-Times,* has published several interviews with Cronkite and articles about him. His admiration for the grand old man is ever evident. Powers recognizes Cronkite's skill as a journalist, family man, and human being and has successfully summarized the feelings of Cronkite fans. The following excerpt from a 1973 *Quill* article written during the height of Cronkite's battle with the Nixon White House serves as a pointed contrast to the subjects of Hoving's essay and pays honor and tribute to the uncontested Dean of Journalism.

The Essential Cronkite

Newspapers convey facts, but little if anything about the nature of the people who report them. It is easy, for instance, to read the Watergate stories in the *Washington Post* without stopping at all to consider the fact that they were typed out on copy paper, probably triple-spaced, by human beings with sweaty fingers.

Television is humanity. It may not be much longer, if they keep making all those situation comedies where a chimpanzee does something cute and a laugh machine responds, but for right now, we'll say that television is humanity. And Walter Cronkite, who ironically has tried harder than almost anybody in the history of broadcasting to keep personality out of his on-air image, has provided Americans with a continuing sense that a fellow taxpayer and shredded-wheat eater, rather than some pre-programmed propagandistic humanoid, is reading the news into the camera—and is just as wrought up over things as they are.

Not that Cronkite is all father-image and no substance— a sort of newsroom Robert Young to Dan Rather's James Brolin. He is a newsman of consummate skill and persistence. His special report on the then-emerging Watergate scandal, put together last summer just after he returned from covering President Nixon's trip to Russia, was among the first and best video efforts to bring that complicated story to light.

His two Emmy awards for coverage of America's space program, his two Emmy awards this year (one for the Watergate piece, another for CBS News' coverage of the shooting of Gov. Wallace), his 22 years of reportage and interviews at CBS—including the now-classic series with Lyndon Johnson shortly before his death—and his eye-witness dispatches for

United Press during World War II leave little further question of Cronkite's journalistic excellence.

But his impact on American Journalism, and his significance in the post-Watergate relationship between public and press, go far beyond Cronkite's reporting ability.

It has to do with a fortuitous mysticism, a mysticism of face and voice. Cronkite himself senses it—as I learned last February, while conducting a series of conversations with him that appeared in the June issue of *Playboy* as the "*Playboy* Interview"—but does not trouble himself to explain it.

But it goes, I think, something like this: somewhere in the collective consciousness of people in this country is the ideal composite face and voice of the American man . . .

It may be a weird blend of cultural contrasts. . . . Whatever it is, Cronkite has it. And that generation—now referred to as Middle America, and the target group for the post public-relations blitz from the White House against the press—hasn't forgotten its main man.

There is more yet to the mysticism: the voice. You don't have to remember the war nor be middle-aged to be affected by the hypnotic cadence of Cronkite's basso delivery. I have interviewed television performers of various levels of fame for three years, and very quickly caught on that they were not exactly in the same class as those folks in togas who ride chariots through the sky and change maidens into cows. And yet when I sat down in front of Cronkite in his office for the first time, popped a question, and heard that vocal drum-roll coming back at—not the whole nation, but ME—I got a bad case of the clams. What's worse, I had the distinct impression that my own voice, by comparison, was doing a sensational if involuntary imitation of Porky Pig. It took several sessions for that feeling to go away.

So much for mysticism. Getting down to practicalities (where Cronkite himself is most comfortable), a major item in his credibility during the dark days of the press's reputation was that he confounds stereotypes. This is not some Sevareidean liberal accusing the Nixon administration of a "crime against the people" by trying to keep reporters from doing their jobs. Nossir. It's Walter, the guy who loves America's system of law so much that he feels civil disobedience is not justified, even when administered by a Martin Luther King, a man Cronkite admired.

. . . He would not, in his capacity as managing editor of CBS News, have sent a reporter to uncover the Pentagon papers, yet he believes in publishing them once they have been uncovered and salutes Daniel Ellsberg's courage. He was enthusiastic ("Oh Boy!") about the space program, yet critical on the air about its cost over-runs. In short, he manages the delicate feat of being a quintessential Middle American without being a cliché.

What this means in practical terms is that viewers have a great deal of trouble dismissing Cronkite's newscasts as this or that shade of propaganda. The humanity he works so hard to suppress pervades this every syllable with a quality of—tired, deflated word—decency."

Afterword

ONE OF THE GOALS I set for myself in writing about the journalistic career of Walter Cronkite was to be as objective as I believe he has been. I feel I was reasonably successful. Being as opinionated at the next person, however, I can't let this opportunity pass without expressing some very subjective and personal thoughts. I readily admit what follows might be considered merely "getting in my licks," but I feel what I have to say bears reflection at least.

I have already made clear that I am a great admirer of Walter Cronkite, and it should come as no surprise to learn that I am not pleased with the direction in which television news broadcasting has gone since his retirement. I heartily concur with Thomas Hoving's "Wynken, Blynken, and Nod" analogy of the status of the second-generation "big three" newscasters. I believe the cause for what has occurred in the demise of televised newscasting, to a large extent, can be traced to the upheaval in the American family structure and the current American public's "bread and circuses" mentality. Network executives are frankly giving the people what they want. I am wondering, though, if we should give pablum to people who need red meat.

Permit me to wax philosophical. Throughout the history of mankind, the Family of Man has gathered where the warmth is. For thousands or, perhaps, millions of years, fire has provided light for illumination and heat for comfort and cooking. For those eons, members of families were drawn to the open fire in caves, teepees, and huts and in the fireplaces of log cabins and frame structures. At the heart of the activity was Mother, doing the things mothers traditionally did.

In the more recent past, however, the wood-burning ranges in thousands of city or farm kitchens baked the bread and warmed the bath water as well as the room where the family ate and gathered for sewing, socializing, doing homework, or pulling taffy ("No matter where I serve my guests, It seems they like my kitchen best"). As women became liberated, for good or for ill, and as single-parent households grew in number and complexity, the "family" structure shifted and fragmented as parents married, divorced, and remarried. Real estate as well as people were shifted back and forth between parents and step-parents, children and step-children. Since the 1970s, following Watergate and the Vietnam War—watersheds in the affairs of the United States—the scene shifted from Mother's kitchen to the comforts of the "family room," where tables were set up before the "warmth" of the ubiquitous television set.

In 1989, 36,000,000 Americans surveyed listed watching television as the activity they most look forward to every day. American children who have grown up with television—the great baby-sitter—will spend nine years of watching it in their lifetimes. The only activity American high school graduates have done more than watching television is sleeping.

Even though I have no statistics to prove it, I would suggest that children today spend more time "communicating" with television than they do with parents or other family members. I do know that the average "quality time" American fathers spend with each child is about fifteen minutes; mothers, of course, spend more, but the hours before the tube greatly exceed the minutes spent with parents. That thought is frightening, for by age sixteen, the average American child has seen 18,000 murders on the tube. If values are being taught, it is likely that television is teaching them. Is there any question why our culture is suffering the way it is today? Reading those television ads in old World War II *Life* magazines—you know, the ones that promised us cultural events, news, and enlightenment—we realize that television has not gone the way it was intended. Let's face it, television today is, as they say, "Where it's at." As latch-key kids and single and working parents come and go at irregular hours, television offers mindless instant companionship, entertainment, and gratification for people who are alone together or simply alone.

Our world is television-oriented. Jesus said it first: "Where your heart is, there will your treasure be also." There is no question today where our hearts are. Our social schedules, eating habits, even visits to the toilet are determined by television. In 1988–89, Nielsen Media Research reported, U.S. households had a television set turned on for an average of seven hours and two minutes a day; that's up from six hours and twenty-six minutes ten years ago. We pay enormous salaries to athletes to perform for us and to actors and comedians and musicians to entertain us. Our lives are divided between the artificial environment of the rectangular electronic box and the artificial, controlled environment of the steel and glass suburban mall where we buy what we are told on television we cannot live without.

Along with the inflated salaries of athletes and other entertainers have come seven-figure salaries for newscasters. It began with Barbara Walters, whom ABC hired away from NBC. There she was, on the Today show, talking to Mamie Eisenhower about her inner-ear and equilibrium problems and selling gloves between interviews and reading the news. Suddenly, she was being paid $3,000,000 to interview Richard Nixon and she didn't have to plug the sponsors' products any more. It wasn't long before all the big-three networks boasted big-buck broadcasters. Are these readers of the day's news worth the multi-million dollar contracts their networks pay them? Probably not. But the charade goes on and the salaries go even higher. Cronkite regrets the celebrity status and high salaries that seem to go with network journalists. He told a *U.S. News and World Report* interviewer, "When people ask if Barbara Walters, Dan Rather or any of us are worth seven-figure salaries, I have to ask: Compared to what?"

Not, he feels, compared to newspaper people, nor teachers. "But compared to other people from whom the network and the local stations are profiting—rock-and-roll singers, for instance—certainly yes."

With the "star" billing night-time newscasters of ABC, NBC, and CBS are now accorded, one might expect the quality of their programs to keep pace with the salaries and hoopla. If anything, I believe the standards have deteriorated. The big three have long attempted to improve their standing by playing what is called "the ratings game." The various gimmicks Dan Rather has tried in an effort to get CBS out of the cellar have already been noted. The Murrows, Cronkites, Chancellors, Huntleys, and Brinkleys would have never given even a fleeting thought to any sort of "slickness" to attract viewers. They idealistically fought for the presentation of news first and were undoubtedly successful in their endeavor.

Realistically, the bottom line has always been, after all, profits. The loss of a single ratings point can mean $150,000,000 to a network that spends $250,000,000 to $350,000,000 a year on its news departments. Granted, that is no small matter; and, in all fairness, the networks' concern for ratings can be appreciated. The means by which ratings are achieved, however, are another matter altogether.

CBS insider and former legal correspondent Fred Graham did not argue with a *USA Today* interviewer who said that "there is no standard in TV news today except profit." He added the title of his book, *Happy Talk*, is "an umbrella term for all the jazz that they have brought into broadcast news, both on the network level and the local level, and it's because of the insatiable scramble for ratings."

In his book, *Happy Talk—Confessions of a TV Journalist*, Graham charges that "flash and trash" have long been the means by which the big three networks have attempted to hold viewers and compete with the cable networks that are eating into their audiences. Executives have introduced "infotainment," a mixture of news and entertainment, to hold audiences. One would think that the disastrous results of CBS's 1954 *Morning Show* would be a lesson to remember.

John Chancellor long ago feared the day when networks hired news readers solely on the basis of "deep voices and hair spray." He and Walter Cronkite both condemned the practice of hiring people with stars in their eyes who wanted to be "on camera" as opposed to being journalists first.

Cronkite believes too many young people today who might have gone on the stage or in the movies in an earlier day are opting for broadcasting. "They're about as interested in journalism as most actors are. They're far more interested in money, personal aggrandizement and a sense of fame.

"They're going through communication schools and learning Trench Coat I, Trench Coat II, and Makeup I and Makeup II. In a lot of schools, as near as I can tell, they're not taking courses that are terribly beneficial—and I don't think they've got the guts or the drive to be newspeople."

The day of hiring attractive people who read the news well, regrettably, has arrived. The hiring of Phyllis George is an early example. CBS admitted she was not a journalist but a pretty face— and one whose appointment helped to bump Fred Graham, he feels, from that network. Regardless of their abilities as journalists, a succession of cheerleader-blond beauties paraded across the television screens: Diane Sawyer and Paula Zahn from CBS and Deborah Norville of NBC are examples of the trend. A new cry (no pun intended) was sounded in 1989 when CNN named 34-year-old Catherine Crier to co-anchor—with former CBS veteran Bernard Shaw—CNN's one-hour news program, *The World Today,* in a time slot opposite Wynken, Blynken, and Nod. Crier is a former college beauty queen who was later elected a judge in Texas. That she had no journalism background at all seems to point the way broadcast news is headed. A pretty face that can read someone else's words is good enough for an American audience satiated by *Sports Illustrated*'s annual swimsuit issue and cheerleaders—real ones— scantily-clad and curvaceous, jiggling on the sidelines during televised (naturally) professional football games. All is fair in love and war and in improving ratings.

In the process of placating television audiences with plastic, alliteristic news readers reminiscent of Gilbert and Sullivan patter-song singers (CNN's leave-'em-smiling "Parting Glances," for example), or the irritating, frequent forced laugh of CNN's Susan Rook, grammar, syntax, and spelling (in graphics) have nose-dived. When I asked Cronkite in 1989 if he is bothered by the misplaced modifiers, dangling participles, incorrect pronoun/antecedent agreement, and reckless use of the word "only," he was quick to respond with a loud and long groan: "Ohhhhh! It just drives me crazy! I went to school in the days when grammar was taught! Three years of it in high school. And we were expected to use it correctly!" As journalism is apparently no longer required as a prerequisite to newscasting, knowledge of the Queen's English has evidently likewise fallen by the wayside.

It seems that "different than" instead of "different from," be-wilderment over the correct usage of the nominative case ("Barbara went to the movies with she and I") and total disregard for the helping verb in past participles (can you believe *Honey, I Shrunk the Kids!* from Walt Disney?) proliferate on the infallible West Coast. Too many reporters today seem to think every boat in the world "sunk." Wrong! "The boat sank!" or, "The boat had sunk."

Walt Disney World in Orlando has recently opened a new "Honey, I Shrunk the Kids" section. Imagine how firmly implanted that incorrect verb is in the minds of all who see it or go through it.

The epidemic of placing "only" before the verb and not before what is to be modified is rampant and is misused by far too many news people. Two recent examples include a CNN report on New York City disk jockey Bruce Morrow which revealed that "He is only on the air four days a week . . ." and the newspaper ads for *The Naked Gun 2 1/2*, which tout, "If You Only See One Movie This Year . . ." Please note, writers of copy, modifiers should be placed near the words they are modifying, in the event you weren't taught that or had forgotten.

Matching pronouns and antecedents seems to have gone the way of the Edsel. What's wrong with "Someone has left his bag on the steps"? Why does it have to be "Someone (one is singular) has left their (plural) bag on the steps?" Somebody, anyone, anybody, everyone, and so forth are all singular and the masculine pronoun has worked for years. Of course if someone wants to say "his or her," I won't argue with that, but give the construction some thought.

I was recently informed by a newspaperman that the Associated Press has ruled that all collective subjects are henceforth and forevermore to receive plural verbs. That means that the British custom of assuming family, club, couple and class are plural (The couple are adopting their first baby, and My family are taking a trip to Canada) will be unwelcomed standard fare for those of us who love our American English, and will cause even more grinding of teeth.

All of the grammatical mistakes I have mentioned, as well as others I have not mentioned, could be corrected if newswriters consulted a ninth-grade grammar text. There is no real mystery to English grammar, but in recent years, Americans, whether professionals or not, have been incredibly lax in their attempts to follow the rules. Unfortunately, far too many listeners think what is read on the air is carved in stone, and careless ad writers undo more than teachers can ever hope to do.

Nor can I ignore the horrendous spelling that so frequently pops up on Ted Turner's various channels. Recent examples include "Aurburn" (for Auburn), and "Czechosovakia," and "travellers" (Britons use two l's; Americans use only one), as well as misspelled titles in promos for upcoming movies. Recently, MGM's *Million Dollar Mermaid* was advertised to be shown on "Thrusday." I'm not sure Thor would approve of that corruption of his name, but that's not unusual on CNN. A network as large and self-laudatory as "Captain Outrageous" Turner's CNN is ("I am the king of cable television!"), should be more careful.

Weather reporters and meteorologists on all television channels forget that compound subjects require plural verbs ("Cold rain and sleet is in the forecast for tomorrow"—Ouch!). Gitano's lovely model croons, "There's my jeans . . ." Why not "There *are* my jeans"? The use of "and" automatically makes a compound subject, which writers too often ignore. "Or," on the other hand, is singular: "Bob or Sue is going with me to the store," is correct.

In 1982 I sent an essay to *TV Guide* in which I expressed my disdain at the sad state of grammar in television. I received a nice note saying essentially, "You're right and your comments are good, but why bother? The malpractice is so widespread, we'll never stop it." Since I have the floor now and you, dear reader, are as concerned about this matter as I am, I have chosen to reproduce that short article here because the principles are the same and needed today as much, if not more, than when it was written.

Lament of an Armchair Newswriter

They are inescapable—those nonstop, jangling, jarring violations of grammar on TV and the radio. The very media which we expect to observe the rules of sentence construction are too often the very culprits in teaching, by application, bad grammar. Local stations might be forgiven their sins because they lack the resources to hire the best, but the networks?

When ad writers, network anchors and other reporters are making six-digit salaries, their public deserves perfection.

Here are some examples of bad ad writing:

A long-running television advertisement for a Mickey Gilley record album brags that Mickey's "amazing array [singular subject] of hit songs are [plural verb] even more spectacular." Subjects and verbs must agree, Mickey. Your "amazing array of hit songs IS even more spectacular."

"Atari, whose family [singular] of games bring [plural] you Superman," could have used a rewrite. Make that "Atari, whose family of games brings you Superman."

Andy Rooney, who is always complaining about something on CBS's *60 Minutes,* recently took on the frequency of commercial breaks during network football games. Andy was unhappy with "every one that were shown." How about a commentary on poor grammar, Andy?

Another problem newswriters seem to have is in deciding what number none is, and how it is used. None is a contraction of not one and is usually singular. "None is going" is correct. Consider CBS's December 22, 1981 broadcast about a mainland Chinese girl who spoke too freely to a Western television interviewer. The reporter concluded that "None of us are as free as we think we are." (The subject is NEVER in a prepositional phrase.) This one is a bit tricky, but think about it before you write about it!

Similarly, networks failed their exams regarding pronouns and their antecedents. A Christmas season *Time* magazine commercial on television implored its audience to "Let someone know how special they are." Someone is not a they, it is a singular person. He is still acceptable as a neutral, singular pronoun, *Time,* Inc.; therefore, your ad should have read, "Let someone know how special he is."

Crest toothpaste: "Crest made their (its) toothpaste tough."

The word each suffers the same fate as none. Each is singular. The incorrect verb and the incorrect pronoun are frequently used and dimpled John Davidson is but one who uses them. On January 4, 1982, on *That's Incredible,* John reminded prospective contestants that "Each school must have their entries in . . ."In this case, it should have been "Each school must have *its* entries in . . ."

Bob Schieffer of CBS has his own personal grammatical hobgoblin going—"what with." He seems to sneak it into every news story he does. On December 3, 1981, he began a piece, "What with all the publicity about Poland . . ."; and less than two weeks later, he filed a report on the U.S. draft, again alluding to the crisis in Eastern Europe, by declaring (shudder), "What with the situation in Poland . . ." On the February 12 *Evening News,* in a story about U.S. battleships, he did it again. What before with is totally unnecessary and totally incorrect. I'm sure your grammar teacher is going mad, Bob, what with all your "what withs."

Networks, ad writers, newspapers, and journals owe their subscribers the best. They should recognize their influential positions as the prime teachers of the day. There is something magical about what is heard on TV or on the radio or read in print. Each utterance, each word becomes, somehow, carved in granite when handed down from Mount Mass Media. "I heard it on TV" becomes synonymous with "It's one of the Ten Commandments" for too many viewers or readers who believe consummately whatever television or radio or print journalism feed them.

Come on, Madison Avenue, Networks, Journalists, Lead! Write! Instruct! But for grammar's sake, do it correctly!"

*   *   *

In summary, and risking sounding like a doomsday crier, newscasting, to a large degree, has sunk (check out that verb, California. You have to have a helping verb before sunk or drunk or shrunk, and so forth) to a new low, having lapsed into what Fred Graham terms "infotainment," "happy talk," "flash and trash," and "Geraldoism."

It is my opinion that, with the possible exception of PBS's *McNeil/Lehrer Report,* there is little indication that serious, straight newscasting is any longer available, although CNN shows great promise, and as it grows and matures may become, in Stephen Randall's words, "The Cronkite Network News." Glitter has held sway so long it is unlikely it will ease its hold on newscasting any time soon. In large measure, the present situation, as has been suggested, reflects the aimless, self-centered, materialistic, and mindless state of the United States and, in all probability, neither an Edward Murrow or even a Walter Cronkite could reverse the trend. Randall goes so far as to suggest the day of the "star" anchor (appropriately a nautical term)is over and even Cronkite would be an anachorism today.

Are the things I have mentioned in this short chapter really important in the overall scheme of things? Probably not. The sun and moon will still rise without Harry Reasoner's rhapsodizing about them, or David Brinkley's rich and wry prose, or Walter Cronkite's sonorous basso-profundo pontificating "That's the way it is." For those of us who are idealistic or perhaps a little bit romantic, what is so ungrammatically and glossily offered up as network news today pales with what we remember.

Is this just another case of an old-timer's (possessive) reminiscing about how much better things used to be? Perhaps. Will those of us who were privileged to be a part of the Murrow, Huntley-Brinkley/Chancellor, Cronkite years simply have to dream of days that used to be and are no more and hope for improvements in the third generation of newscasters? I hope not, but pragmatically we must accept the probability that we have seen the sun set on television newscasting's golden age.

Appendix 1

The chapter entitled "Stringing Up the Western Union Boy" refers to two speeches by then–Vice President Spiro Agnew attacking the news media in general and the television networks in particular. Both speeches are presented here in their entirety, as reported in the *Congressional Record.*

The first speech was delivered before the Mid-West Regional Republican Committee in Des Moines, Iowa, November 13, 1969.

The Des Moines Speech

Tonight I want to discuss the importance of the television news medium to the American people. No nation depends more on the intelligent judgment of its citizens. No medium had a more profound influence over public opinion. Nowhere in our system are there fewer checks on vast power. So, nowhere should there be more conscientious responsibility exercised than by the news media. The question is, are we demanding enough of our television news presentations? And are the men of this medium demanding enough of themselves?

Monday night a week ago, President Nixon delivered the most important address of his administration, one of the most important of our decade. His subject was Vietnam. His hope was to rally the American people to see the conflict through to a lasting and just peace in the Pacific. For 32 minutes, he reasoned with a nation that has suffered almost a third of a million casualties in the longest war in its history.

When the president completed his address—an address, incidentally, that he spent weeks in the preparation of—his words and policies were subjected to instant analysis and querulous criticism. The audience of 70 million Americans gathered to hear the president of the United States was inherited by a small band of network commentators and self-appointed analysts, the majority of whom expressed in one way or another their hostility to what he had to say.

It was obvious that their minds were made up in advance. Those who recall the fumbling and groping that followed President Johnson's dramatic disclosure of his intention not to seek another term have seen these men in a genuine state of non-preparedness. This was not it.

One commentator twice contradicted the president's statement about the exchange of correspondence with Ho Chi Minh. Another challenged the president's abilities as a politician. A third asserted that the president was following a Pentagon line. Others, by the expression on their faces, the tone of their questions and the sarcasm of their responses made clear their sharp disapproval.

To guarantee in advance that the president's plea for national unity would be challenged, one network trotted out Averell Harriman for the occasion. Throughout the president's message, he waited in the wings. When the president concluded, Mr. Harriman recited perfectly. He attacked the Thieu Government as unrepresentative; he criticized the president's speech for various deficiencies; he twice issued a call to the Senate Foreign Relations Committee to debate Vietnam once again; he stated his belief that the Viet Cong or North Vietnamese did not really want a military takeover of South Vietnam; and he told a little anecdote about a "very, very responsible fellow" he had met in the North Vietnamese delegation.

All in all, Mr. Harriman offered a broad range of gratuitous advice—challenging and contradicting the policies outlined by the president of the United States. Where the president had issued a call for unity, Mr. Harriman was encouraging the country not to listen to him.

A word about Mr. Harriman. For 10 months he was America's chief negotiator at the Paris peace talks—a period in which the United States swapped some of the greatest military concessions in the history of warfare for an enemy agreement on the shape of the bargaining table. Like Coleridge's Ancient Mariner, Mr. Harriman seems to be under some heavy compulsion to justify his failure to anyone who will listen. And the networks have shown themselves to give him all the air time he desires.

Now every American has a right to disagree with the president of the United States and to express publicly that disagreement. But the people who elected him, and the people of this country have the right to make up their own minds and form their own opinions about a presidential address without having a president's words and thoughts characterized before they can even be digested.

When Winston Churchill rallied public opinion to stay the course against Hitler's Germany, he didn't have to contend with a gaggle of commentators raising doubts about whether Britain had the stamina to see the war through. When President Kennedy rallied the nation in the Cuban missile crisis, his address to the people was not chewed over by a roundtable of critics who disparaged the course of action he'd asked America to follow.

The purpose of my remarks tonight is to focus your attention on this little group of men who not only enjoy a right of instant rebuttal to every presidential address, but, more importantly, wield a free hand in selecting, presenting and interpreting the great issues in our nation.

First, let's define that power. At least 40 million Americans every night, it's estimated, watch the network news. Seven million of them view ABC, the remainder of them being divided between NBC and CBS. According to Harris polls and other studies, for millions of Americans the networks are the sole sources of national and world news. In Will Rogers' observation, what you knew was what you read in the newspaper. Today for growing millions of Americans, it's what they see and hear on their televisions.

Now how is this network news determined? A small group of men, numbering perhaps no more than a dozen anchormen, commentators and executive producers, settle upon the 20 minutes or so of film and commentary that's to reach the public. This selection is made from the 90 to 180 that may be available. Their powers of choice are broad. They decide what 40 to 50 million Americans will learn of the day's events in the nation and in the world.

We cannot measure this power and influence by the traditional democratic standards, for these men can create national issues overnight. They can make or break by their courage and commentary a moratorium on the war. They can elevate men from obscurity to national prominence within a week. They can reward some politicians with national exposure and ignore others.

For millions of Americans the network reporter who covers a continuing issue—like the ABM or civil rights—becomes, in effect, the presiding judge in a national trial by jury.

It must be recognized that the networks have made important contributions to the national knowledge—for news, documentaries and specials. They have often used their power constructively and creatively to awaken the public conscience to critical problems. The networks made hunger and black lung disease national issues overnight. The TV networks have done what no other medium could have done in terms of dramatizing the horrors of war. The networks have tackled our most difficult social problems with a directness and immediacy that's the gift of their medium. They focused the nation's attention on its environmental abuses—on pollution in the Great Lakes and the threatened ecology of the Everglades.

But it was also the networks that elevated Stokely Carmichael and George Lincoln Rockwell from obscurity to national prominence.

Nor is their power confined to the substantive. A raised eyebrow, an inflection in the voice, a caustic remark dropped in the middle of a broadcast can raise doubts in a million minds about the veracity of a public official or the wisdom of a Government policy.

One Federal Communications Commissioner considers the powers of the networks equal to that of local, state and federal governments all combined. Certainly it represents a concentration of power over American public opinion unknown in history.

Now what do Americans know of the men who wield this power? Of the men who produce and direct the network news, the nation knows practically nothing. Of the commentators, most Americans know little other than that they reflect an urbane and assured presence seemingly well-informed on every important matter.

We do know that to a man these commentators and producers live and work in the geographical and intellectual confines of Washington, D.C., of New York City, the latter of which James Reston terms the most unrepresentative community in the entire United States. Both communities bask in their own provincialism, their own parochialism. We can deduce that these men read the same newspapers. They draw their political and social views from the same sources. Worse, they talk constantly to one another, thereby providing artificial reinforcement to their shared viewpoints.

Do they allow their biases to influence the selection and presentation of the news? David Brinkley states objectivity is impossible to normal behavior. Rather, he says, we should strive for fairness.

Another anchorman on a network news shows contends, and I quote: "You can't expunge all your private convictions just because you sit in a seat like this and a camera starts to stare at you. I think your program has to reflect what your basic feelings are. I'll plead guilty to that."

Less than a week before the 1968 election, this same commentator charged that President Nixon's campaign commitments were no more durable than campaign balloons. He claimed that, were it not for the fear of hostile reaction, Richard Nixon would be giving in to, and I quote him exactly, "his natural instinct to smash the enemy with a club or go after him with a meat axe." Had this slander been made by one political candidate about another, it would have been dismissed by most commentators as a partisan attack. But this attack emanated from the privileged sanctuary of a network studio and therefore had the apparent dignity of an objective statement.

The American people would rightly not tolerate this concentration of power in Government. Is it not fair and relevant to question its concentration in the hands of a tiny, enclosed fraternity of privileged men elected by no one and enjoying a monopoly sanctioned and licensed by Government?

The views of the majority of this fraternity do not—and I repeat, do not—represent the views of America. That is why such a great gulf existed between how the nation received the president's address and how the networks reviewed it. Not only did the country receive the president's address more warmly than the networks, but so also did the Congress of the United States. Yesterday, the president was notified that 300 individual Congressmen and 50 Senators of both parties had endorsed his efforts for peace.

As with other American institutions, perhaps it is time that the networks were made more responsive to the views of the nation and more responsible to the people they serve.

Now I want to make myself perfectly clear. I'm not asking for Government censorship or any other kind of censorship. I'm asking whether a form of censorship or any other kind of censorship already exists when the news that 40 million Americans receive each night is determined by a handful of men responsible only to their corporate employers and is filtered through a handful of commentators who admit to their own set of biases.

The questions I'm raising here tonight should have been raised by others long ago. They should have been raised by those Americans who have traditionally considered the preservation of freedom of speech and freedom of the press their special provinces of responsibility. They should have been raised by those Americans who share the view of the late Learned Hand that right conclusions are more likely to be gathered out of a multitude of tongues than through any kind of authoritative selection.

Advocates for the networks have claimed a First Amendment right to the same unlimited freedoms held by the great newspapers of America. But the situations are not identical.

Where the *New York Times* reaches 800,000 people, NBC reaches 20 times that number on its evening news. The average weekday circulation of the *Times* in October was 1,012,367; the average Sunday circulation was 1,523,558.

Nor can the tremendous impact of seeing television film and hearing commentary be compared with reading the printed page. A decade ago before the network crews acquired such dominance over public opinion, Walter Lippman spoke to the issue. He said there's an essential and radical difference between television and printing. The three or four competing television stations control virtually all that can be received over the air by ordinary television sets. But besides the mass circulation monthlies, out-of-town newspapers, and books. If a man doesn't like his newspaper, he can read another from out of town or wait for a weekly news magazine. It's not ideal, but it's infinitely better than the situation in television.

Now it's argued that this power presents no dangers in the hands of those who have used it responsibly. But, as to whether or not the networks have abused the power they enjoy, let us call as our first witness former Vice-President Humphrey and the City of Chicago. According to Theodore White, television's intercutting of the film from the streets of Chicago with the current proceedings on the floor of the convention created the most striking and false political picture of 1968—the nomination of a man for the American Presidency by the brutality and violence of merciless police.

If we are to believe a recent report of the House of Representatives Commerce Committee, then television's presentation of the violence in the streets worked an injustice on the reputation of the Chicago police. According to the committee findings, one network in particular presented, and I quote, "a one-sided picture which in large measure exonerates the demonstrators and protesters. Film of provocations of police that was available never saw the light of day while the film of a police response which the protesters provoked was shown to millions."

Another network showed virtually the same scene of violence from three separate angles without making clear it was the same scene. And, while the full report is reticent in drawing conclusions, it is not a document to inspire confidence in the fairness of the network news.

Our knowledge of the impact of network news on the national mind is far from complete, but some early returns are available. Again, we have enough information to raise serious questions about its effect on a democratic society. Several years ago Fred Friendly, one of the pioneers of network news, wrote that its missing ingredients were conviction, controversy and a point of view—the networks have compensated with a vengeance.

And in the networks' endless pursuit of controversy, we should ask: What is the end value—to enlighten or to profit? What is the end result—to inform or to confuse? How does the ongoing exploration for more action, more excitement, more drama serve our national search for internal peace and stability?

Gresham's Law seems to be operating in the network news. Bad news drives out good news. The irrational is more controversial than the rational. Concurrence can no longer compete with dissent. One minute of Eldridge Cleaver is worth 10 minutes of Roy Wilkins. The labor crisis settled at the negotiating table is nothing compared to the confrontation that results in a strike—or better yet, violence along the picket lines.

Normality has become the nemesis of the network news. Now the upshot of all this controversy is that a narrow and distorted picture of America often emerges from the televised news. A single dramatic piece of the mosaic becomes in the minds of millions the entire picture. And the American who relies upon television for his news might conclude that the majority of Americans feel no regard for their country. That violence and lawlessness are the rule rather than the exception on the American campus.

We know that none of these conclusions is true. Perhaps the place to start looking for a credibility gap is not in the offices of the Government in Washington but in the studios of the networks in New York.

Television may have destroyed the old stereotypes, but has it not created new ones in their places? What has this passionate pursuit of controversy done to the politics of progress through local compromise essential to the functioning of a democratic society?

The members of Congress or the Senate who follow their principles and philosophy quietly in a spirit of compromise are unknown to many Americans, while the loudest and most extreme dissenters on every issue are known to every man in the street. How many marches and demonstrations would we have if the marchers did not know that the ever-faithful TV cameras would be there to record their antics for the next news show?

We've heard demands that Senators and Congressmen and judges make known all their financial connections so that the public will know who and what influences their decisions and their votes. Strong arguments can be made for that view. But when a single commentator or producer, night after night, determines for millions of people how much of each side of a great issue they are going to see and hear, should he not first disclose his personal views on the issue as well?

In this search for excitement and controversy, has more than equal time gone to the minority of Americans who specialize in attacking the United States—its institutions and its citizens?

Tonight I've raised questions. I've made no attempt to suggest the answers. The answers must come from the media men. They are challenged to turn their critical powers on themselves, to direct their energy, their talent and their conviction toward improving the quality and objectivity of news presentation. They are challenged to structure their own civic ethics to relate their great feeling with the great responsibilities they hold.

And the people of America are challenged, too, challenged to press for responsible news presentations. The people can let the networks know that they want their news straight and objective. The people can register their complaints on bias through mail to the networks and phone calls to local stations. This is one case where the people must defend themselves; where the citizen not the Government, must be the reformer; where the consumer can be the most effective crusader.

By way of conclusion, let me say that every elected leader in the United States depends on these men of the media. Whether what I've said to you tonight will be heard and seen at all by the nation is not my decision, it's not your decision, it's their decision.

In tomorrow's edition of the *Des Moines Register* you'll be able to read a news story detailing what I've said tonight. Editorial comment will be reserved for the editorial page where it belongs. Should not the same wall of separation exist between news and comment on the nation's networks?

Now, my friends, we'd never trust such power, as I've described, over public opinion in the hands of an elected Government. It's time we questioned it in the hands of a small and unelected elite. The great networks have dominated America's airwaves for decades. The people are entitled to a full accounting of their stewardship.

A week later, on November 20, 1969, Agnew delivered another speech in Montgomery, Alabama. The text below picks up the speech after three pages of effusive introductory remarks.

The Montgomery Speech

One week ago tonight I flew out to Des Moines, Iowa, and exercised my right to dissent. This is a great country—in this country every man is allowed freedom of speech, even the vice-president. Of course, there's been some criticism of what I said out there in Des Moines. Let me give you a sampling.

One Congressman charged me with, and I quote, "a Creeping Socialistic scheme against the free enterprise broadcast industry." Now this is the first time in my memory that anyone ever accused Ted Agnew of having socialistic ideas.

On Monday, largely because of that address, Mr. [Hubert] Humphrey charged the Nixon administration with a "calculated attack" on the right of dissent and on the media today. Yet it's widely known that Mr. Humphrey himself believes deeply that the unfair coverage of the Democratic convention in Chicago, by the same media, contributed to his defeat in November. Now his wounds are apparently healed, and he's casting his lot with those who were questioning his own political courage a year ago. But let's leave Mr. Humphrey to his own conscience. America already has too many politicians who would rather switch than fight.

There were others that charged that my purpose in that Des Moines speech was to stifle dissent in this country. Nonsense. The expression of my views has produced enough rugged dissent in the last week to wear out a whole covey of commentators and columnists.

One critic charged that the speech was disgraceful, ignorant and base; that leads us as a nation, he said, into an ugly era of the most fearsome suppression and intimidation. One national commentator, whose name is known to everyone in this room, said: "I hesitate to get in the gutter with this guy." Another commentator charges that "it was one of the most sinister speeches that I've ever heard made by a public official."

The president of one network said that it was an unprecedented attempt to intimidate a news medium which depends for its existence upon government licenses. The president of another charged me with an appeal to prejudice, and said that it was evident that I would prefer the kind of television that would be subservient to whatever political group happened to be in authority at the time.

And they say I have a thin skin.

Here indeed are classic examples of overreaction. These attacks do not address themselves to the questions I raised. In fairness, others, the majority of the critics and commentators, did take up the main thrust of my address. And if the debate that they have engaged in continues, our goal will surely be reached, our goal which of course is a thorough self-examination by the networks of their own policies and perhaps prejudices. That was my objective then, and that's my objective now.

Now let me repeat to you the thrust the other night and perhaps make some new points and raise a few new issues. I'm opposed to censorship of television, of the press in any form. I don't care whether censorship is imposed by government or whether it results from management in the choice and presentation of the news by a little fraternity having similar social and political views. I'm against, I repeat, I'm against media censorship in all forms.

But a broader spectrum of national opinion should be represented among the commentators in the network news. Men who can articulate other points of view should be brought forward and a high wall of separation should be raised between what is news and what is commentary. And the American people should be made aware of the trend toward the monopolization of the great public information vehicles and the concentration of more and more power in fewer and fewer hands.

Should a conglomerate be formed that tied together a shoe company with a shirt company, some voice will rise up righteously to say that this is a great danger to the economy and that the conglomerate ought to be broken up. But a single company, in the nation's capital, holds control of the largest newspaper in Washington, D.C., and one of the four major television stations, and an all-news radio station, and one of the three major national news magazines— all grinding out the same editorial line—and this is not a subject that you've seen debated on the editorial pages of the *Washington Post* or the *New York Times*.

For the purpose of clarity, before my thoughts are obliterated in the smoking typewriters of my friends in Washington and New York, let me emphasize that I'm not recommending the dismemberment of the *Washington Post* Company, I'm merely pointing out that the public should be aware that these four powerful voices hearken to the same master. I'm raising these questions so that the American people will become aware of—and think of the implications of—the growing monopoly that involves the voices of public opinion, on which we all depend for our knowledge and for the basis of our views.

When the *Washington Times-Herald* died in the nation's capital, that was a political tragedy; and when the *New York Journal-American,* and the *New York World-Telegram* and *Sun,* the *New York Mirror* and the *New York Herald-Tribune* all collapsed within this decade, that was a great, great political tragedy for the people of New York. The *New York Times* was a better newspaper when they were all alive than it is now that they are gone.

And what has happened to the City of New York has happened in other great cities of America. Many, many strong, independent voices have been stilled in this country in recent years. And lacking the vigor of competition, some of those who have survived have—let's face it—grown fat and irresponsible.

I offer an example: when 300 Congressmen and 59 Senators signed a letter endorsing the president's policy in Vietnam, it was news—and it was big news. Even the *Washington Post* and the *Baltimore Sun*—scarcely house organs for the Nixon administration—placed it prominently in their front pages. Yet that morning the *New York Times*, which considers itself America's paper of record, did not carry a word. Why? Why?

If a theology student in Iowa should get up at a PTA luncheon in Sioux City and attack the president's Vietnam policy, my guess is, that you'd probably find it reported somewhere in the next morning's issue of the *New York Times.* But when 300 Congressmen endorse the president's Vietnam policy, the next morning it's apparently not considered news fit to print.

Just this Tuesday when the Pope, the spiritual leader of half a billion Roman Catholics, applauded the president's effort to end the war in Vietnam, and endorsed the way he was proceeding, that news was on page 11 of the *New York Times.* The same day a report about some burglars who broke into a souvenir shop at St. Peter's and stole $9,000 worth of stamps and currency—that story made page 3. How's that for news judgment?

A few weeks ago here in the South I expressed my views about street and campus demonstrations. Here's how the *New York Times* responded:

"He [that's me] lambasted the nation's youth in sweeping and ignorant generalizations, when it's clear to all perceptive observers that American youth today is far more imbued with idealism, a sense of service and a deep humanitarianism that any generation in recent history, including particularly, Mr. Agnew's generation."

That's what the *New York Times* said. Now that seems a peculiar slur on a generation that brought America out of the great depression without resorting to the extremes of communism or facism. That seems a strange thing to say about an entire generation that helped to provide greater material blessings and more personal freedom—out of that depression—for more people than any other nation in history. We have not finished the task by any means—but we are still on the job.

Just as millions of young Americans in this generation have shown valor and courage and heroism fighting the longest, and least popular, war in our history, so it was the young men of my generation who went ashore at Normandy under Eisenhower, and with MacArthur into the Philippines. Yes, my generation, like the current generation, made its own share of great mistakes and blunders. Among other things, we put too much confidence in Stalin and not enough in Winston Churchill.

But whatever freedom exists today in Western Europe and Japan exists because hundreds of thousands of young men of my generation are lying in graves in North Africa and France and Korea and a score of islands in the Western Pacific. This might not be considered enough of a sense of service or a deep humanitarianism for the perceptive critics who write editorials for the *New York Times,* but it's good enough for me. And I'm content to let history be the judge. Now, let me talk briefly about this generation of young Americans. Like Edmund Burke, I wouldn't know how to draw up an indictment against a whole people. After all, they're our sons and daughters. They contain in their numbers many gifted, idealistic and courageous young men and women. But they also list in their numbers an arrogant few who march under the flags and portraits of dictators, who intimidate and harass university professors, who use gutter obscenities to shout down speakers with whom they disagree, who openly profess their belief in the efficacy of violence in a democratic society.

Oh, yes, the preceding generation had its own breed of losers and our generation dealt with them through our courts, our laws and our system. The challenge is now for the new generation to put its house in order.

Today, Dr. Sydney Hook writes of "storm troopers" on the campus; that "fanaticism seems to be in the saddle." Arnold Beichman writes of "young Jacobins" in our schools who "have cut down university administrators, forced curriculum changes, halted classes, closed campuses and sent a nationwide chill of fear all through the university establishment." Walter Laqueur writes in *Commentary* that "the cultural and political idiocies perpetuated with impunity in this permissive age have gone clearly beyond the borders of what is acceptable for any society, however liberally it may be constructed."

George Kennan has devoted a brief, cogent and alarming book to the inherent dangers of what's taking place in our society and in our universities. Irving Kristol writes that our "radical students find it possible to be genuinely heartsick at the injustice and brutalities of American society, at the same time they are blandly approving of injustice and brutality committed in the name of 'the revolution.' Or, as they like to call it, 'the movement.' "

Now those are not names drawn at random from the letterhead of the Agnew-for-Vice-President committee. Those are men more eloquent and erudite than I, and they raise questions that I've tried to raise.

For we must remember that among this generation of Americans there are hundreds who have burned their draft cards and scores who have deserted to Canada and Sweden to sit out the war. To some Americans, a small minority, these are the true young men of conscience in the coming generation. Voices are and will continue to be raised in the Congress and beyond asking that amnesty—a favorite word—amnesty should be provided for these young and misguided American boys. And they will be coming home one day from Sweden and from Canada and from a small minority of our citizens they will get a hero's welcome.

They are not our heroes. Many of our heroes will not be coming back home; some are coming back in hospital ships, without limbs or eyes, with scars they shall carry for the rest of their lives. Having witnessed firsthand the quiet courage of wives and parents receiving posthumously for their heroes Congressional Medals of Honor, how am I to react when people say, "Stop speaking out, Mr. Agnew, stop raising your voice"?

Should I remain silent while what these heroes have done is vilified by some as "a dirty, immoral war" and criticized by others as no more than a war brought on by the chauvinistic anti-communism of presidents Kennedy, Johnson and Nixon? These young men made heavy sacrifices so that a developing people on the rim of Asia might have a chance for freedom that they obviously will not have if the ruthless men who rule in Hanoi should ever rule over Saigon. What's dirty or immoral about that?

One magazine this week said that I'll go down as the "great polarizer" in American politics. Yet, when that large group of young Americans marched up Pennsylvania Avenue and Constitution Avenue last week, they sought to polarize the American people against the president's policy in Vietnam. And that was their right. And so it is my right, and my duty, to stand up and speak out for the values in which I believe.

How can you ask the man in the street in this country to stand up for what he believes if his own elected leaders weasel and cringe? It's not an easy thing to wake up each morning to learn that some prominent man or some prominent institution has implied that you're a bigot or a racist or a fool. I'm not asking immunity from criticism. This is the lot of a man in politics; we wouldn't have it any other way in a democratic society.

But my political and journalistic adversaries sometimes seem to be asking something more—that I circumscribe my rhetorical freedom while they place no restriction on theirs.

As President Kennedy observed in a far more serious situation: this is like offering an apple for an orchard.

We do not accept those terms for continuing the national dialogue. The day when the network commentators and even the gentlemen of the *New York Times* enjoyed a form of diplomatic immunity from comment and criticism of what they said is over. Yes, gentlemen, the day is passed.

Just as a politician's words—wise and foolish—are dutifully recorded by press and television to be thrown up at him at the appropriate time, so their words should be likewise recorded and likewise recalled. When they go beyond fair comment and criticism they will be called upon to defend their stalemates and their positions just as we must defend ours. And when their criticism becomes excessive or unjust, we shall invite them down from their ivory towers to enjoy the rough and tumble of public debate.

I don't seek to intimidate the press, or the networks or anyone else speaking out. But the time for blind acceptance of their opinions is past. And the time for naive belief in their neutrality is gone. As to the future, each of us could do worse than to take as our own the motto of William Lloyd Garrison who said, and I'm quoting, "I am in earnest. I will not equivocate. I will not excuse. I will not retreat a single inch. And I will be heard."

Appendix 2

Walter Cronkite's Chronology

1916   Born, St. Joseph, Missouri, November 4

1928   Moves with family to Houston, Texas

1933   Graduates from San Jacinto High School; Enters University of Texas, Austin

1936   Drops out of college; Employed by radio station KCMO, Kansas City, Kansas

1937   Begins "Wanderings," taking jobs all over Southwest

1939   Rejoins United Press

1940   Marries Mary Elizabeth (Betsy) Maxwell

1942   Made U.P. war correspondent, assigned to European theatre

1945   Germany surrenders; Reopens U.P. bureaus in Lowlands

1945   Chief correspondent at Nurenberg Nazi War Trials

1946   Brief return to U.S.; Accepts assignment to Moscow

1948   Returns to U.S.; Resigns from U.P; begins lecture tour through Southwest; accepts reporting position in Washington, D.C., for mid-Western radio station KMBD

1950   Recruited by Edward Murrow to CBS-TV, WTOP, Washington, D.C.

1952   Selected by CBS to cover first televised presidential conventions; Covers Queen Elizabeth II's coronation

1953   Transferred to New York; Hosts *The Twentieth Century, You Are There*

1954   Disastrous *Morning Show*

1956   CBS anchorman for political conventions

1960   Anchors political conventions

1961   Named "Broadcaster of the Year"; covered first space shot, of Alan B. Shepard

1962   Receives George Foster Peabody Award; Replaces Douglas Edwards as anchor for CBS *Evening News*

1963   Anchors first live transatlantic Telstar satellite transmission; Doubles *Evening News* in length, from fifteen minutes to thirty minutes; Teamed with former astronaut Wally Schirra for space coverage

1964   Replaced by Robert Trout and Roger Mudd between conventions; Reports *Evening News* broadcasts from Atlantic City for duration of convention

1968   Anchors political conventions

1969   Nixon White House opens attack on press with Vice-President Agnew's Des Moines and Montgomery speeches; First broadcast journalist to receive the William Allen White Award for Journalistic Merit

1970   Cronkite defends First Amendment rights with speech before Economic Club of Detroit; Anchors political conventions; Honored by American Civil Liberties Union for "distinguished public service in the defense and practice of the First Amendment"

1971   Awarded George Polk Memorial Award for Outstanding Achievement in Journalism; Defends, interviews Daniel Ellsberg; Named "Broadcaster of the Year"; Freedom of Press Award for "resisting a White House attempt to discredit CBS News' disclosure of an atrocity at Bau Me, South Vietnam"

1972   Hosts political conventions; Exposes Watergate break-in

1973   Receives Emmys for CBS *Reports*: "The Rockefellers"; *Evening News* coverage of the resignation of Vice-President Agnew and Watergate bread-in 1974 Anchors political conventions; Receives Emmys for CBS Special "Solzhenitsyn," and "Watergate: The White House Transcripts"

1980   Hosts last political convention for CBS

1981   Accepts Presidential Medal of Freedom from Jimmy Carter: Receives special George Foster Peabody Award for three decades of contributions to broadcast journalism; Retires as Managing Editor of Evening News, becoming "Special Correspondent"

1982   Received the National Association of Broadcaster's Distinguished Service Award

1985   Inducted into Academy of Television Arts and Sciences "Hall of Fame"

Selected Bibliography

Books

Andrus, Burton C. *I Was the Nuremberg Jailer*. New York: Coward-McCann, Inc., 1969.

Bernstein, Carl and Woodward, Bob. *All the Presidents Men*. New York: Delacorte Press, 1968.

Bustom, Frank and Owen, Bill. *The Big Broadcast*. New York: The Viking Press, 1972.

Brinkley, David. *Washington Goes to War*. New York: A.A. Knopf, 1988.

Cameron, Gail. *Rose*. New York: G.P. Putnam's Sons, 1971.

Churchill, Winston S. and the Editors of *Life*. *The Second World War*. New York: Time, Inc., 1959.

_____. *Triumph and Tragedy*. Boston: Houghton Mifflin Company, 1953.

Esame, H. *Patton: A Study in Command*. New York: Charles Scribner's Sons, 1974.

Friendly, Fred W. *Due to Circumstances Beyond Our Control....* New York: Random House, Inc., 1967.

Kendrick, Alexander. *Prime Time*. Boston: Little, Brown and Company, 1969.

Lasky, Victor. *JFK: The Man and the Myth*. New York: The MacMillan Company, 1963.

Lessing, Lawrence. *Man of High Fidelity*. Philadelphia: Bantam Books, 1970.

McGinniss, Joe. *The Selling of the President, 1968*. New York: Simon and Schuster, 1970.

Minor, Dale. *The Information War*. New York: The H. W. Wilson Company, 1975.

Morris, Joe Alex. *Deadline Every Minute*. New York: Greenwood Press, 1968.

Rather, Dan and Gates, Gary Paul. *The Palace Guard*. New York: Warner Paperback Library, 1975.

Ryan, Cornelius. *A Bridge Too Far*. New York: Simon and Schuster, 1974.

Shirer, William L. *The Rise and Fall of the Third Reich*. New York: Simon and Schuster, 1960.

Stein, Meyer L. *Under Fire*. New York: Simon and Schuster, 1968.

White, Theodore H. *The Making of the President, 1960*. New York: Mentor Books, 1967.

_____. *The Making of the President, 1964*. New York: New American Library, 1965.

Wilbur, Ted. *Space and the United States Navy*. Washington, D.C.: United States Government Printing Office, 1970.

Journals

American Home. September, 1968.

Atlantic Monthly. October 1, 1943.

Better Homes & Gardens. September, 1960.

Connoisseur. September, 1989.

Current. May, 1981.

Current History. August, 1974.

Diversions. August, 1991.

Editor and Publisher. April 23, 1988.

Esquire. April, 1973.

_____. April, 1974.

_____. December, 1975.

Family Weekly. February 10, 1980.

_____. March 8, 1981.

Fortune. January, 1940.

Gentleman's Quarterly. February, 1991.

Good Housekeeping. May, 1958.

_____. July, 1972.

Life. August, 28, 1964.

_____. July 24, 1971.

_____. October 24, 1966.

_____. October 3, 1971.

_____. November, 1980.

Look. September 11, 1962.

_____. July 24, 1971.

_____. October 24, 1966.

_____. October 3, 1970.

McCall's. November, 1977.

Modern Maturity. August-September, 1975.

Motor Boating. August, 1965.

Motor Boating and Sailing. November, 1976.

Nation. February 27, 1967.

National Geographic. July 1991.

National Review. June 2, 1964.

Newsweek. October 4, 1943.

_____. February 9, 1953.

_____. May 15, 1961.

_____. February 5, 1961.

_____. March 26, 1962.

_____. September 23, 1963.

_____. June 1, 1964.

_____. August 10, 1964.

_____. March 11, 1968.

_____. November 12, 1973.

New Yorker. November 5, 1966.

_____. April 3, 1965.

_____. September 17, 1973.

Parade. March 23, 1980.

_____. October 18, 1981.

People. July 21, 1975.

Playboy. June, 1973.

_____. November, 1990.

Saturday Evening Post. March 16, 1963.

Saturday Review. December 12, 1970.

Senior Scholastic. April 27, 1952.

Smithsonian. June, 1989.

Theatre Arts. November, 1952.

Time. August 7, 1964.

_____. October 14, 1966.

_____. May 31, 1971.

_____. September 10, 1973.

_____. February 2, 1976.

_____. September 24, 1990.
_____. March 8, 1981.
Today's Health. February, 1972.
TV Guide. June 29, 1963.
_____. July 2, 1963.
_____. October 12, 1968.
_____. July 19, 1969.
_____. March 4, 1972.
_____. January 31, 1976.
_____. April 21, 1979.
U.S. News and World Report. March 16, 1981.

Newspapers

Christian Science Monitor. July 19, 1974
Dallas Morning News. May 6, 1990.
Kansas City Journal. April 17, 1940.
New York Herald-Tribune. June 7, 1944.
New York Times. November 28, 1942.
_____. November 28, 1942.
_____. June 7, 1944.
_____. September 2, 1944.
_____. November 27, 1944.
_____. December 29, 1944.
_____. December 30, 1944.
_____. December 31, 1944.
_____. August 18, 1945.
_____. August 21, 1945.
_____. November 11, 1945.
_____. December 4, 1945.
_____. October 13, 1946.
_____. July 20, 1952.
_____. March 14, 1954.
_____. December 10, 1956.
_____. November 8, 1962.
_____. May 2, 1962.
_____. September 3, 1963.
_____. August 15, 1945.

_____. June 6, 1964.

_____. August 9, 1964.

_____. September 15, 1964.

_____. September 8, 1967.

_____. August 28, 1968.

_____. August 29, 1968.

_____. September 21, 1968.

_____. May 6, 1969.

_____. July 21, 1969.

_____. July 24, 1969.

_____. November 26, 1969.

_____. December 19, 1969.

_____. May 22, 1970.

_____. November 17, 1970.

_____. February 17, 1971.

_____. March 19, 1971.

_____. March 20, 1971.

_____. March 24, 1971.

_____. March 25, 1971.

_____. March 27, 1971.

_____. May 8, 1971.

_____. May 13, 1971.

_____. August 4, 1971.

_____. September 29, 1971.

_____. January 5, 1972.

_____. November 4, 1972.

_____. November 21, 1972.

_____. February 26, 1973.

_____. May 11, 1973.

_____. May 23, 1973.

_____. August 23, 1973.

_____. September 1, 1973.

_____. November 2, 1973.

_____. November 13, 1973.

_____. January 24, 1974.

_____. February 12, 1974.

_____. February 24, 1974.

_____. June 18, 1974.

_____. June 19, 1974.

Providence Journal. June 15, 1975.
_____. July 3, 1975.
USA Today. March 8, 1990.
Washington Post. May 6, 1979.